Education's for Other People

Access to Education for Non-Participant Adults

A Research Report

Veronica McGivney
(Research Associate, NIACE)

National Institute of Adult Continuing Education

First published in 1990 by the National Institute of Adult Continuing Education (England and Wales), 19B De Montfort Street, Leicester LE1 7GE.
© NIACE 1990
Reprinted 1991

British Library Cataloguing in Publication Data

McGivney, Veronica
Education's for other people: access to education for non-participant adults: a research report.
1. Great Britain. Adult education
I. Title
374.941
ISBN 0 900559 93 4

Printed and bound in Great Britain by The Eastern Press Ltd, Reading
Cover design by Prakash Rathod

Contents

Section 2: Access for Non-Participant Groups: Stages, Issues and Approaches

Section 3: The Non-Participant Groups

Contents

Section 4: Education Providers: Policy and Institutional Innovation

Contents

Section 5: Concluding Observations

Preface and Acknowledgements

This report is based on research funded by the Economic and Social Research Council (ESRC), reference number: COO232392.

This book is aimed at practitioners, policy-makers and anyone with an interest in equal opportunities in education. It is intended as a guide to some of the main issues in widening access. Much of the information on which the sections are based was provided by education organisers and teaching staff, with whom interviews inevitably elicited views and perceptions as well as factual information. Since internal problems were often frankly expressed, it was necessary to promise complete confidentiality. To avoid identification of informants, some comments have been used to illustrate general issues, without mentioning the names of specific institutions or organisations.

It proved impossible to obtain data on the number of individuals from non-participant categories in general (untargeted) provision. Detailed information on the student body (age, ethnic origin, occupational status, educational background and pos- school participation) is not routinely recorded by many education providers and, at the time the research was conducted, there had been few attempts in institutions, other than residential colleges, to analyse the composition of adult student clienteles.

A wide range of educational processes are involved in "access" but these cannot be examined in depth in this report. Detailed investigations of areas such as educational guidance and assessment of prior learning are available elsewhere.

During the research, a large number of people provided written information and gave up considerable time to discuss their experience and relevant issues during visits and over the telephone. To all of these people I am very grateful. Their names are listed in Appendix 1. Particular thanks to Beryl and Geoff Bateson, Pam Cole and Dania Leslie for their great help and hospitality; to Les Brook, Cliff Burgess, Julia Carter, Sheila Clarke, Eric Higginson, Sheila Morton, Jenny Reeves, Tony Tovell and Brian Wicker for arranging visits and interviews; to Geoff Bateson, Cathy Brophy, Sheila Clarke, Jan Eldred and John Leahy for organising and conducting interviews with "non-participants"; to Ann Bell, Faith Mann and Bob Pitt for conducting surveys of students, and to Alan Charnley for analysing a large number of completed questionnaires. Finally, many thanks to Alan Charnley and Russell Gibbon for reading and commenting on the text.

Key to acronyms

ALBSU: Adult Literacy and Basic Skills Unit
CNAA: Council for National Academic Awards
DES: Department of Education and Science
ESF: European Social Fund
ESG: Education Support Grant
ESL/ESOL: English as a Second Language; English for Speakers of Other Languages
ERA: Education Reform Act
ET: Employment Training
FEU: Further Education Unit
GRIST: Grant-related in-service training
ILEA: Inner London Education Authority
LEA: Local Education Authority
NAB: (former) National Advisory Body for public sector higher education
NAFE: Non-advanced further education
NCVQ: National Council for Vocational Qualifications
PCFC: Polytechnics and Colleges Funding Council
REPLAN: the DES programme for the adult unemployed
TAPs: Training Access Points
TVEI: Technical and Vocational Education Initiative
UDACE: Unit for the Development of Adult Continuing Education
UFC: Universities Funding Council
WRNAFE: Work-related non-advanced further education

Note: Specific references, citations and sources are given in the text in the form of numbered notes at the end of each section. Where an author/date reference is given, the details of the publication will be found in the bibliography on page 184.

Introduction

Large sections of the population do not voluntarily engage in any forms of learning after school. The non-participation issue, as it has been termed, has long been a matter of concern in this country and throughout the industrial world. In Britain, there have been a number of initiatives to recruit new clienteles to post-compulsory education, but these have been geographically patchy and have met with varying degrees of success. This project was designed to investigate the problem of adult non-participation and to identify ways in which education providers can attract and provide appropriate activities for the most hard-to-reach adult groups. The research was conducted between November 1987 and April 1989.

Aims

The primary aims of the project were to:

☐ identify typologies of non-participants
☐ identify the attitudes, perceptions and learning requirements of such groups and the factors that inhibit them from participating in educational activities
☐ identify effective methods of recruiting non-participant groups to formal and informal learning programmes
☐ identify appropriate initial learning opportunities and support mechanisms for such groups
☐ identify appropriate progression routes from introductory to other forms of learning
☐ identify the processes of institutional change arising from work with non-traditional student groups.

Objectives

In order to achieve these aims the project set out to:

☐ examine existing research on adult participation and non-participation in organised educational activities
☐ investigate some of the recruitment strategies and first-stage learning programmes designed for such groups in different education sectors in different parts of the country
☐ establish the key issues involved in reaching and negotiating with the

different sub-groups and in improving their access to different types of educational opportunities
- ☐ investigate the outcomes of participation for the groups concerned and for the providing agencies
- ☐ investigate the nature and extent of progression routes to further and higher education and the problems involved in transition from informal to formal learning.

Some Definitions

- ☐ Adults are defined as people over 19 (excluding conventional full-time students).
- ☐ Adult education is used throughout as a convenient shorthand for the whole spectrum of learning activities engaged in by adults, including part-time or full-time, formal or informal, credit or non-credit, vocational or non-vocational learning.
- ☐ access (with a small "a") is used as a general term referring to the processes and conditions that enable people to gain entry to appropriate learning opportunities and derive maximum benefit from them. Access or Access course (with a capital "A") is a more limited term, referring only to the type of course specifically designed as an alternative route into higher education.

Methods

A triangulation approach was employed, using primary and secondary data. The methodology involved the following sequence:

- ☐ Literature search of British and non-British research and other published and unpublished materials on participation and non-participation.
- ☐ Correspondence with staff in a wide range of educational organisations and institutions throughout England and Wales.
- ☐ Unstructured telephone interviews with education staff working with the groups identified as non-participant.
- ☐ Unstructured face-to-face interviews with staff and some current students in a range of education institutions and organisations in different parts of the country.
- ☐ Structured interviews (using questionnaires) with purposive samples of the public (people belonging to non-participant categories).
- ☐ Surveys of first-time students (former non-participants) attending mainstream and special development programmes.
- ☐ Case studies of centres/institutions which have introduced new clienteles.

The Scope of the Enquiry

Geographical spread

Although the original intention had been to restrict the investigation to a limited number of contrasting geographical areas in England and Wales, so much information was received in response to the preliminary trawl, including data from Scotland, that it was decided to follow up those providers with the most relevant experience, taking care to include a range of organisations and institutions in urban, suburban and rural settings.

Providing agencies

Because of the breadth of the subject and the limited time available, some constraints had to be introduced into the project at an early stage to keep it to manageable proportions. Since educational opportunities for adults and the agencies providing them are extremely diverse, it was decided to restrict investigation to the main statutory and some voluntary providers of organised educational activities. No examples of private providers, employers or distance education schemes were therefore included. Information was obtained from LEAs and individual adult education centres and institutes; WEA districts; further education and community colleges; community schools; community education projects; short-term development projects (REPLAN and ALBSU); polytechnics; universities; and voluntary organisations. (A full list of all the organisations and institutions that provided information for the research is provided in Appendix 1.)

Non-participant groups

The number of identified non-participant typologies turned out to be large and it was considered practical in the time available to focus mainly on those sections of the community with broadly similar difficulties of access, namely: unskilled and semi-skilled manual workers; the unwaged and unemployed; women with dependent children; ethnic minority groups; and older adults (aged 55-plus). As these comprise very large sections of the community, a narrower focus was required in some cases, notably in the ethnic minority category, where it was decided to concentrate on Asian and Afro-Caribbean groups. Arrangements for groups with special needs were not investigated during the project.

Rate of Change

During the time the research was conducted, changes were taking place in education at all levels. This meant that it was almost impossible to obtain a reliably stable picture of provision at any given time, a problem exacerbated by local reorganisations (LEA and staff changes) and the fact that developmental work is often experimental and short-term. The examples of special access measures and targeted provision cited in this report were recorded before the changes introduced by the Education Reform Act of 1988. Some of the projects and initiatives reported have subsequently changed or ceased altogether. As a result, this report cannot be an exhaustive account but only a snapshot of the kinds of approaches that have been employed with new adult clienteles and some of the central issues arising from such work.

The Research

The first task of the research was to establish the main non-participant typologies. This was done through an extensive literature search which revealed that throughout the industrialised world, adults who do not engage in learning tend to fall into large, often overlapping categories:

☐ people with no or few educational qualifications
☐ people with basic education needs
☐ low income groups, the unwaged, unemployed, and people dependent on state benefits
☐ people in unskilled or semi-skilled manual occupations
☐ ethnic minority groups
☐ older adults (aged over 50)
☐ women with young children
☐ people with mental or physical handicap
☐ people living in certain rural areas.

The next stage was to explore the obstacles individuals in the largest non-participant groups face in gaining access to educational opportunities. Research has identified a whole range of interacting deterrent factors, many of them to do with people's situational and material circumstances. However, surveys of non-participant sections of the public conducted during the project suggest that, while each group experiences a specific set of obstacles, the most powerful barrier to access is attitudes and expectations. Education is simply not part of the value system and behaviour pattern of a disturbing number of people. To change this requires a fundamental shift in societal values and mores towards a perception of education as an enabling service for the whole community, rather than just for a small, academically-oriented elite.

The main part of the project, involving substantial contact with education providers, showed that to a small but significant degree, the attitude barrier has been breached. In some areas people from non-participant categories have been attracted to a range of learning activities as a result of innovative recruitment and programming strategies. However, their recruitment has depended on the readiness and ability of education staff to change from a traditional provider-led educational model to one that is more responsive to the particular circumstances, interests and requirements of different client groups. This shift is still the exception rather than the norm, even in a system ostensibly evolving towards greater client responsiveness.

Background to the Research

During the time the research was conducted, a number of developments took place in quick succession – the new Education Reform Act (ERA); the demise of MSC and its replacement by the Training Commission and, subsequently, the Training Agency; the introduction of Employment Training (ET) and the decision to make training the responsibility of employer-led Training Enterprise Councils (TECs); the announcements of a loan scheme for students in higher education and fundamental changes in higher education funding. These developments took place against a background of social, economic and demographic change, rising skill shortages and continuing long-term unemployment. One factor in particular – the declining number of 16–19-year-olds – contributed to a heightened awareness of the exclusivity of our post-school education system and prompted widespread calls for educational change. The rhetoric, arising more from concern about labour and skill shortages than a desire to bring about greater equity in education, centred on opening up the advanced sector of post-compulsory education and it is in higher education that measures to widen access have been concentrated. In 1988 and 1989, central Government and a plethora of national bodies joined in an ever-louder chorus of calls on higher education to adopt more flexible entry procedures for "non-standard" students (those without A-levels), by accelerating the introduction of innovations already pioneered in some institutions: assessment of prior learning, the development of modular and part-time courses, and credit transfer schemes.

In other parts of post-compulsory education, developments to improve access for under-represented groups had been gathering momentum on a broader scale. By 1988 a growing number of LEAs and education institutions had adopted equal opportunities policies, and a variety of initiatives had been launched to expand opportunities for adult learners:

☐ curricular developments (adult basic education programmes, English for speakers of another language, Second Chance and Access programmes, special learning programmes for the unemployed)
☐ the expansion of information and guidance services
☐ the establishment of the National Council for Vocational Qualifications (NCVQ), the PICKUP updating scheme and new assessment systems
☐ increasing opportunities for flexi-study, open- and distance-learning.

Alongside these developments, a growing tendency has been for different sectors, organisations and institutions to make collaborative arrangements in providing educational opportunities for new adult learners.

Cumulatively, these developments suggest that radical changes are taking place which could herald the evolution of the post-school education system from a body supplying ready-made "packages" into an age-segmented clientele to a more responsive service facilitating movement between different types and levels of education at all stages of people's lives. The reality, as always with education, is that change is taking place in a patchy and uneven manner across the country.

Variations In Practice

The research found that in some areas opportunities for educationally disadvantaged adult groups were opening up, while in others they were closing down. Much depended on who had made the decision to target different sections of the community and why. Thus, issues that proved pertinent to the enquiry were the reasons for innovation and the ways in which new practices had been introduced into organisations or institutions. Information received from a range of formal and informal education providers during the project revealed that people in adult, further and higher education have been trying to create opportunities for a wider cross-section of the community for a variety of reasons: ethical, because it is morally right; practical, to fill empty spaces and to meet specific demand; opportunistic, because special funding is available; or (frequently) a mixture of the three. The researcher encountered examples both of the bottom-up approach, where work with new groups was gradually spreading through an institution as a result of the efforts of energetic development staff, and the top-down approach, where principals were trying to introduce whole-institution changes in establishments with long-established procedures and traditional student clienteles.

The research also revealed sharp contrasts in policy and practice between different geographical areas and education authorities; between different institutions and organisations; between different departments in institutions, and between educators engaged in mainstream and those engaged in development work. Hence there are some areas and institutions where there has been evolution and innovation, and others where the system seems caught in a time warp: where "Adult Education" is restricted to the traditional evening provision with which the term is usually associated, and where the further education sector continues to provide the same courses for the same cohort (predominantly white and male, aged 16–19), within the same discrete departmental system as 20 or 30 years ago. In such areas, any changes exist only at the margins and any developmental incursions into mainstream are fiercely resisted, as is the notion that the nature of the student body might change. Even in areas with pockets of high deprivation, there are local education authorities and institutions with no equal opportunities policies, no fee remission policies, few outreach facilities or staff, no community needs/wants analysis, nor any perception that these might be desirable. Several times the researcher was told that as courses in centres and institutions are "open to all members of the community", no special measures need be taken to facilitate the participation of specific groups. Another view frequently encountered was that the adoption of an equal opportunities policy automatically (and miraculously) improves access for groups such as women and black people. In such cases the gap between rhetoric and practice can be alarmingly wide. One interviewee had asked staff in a higher education institution how policy and practice had changed in relation to women. She was told that this had been "fully" taken care of: a memo had been sent to all teaching staff asking them to "pay attention to gender issues in their teaching". The research also indicated that fears about diminishing numbers of traditional students do not necessarily stimulate policies in favour of adults: a number of further and higher education institutions had plans to recruit high-fee-paying overseas students to compensate for shortfalls in conventional student numbers.

Improving Access for Non-participant Adults: Methods and Issues

The research started from the premise that inequities in educational access and the problem of non-participation need to be tackled not at the top of the educational ladder (although there is much work to be done there) but, more relevantly, at the bottom. It is unrealistic to expect many individuals from those sections of the community least well-served by the education system to be attracted to the sector that has hitherto demonstrated the most exclusivity, higher education. It soon became clear that it would be just as unrealistic to look at the first stages of access in isolation, since genuine access to education involves a continuum of process and conditions. In consequence, the research focused on four consecutive stages:

☐ contact, negotiation and recruitment
☐ prgramme development and support mechanisms
☐ transition from introductory to more advanced learning activities
☐ transition from community-based activities to formal educational institutions.

Information received during the research confirmed that at community or neighbourhood level, there are numerous examples of innovative learning programmes, developed by voluntary, LEA and community education workers, which demonstrate that even those most resistant to education can be attracted to learning activities when they are presented, delivered and organised in ways that are substantially different from the compulsory, formal learning experience.

Information received during the research confirmed, repeatedly, that the first-stage learning programmes that are most effective in attracting and retaining new groups and helping them to move on in various ways have the following characteristics:

☐ Thorough preparatory groundwork and personal contacts in the community.

☐ Negotiation of curricula and all aspects of programmes with the groups concerned.

☐ Informal settings and teaching/learning styles.

☐ Student support mechanisms (especially guidance) at every stage of the access process.

☐ Availability of progression routes and help with transition to other forms and levels of learning.

The research found examples of good practice in all these areas, but because of the diversity of practice in post-school education, there can be problems relating to the "transferability" of models. Moreover, work targeting specific groups is very unevenly distributed across the country as a whole.

A cursory glance at some 1989–90 area prospectuses of programmes specifically for adults reveals that a wide range of intellectual and leisure interests are catered for. However, one can search hard for evidence of work targeting specific or "disadvantaged" categories of students. Courses and other learning activities for groups such as the unemployed, people with basic education needs, speakers of other languages, the elderly and women returners, are often separately listed as specially-funded programmes, a fact which simultaneously labels them as priority areas and as areas peripheral to "normal" or staple adult provision. The "Catch 22" in this is that without special funding such groups might not be catered for, but the availability of special funding provides an excuse for not targeting them within "normal" programming. For example, most of the initiatives with ethnic minority groups reported to this project were Section XI-funded and a great deal of the most innovative work with unemployed adults was REPLAN-funded. This prompts the question: how often is such work integrated into mainstream after the life-span of special funding or projects? Although special funding has spearheaded innovation in many areas, in others it has led to work with non-traditional groups remaining marginal, "ghettoised" and not integrated with mainstream.

Policy Changes

The effects, on work with adults, of the changes initiated by ERA have yet to be assessed but the research suggests that there is a major contradiction embodied in policy: namely, the tension between the principles of "equity" and wider access and the requirement to make adult, further and higher education services more subject to market forces. To improve access for the most under-represented groups requires substantial intervention by education providers, involving outreach approaches, greater flexibility and relaxation of rules and procedures, as it may take time to build up to the required minimum numbers: in other words, wide-ranging changes in practice and resource allocation. Work with non-participant groups is, inevitably, more time-consuming, more labour-intensive and hence more expensive than catering for a known and established clientele.

The challenge, then, is to match word with deed. DES Circular 19/89 gives the adult education service a secure statutory framework in which to meet local needs and requires LEAs to take into account "the need to secure an appropriate range of opportunities for disadvantaged adults including those with special education needs, those requiring basic skills or language support, and the unemployed." To date, however, as this ESRC-funded research suggests, a characteristic of work with these groups is its vulnerability. In the Local Authorities, institutions and centres visited during the project, staff invariably referred to the threats to innovation posed by the problem of actual or anticipated cutbacks. Some innovative approaches which had proved effective with educationally disadvantaged groups were under threat as funding came to end or changes in regulations and criteria were announced, at short notice, by outside funding bodies. There were widespread fears that much of the acclaimed work with disadvantaged adults in the ILEA would be lost after the dispersal of education services to the London boroughs. Some successful initiatives reported during the research came to an end only a few months after the project was completed. It is against this background of change, insecurity, uncertainty and financial pressure that the work undertaken with non-participant groups reported in the following sections should be judged.

Section 1

Participation and Non-Participation: A Review of the Literature

Research on participation and non-participation has been prolific, particularly in the United States. However, participation is a complex field of enquiry and it is worth signalling from the outset some of the misgivings that have been expressed about this kind of research. First, the sheer size, diversity and complexity of post-school education makes the concept of participation impossible to pin down:

> The concept of participation may be a different species for different strata of society ..."Adequate" or "successful" participation is a chameleon set against a background of quick-changing groups, courses, centres, areas and times. Lack of participation is an equally elusive reptile flitting across the same institutional neon (1).

Second, in view of the diversity and complexity of human beings and their circumstances, there is no single theory that can satisfactorily explain participation or non-participation:

> We are presented with a set of partial and overlapping existing explanations in which the different approaches each offer plausible suggestions for lines of enquiry – in effect they are investigative pointers rather than testable propositions (2).

For the purposes of this short project, however, some of the main findings of existing research have been taken on trust in order to provide a general starting point.

Who Are the Participants?

The first task of the research was to establish the main participant and non-participant typologies and to examine the reasons put forward for their involvement or non-involvement in educational activities.

Participation surveys inevitably vary enormously in methods and terms of reference. The definition of "adult" can vary from anyone aged 17 or over to anyone aged over 20, and estimates of adult student numbers fluctuate widely, according to whether learning activities are defined as all voluntary learning efforts (Tough, 1979) or institutionally-based activities and courses taken part-time. This divergence suggests that survey results should be treated with caution. Nevertheless, there is enough consistency in research findings to take them as a reasonably reliable guide. In Britain, for example, most of the larger-scale surveys suggest that, discounting school-leavers who go straight into further or higher education, adult participation in organised education usually lies somewhere between 10% and 15% at any given time, although this figure would be much higher – over 40% – if *any* participation since leaving school is taken into account (ACACE, 1982*b*). A 1987 FEU survey of participation in adult and continuing education in three different English locations suggested that 14% of adults were currently participating and 32% had done so at some time in the past (3). Research in Scotland (1988) came up with a higher figure: approximately 42% of a sample of 2000 had returned at least once after leaving school to organised education, defined here as courses or systematic programmes of learning lasting for seven hours or more within a three-month period (4).

Participant typologies

"Mature students do not represent a cross-section of the adult population ... adult education is largely the preserve of the middle classes" (5). This conclusion, based on the results of a survey of mature students attending qualifying and non-qualifying courses in England and Wales, confirms the findings of virtually all British national and regional surveys in the last 20 years. The NIAE (1970) study *Adequacy of Provision* showed that while the non-vocational adult education service had expanded, it had chiefly benefited younger, better educated and higher income groups. A decade later the ACACE (1982*a*) survey showed little change:

> *All the indications show that those with the longest initial education,*
> *those who are in the higher social classes, the young, men, and those*
> *seeking vocational education are consistently better able to take*
> *advantage of the existing opportunities for continuing education (6).*

The 1987 FEU survey, *Marketing Adult Continuing Education*, also found participation skewed towards the young, higher social grades, owner occupiers and those with access to a car, while the Munn and MacDonald survey in Scotland (1988) reported that adult "returners" – people over 20 who had been out of full-time education for at least two years – were predominantly in socio-economic groups A and B. Unsurprisingly, an investigation into use of education information, advice and guidance services also found that people seeking advice and guidance about education, training or jobs were more likely to be young, male, from the higher socio-economic groups and in possession of some educational qualifications (7). Smaller local surveys confirm this general picture.

Thus, despite their diversity, studies of participation in the UK reveal a striking consistency in the composite picture they yield of the typical participant body:

> *The empirical evidence ... consistently shows that adult education of all kinds recruits disproportionately from certain parts of the adult population: those of working age rather than the retired; those in non-manual rather than manual occupations; and those with more than minimal previous educational success (8).*

This phenomenon is not confined to the UK. Similar findings have been reported in OECD countries and in New Zealand, where Boshier (1971) referred to participants in adult education as "A narrow *creme de la creme* segment of the population". Moreover, the general profile of adult participants appears to be consistent across all levels of education.

Major characteristics

Thus, the available evidence indicates that the main attributes associated with adult participation are:

AGE: Anderson and Darkenwald (1979) consider this to have a more significant impact on participation than variables such as gender or race. Young adults are more likely to engage in learning than those over the age of 50.

EDUCATIONAL BACKGROUND AND ATTAINMENT: The extent and experience of initial schooling is widely considered to be the most important predictor of adult participation. According to American research, school leaving age is more highly associated with participation in continuing education in that country than any other characteristic. The same finding has been reported in France. Christian de Montlibert (1973), for example, maintains that even among people belonging to the same professional and social categories, those with longer schooling consistently participate more in educational and cultural activities than those who left school early. This, according to de Montlibert, indicates that initial education plays a greater role than current socio-economic status in determining participation behaviour. In the UK, all the large-scale surveys have found that the main beneficiaries of continuing education are those who have had the longest initial educational experience. This has been described as the "iron law of education: the more education people have had, the more likely they are to want more and the more competent they will be at getting it" (9).

SOCIO-ECONOMIC STATUS: As the ACACE report (1982b) observed: "The phenomenon of social class as it affects education in this country is extremely powerful" (10). Typical adult participants in post-school education are employed and in the higher socio-economic groups – IPA categories A, B, C1 and C2. Thus, in spite of developments such as comprehensive schools and polytechnics and repeated calls for improved access, inequalities in access to post-school education have not been eliminated.

It has been observed that, even in lower occupational groups, the same general characteristics distinguish participants from non-participants. This became evident in a French study of participation in targeted programmes in several mining communities (11). Confirming the findings of other French researchers, this enquiry demonstrated that participation in education within working-class groups is governed by exactly the same sociological factors that create inequalities in access between different classes and social levels. Jacques Hedoux, the author of the study, discovered that participants in the programmes comprised an "active social minority" characterised by certain favourable attributes, namely: *good material circumstances* (higher income and occupational levels); *greater mobility* (ability to anticipate and instigate social change); *cultural familiarity* (higher level of schooling, extended social relationships and cultural practices).

Involvement in social, community and cultural activities

Hedoux observed that educational participation was strongly connected with the extent of an individual's integration into community life. Participants were generally leading a more diverse and intense social life than non-participants, and tended to be more involved in voluntary groups, political parties, unions, churches, and local cultural activities. In consequence they had more contact with key local figures (*notables*), such as teachers, religious leaders, council members and people in management positions.

He found that whereas participants and non-participants engaged equally in *mass culture* (newspapers, TV, holidays), participants and their families were significantly more engaged in cultural practices such as reading, and visiting cinemas, theatres, museums and exhibitions. For Hedoux this implied "a dynamic of cultural development within families which reinforces the positive thrust towards education". He concluded that participation in adult education arises from "particularly tenacious social differentiations" and that voluntary participation in education in itself constitutes a strong discriminating variable in the working-class population. This contention was widely confirmed by other research reports and the information collected during this project.

Who Are the Non-Participants?

There are substantial numbers of people who have been defined as failures by the schooling system and who remain outside the world of adult education. The lower you go down the social hierarchy, the more there are (12).

The ACACE national survey of 1982 estimated that 51% of the adult population of England and Wales had not engaged in any kind of education or training since leaving school. The more recent survey in Scotland (Munn and MacDonald, 1988) found a slightly higher proportion – 58% of the sample population – to be non-participants. An OECD conference report (1977) referred to non-participation as an international phenomenon: "Irrespective of their political ideologies, technologically advanced and industrially backward countries alike testified at the Tokyo conference that the overwhelming majority of their populations were not participating in adult education" (13).

Major characteristics

As one would expect from the profile of typical participants (pages 12–13), the characteristics that distinguish non-participants from participants are age, educational experience and attainment, and socio-economic status.

AGE: Older adults are less likely to participate than younger ones and most available research shows a fall-off at retirement age, particularly among men.

EDUCATIONAL BACKGROUND: Non-participation in education in adult life is closely linked with initial educational experience. Virtually all the British and non-British survey reports consulted for this research show that people who do not participate in any form of continuing education or training tend to be those with the least initial education. The ACACE national survey (1982a) revealed that the majority of non-participants had left school at the minimum leaving age; in the 1988 Scottish survey, 80% of non-returners had left school at age 16 or under.

SOCIO-ECONOMIC STATUS: Socio-economic status (which is often linked with experience of and attitudes to initial schooling) also contributes significantly to non-participation. One of the "most persistent" findings of a large-scale survey in the USA was "the great disparity in involvement in continuing education of segments of the population situated at different levels of the social hierarchy" (14). An OECD report (1979) referred to the striking under-representation of unskilled manual workers in learning activities in the USA, Denmark, France, Italy, the Netherlands, Spain and the UK (15). In England and Wales, the low proportion of participants from working-class backgrounds and occupations in all levels of post-compulsory education frequently arouses comment. A study of post-initial education in the north-west of England (Percy, 1983) found that only 18% of participants were working class, and a wider national survey (Woodley et al., 1987) concluded that working-class people, particularly women, are "massively under-represented" throughout post-school education. The close relationship between occupational status and participation is stressed in the Woodley survey, in the findings of the American researchers, Anderson and Darkenwald (1979), and in the work of de Montlibert (1973), whose study of paid educational leave in France highlights glaring disparities in access between different occupational groups.

Non-participant groups

Cumulatively, the evidence implies that irrespective of location or educational setting, certain sections of the community tend not to engage in any form of educational activity after leaving school – older adults; less well-educated people in lower social, economic and occupational strata; women with dependent children; ethnic minority groups; and people living in rural areas. These groups, which were singled out in the large American survey in the 1960s (Johnstone and Rivera, 1965) have remained virtually unchanged in two succeeding decades. The 1977 OECD report, for example, identified the following non-participant typologies:

☐ unemployed young adults (especially premature school leavers)
☐ some rural populations
☐ immigrants
☐ the aged
☐ urban poverty groups
☐ unemployed and underemployed workers with little education
☐ unskilled and semi-skilled workers
☐ some groups of women (housebound mothers, women from lower socio-economic groups)
☐ people with linguistic problems.

Taken together, these groups add up to a large majority, whose main characteristic, according to the OECD report, is social and economic deprivation. There is a certain amount of crossover between groups: the least educated are often unemployed or in unskilled occupations and have low incomes; people on the lowest incomes are likely to be found among the elderly, immigrant groups and women. However, each of the categories listed is a large and heterogeneous section of society and each contains many sub-groups, some of which are more likely than others to engage in voluntary learning.

Non-participant categories vary according to different geographical, demographic and cultural situations. In the US, research shows that women, especially young mothers, are particularly educationally disadvantaged. In France, a survey of participation in specially targeted programmes in mining communities revealed two sets of non-participants: a group mixed in age and gender who knew about the programmes and were favourably disposed to them but still chose not to participate, and a hard core of non-participants (*radical non-public*) made up of unwaged married women, older adults, non-qualified manual workers and people on the lowest incomes who claimed to have absolutely no knowledge of the programmes, even after 10 years of intensive and widespread publicity (16). In the Republic of Ireland, rural dwellers are likely to be non-participants, while in England and Wales, several groups have been identified as persistently under-representedin post-school education: ethnic minorities, women, physically and mentally handicapped adults, manual workers, and the elderly.

The Focus of the Research

To check the validity of the identified typologies, the education providers and teaching staff contacted during the course of this research were asked which sections of the community they were not attracting or found it particularly difficult to recruit. Working-class people in general, ethnic minority groups, the elderly, and groups which one informant referred to as "severely culturally defined", such as some married women, were frequently mentioned. The majority of respondents also commented on the acute difficulties they experienced in attracting men, particularly the unemployed and manual workers. The general consensus, therefore, was that the typologies are still generally accurate, although much depends on the location and the extent of outreach opportunities available. In view of this and the limited time available, it was decided to focus on five large (sometimes overlapping) non-participant sections of the community: manual workers; the unemployed and unwaged; women with childcare responsibilities; older adults; and ethnic minority groups. As many individuals within these groups left school at the minimum leaving age and possess few qualifications, it was decided not to treat people without qualifications as a separate category.

Before investigating how these groups might be attracted to organised educational activities, it was necessary to explore the reasons that have been identified for participation and non-participation in voluntary educational activities.

What are the Reasons for Non-Participation?

Lack of information

A common finding in participation research is that non-participants have little or no knowledge of the educational opportunities available. A British review of research into disadvantaged adult groups (17) estimated that up to two-thirds of non-participants simply did not know what learning opportunities exist. A reason for this was suggested by the French researcher

Hedoux (1981). He observed that the most striking feature separating the *radical non-public* from participants in the targeted learning programme *Action Collective de Formation* was their general lack of involvement in communal life. This led him to infer a probable link between social and communal involvement and people's knowledge of educational opportunities. People involved in social and cultural activities are in information networks, and are therefore more likely to be aware of existing educational opportunities. However, there is little evidence that simply knowing what is on offer leads to participation. Hedoux' research identified a second population of non-participants: people who knew about the targeted learning scheme and were favourably disposed towards it but still failed to participate. It is clear, then, that while a positive image of a learning programme and all the necessary information to enrol are essential pre-requisites of participation, by themselves they are not sufficient to bring about enrolment.

Identified deterrents to participation

The reasons for participation and non-participation are numerous, complex and much debated. There has been a great deal of research into the factors that deter people from engaging in voluntary learning, particularly in the US, where the "deterrent concept" is seen as an effective way of explaining variance in adult participation (Scanlan and Darkenwald, 1984). However, some reservations have been expressed regarding the value of surveys conducted to identify barriers to participation. While conceding that there is a certain consistency in their findings, Scanlan (1986) points out that they usually require respondents to select deterrent factors from a list predetermined by the researchers, and this can result in distortions. Results can also be skewed as a result of sampling methods and respondents' desire to answer in a socially acceptable way. Moreover, such surveys are based on the assumption that people can readily recall and analyse their own behaviour.

In her synthesis of American research, Cross (1981) divided deterrents to participation into three now-familiar categories – situational, institutional and dispositional. Although they have been described as oversimplified, these categories provide a useful starting point for considering the problem of non-participation.

Situational barriers

TIME: The obstacle most frequently mentioned by adults in American and British surveys is lack of time for participation in education, a constraint arising from family responsibilities and work schedules, with people working part-time or shift work at unsociable hours reporting the most difficulties.

Nonetheless, most research findings show that the majority of participants in part-time education programmes are in paid employment, and people without job-related obligations are less likely to take advantage of learning opportunities. Thus an increase in leisure time does not necessarily lead to a boom for adult education. A time budget study in the US revealed that a general increase in leisure hours was almost entirely absorbed by increased television viewing, mostly for non-educational purposes (18).

COSTS: A comparison of stated deterrents in Great Britain and the US (19) revealed that the financial costs of participation were rated of low importance by the American sample, but considered a significant deterrent by British respondents: a difference which undoubtedly reflects the income gap between the two populations. The ACACE survey (1982a) found that cost was a major perceived barrier by both men and women, and there is some evidence that economic factors have had a negative impact on wider participation in Great Britain country. Both the NIAE (1970) and ACACE (1982b) national reports described how increased participation in adult education by people from the lower socio-economic groups was abruptly reversed as a result of "frequent and steep" fee increases in the second half of the 1970s. Local surveys have confirmed this effect. One conducted in south-east Derbyshire (20) revealed that sharp fee increases resulted in a 28% fall in enrolments among those with relatively less disposable incomes. Similarly, a study in Newcastle-upon-Tyne showed that a 65% increase in LEA fees between 1979 and 1983 led to a 22% fall, particularly in neighbourhoods considered priority areas, while a survey of adult students in the north-west suggested that increased costs would be a strong deterrent to those already participating (21). However, while there is no doubt that increased fee levels affect the most economically disadvantaged groups, the evidence overall is inconclusive and contradictory. In the interviews with non-participants conducted during this research, cost was cited as a reason for non-participation by less than 9% of respondents. Moreover, the information received from LEA providers collectively suggests that costs may be less of a barrier than is generally supposed, although groups such as the elderly, those receiving Social Security benefits, and the unemployed clearly require some financial concessions or assistance. It has frequently been found that non-participants who cite expense as an obstacle have little idea of the actual cost of learning activities. This has led some researchers to suspect that cost, like lack of time, may serve as a socially acceptable or face-saving reason for not participating, camouflaging more complex and possibly unrecognised reasons.

Institutional barriers: the unresponsive system

One of the principal reasons for non-participation is the education system itself. The middle-class character of adult education is a well-documented, international phenomenon. In 1978, Wiltshire and Mee (22) estimated that only 5% of education provision for adults was targeted at educationally or socially disadvantaged groups. Over a decade later, although there have been a variety of targeted initiatives supported by special funding, locally-organised LEA, WEA or university programmes for adults have retained a strong middle-class ethos. With current pressures on services to become more market-oriented and self-financing, this situation looks likely to persist: "The reality is that demands determine supply even when there is an underlying intention to reach a more equitable situation" (23).

Imbalances in the nature of participation are even more evident in the other post-school sectors. Further and higher education institutions have traditionally catered for a young, white, middle-class and predominantly male section of the population. "Non-traditional" students who do succeed in gaining entry to such institutions often experience a range of problems. O'Shea and Corrigan (24) have given a graphic description of the tremendous cultural conflicts experienced by adults from working-class backgrounds who enrol in higher education. Moreover, there is widespread evidence that ethnic minority individuals feel even more alienated in white, middle-class learning environments where the curriculum, in some subject areas, is essentially ethnocentric (25). Until relatively recently, the system has done little to support non-traditional students in further and higher education. As one report comments: "If institutions do not cope adequately with mature students' needs, another barrier to participation is created. In the graphic phrase of the Open University, the open door will become a revolving door" (26).

Paid educational leave (PEL) completes the picture of middle-class dominance. Traditionally, this has mainly benefited higher status workers, and men in particular. Even when such opportunities are increased, the evidence in most industrial countries suggests that the chief beneficiaries are people in more advantaged circumstances. In France it was observed (Dubar, 1977) that the workers who took most advantage of the new opportunities offered by the 1971 law on PEL were those with most qualifications and "cultural capital". Indeed, de Montlibert (1973) asserts that increased PEL in France strengthened previously established inequalities and reinforced the gaps between participants and non-participants: "It is those in higher grade positions who take to education like ducks to water". This process is well documented and has been described as "the phenomenon of second creaming: an increase in services principally benefits those who just failed to profit from what already existed, leaving others relatively worse off" (27). But why is this the case?

Education and social selection

O'Shea and Corrigan (1979) maintain that other groups hold back not because of low motivation, but because of powerful constraints arising from cultural and social class divisions. Many educationists and researchers have observed that adult participation in education is the continuation of a process which starts at school. School creates (or reinforces) sharp divisions in society, by conditioning children to accept different expectations and status patterns according to their academic "success" or "failure". Through the use of imposed standards and selection, the education system traditionally rejects or excludes large numbers of the population, many of whom subsequently consider themselves as educational failures (Hopper and Osborn, 1975). To a significant degree, post-school education perpetuates the values and status patterns embedded in the school system. Many further and higher education institutions still retain the ethos and procedures of the compulsory school system, with people being ranked or excluded according to their ability to reach imposed sets of standards. Thus, post-school education can all too easily reinforce inequalities that commenced early in childhood. It is not surprising, therefore, that amid all the identified reasons for non-participation, one factor consistently stands out. People who have ostensibly "failed" in the school system do not wish to repeat that failure. Many are consequently suspicious of education in any form, even informal learning opportunities specifically designed for them.

Reference groups

De Montlibert (1973) has described how a new centre offering educational opportunities to redundant steel workers in Lorraine attracted only 10 enrolments. The same thing happened in the Vosges region when a textile factory was due to be closed. Enquiries revealed that the concept of education was perceived as totally alien and irrelevant by the workers threatened with redundancy: "'Culture isn't for us', said one worker, to the approval of all his colleagues". De Montlibert interpreted this reaction as a "quasi-political revolt" against a situation of which people saw themselves as victims. However, it could also be viewed as a gesture of class solidarity. The process of "social stratification" achieved, cumulatively, through the influences of family background, school and work, results in education becoming part of the value system of some groups but not of others. The importance of peer or reference groups in shaping behaviour and attitudes cannot be overestimated. It has been observed (Gooderham, 1987) that whereas professional, white collar workers tend to be influenced by a much wider network than just their co-workers, manual workers form very strong peer pressure groups which have a determining influence on norms and behaviour. This is strongly borne out in the French research. The French steel worker who dismissed learning was expressing a consensus view of a group whose normal behaviour patterns exclude voluntary participation in education. Similar reactions have been encountered in this country by people initiating work with unemployed men. A report on the education and training scheme for redundant steel-workers at Consett (Holmes and Storrie, 1985) observed that men found returning to education without a purely instrumental aim difficult to justify to their co-workers. There is substantial evidence that many people from working-class communities are acutely conscious of the fact that attending classes renders them conspicuous and an oddity among their neighbours. Some face hostility and lack of support from spouses, relatives and friends, many of whom perceive their participation as a kind of class betrayal. Hostility or disapproval can be particularly strong if participation is seen to threaten accepted gender roles: "It is not uncommon to find friends and co-workers who want the learner to remain in the fold ... there are spouses who fear their mate's educational endeavours will affect the relationship and family members who are concerned that household responsibilities will be traded-off against school obligations" (28).

It could be argued, therefore, that certain sections of the community do not readily participate in education or training partly because of constraints arising from their personal circumstances, but primarily because voluntary learning is perceived to be part of the culture pattern of higher socio-economic groups. Middle-class dominance in education is a difficult circle to break: members of higher socio-economic groups tend to live and work in environments where they have more scope for influencing their situation than those in lower income groups; where they have access to education or training opportunities; and where there is a positive orientation to education. They often come from families in which education was valued, have themselves been "successful" in educational terms and have consequently passed on positive attitudes to education to their own children.

Dispositional barriers

As this suggests, reluctance to engage in education may have more to do with attitudes, perceptions and expectations than with any practical barriers. The authors of the ACACE (1982b) report claim that the major "unstated barrier" to participation is to do with attitude. This problem may have been underestimated, partly because research instruments tend to have a bias towards situational and institutional barriers; partly because respondents may not recognise, or wish to admit to, negative feelings towards education. Nevertheless, a number of studies confirm that attitudes and perceptions play a significant role in non-participation. Notably, these include perceptions of inappropriateness and lack of relevance; no awareness of learning needs; hostility towards school; the belief that one is too old to learn; and lack of confidence in one's ability to learn. These have all been repeatedly identified as major reasons for non-participation, particularly among older adults, people of low educational attainment and those on low incomes. In Britain, it is indisputable that a large proportion of the adult population considers education as totally irrelevant: "For those who believe that education ends with school and real life begins with work the whole concept of adult learning is novel" (29).

In the surveys conducted for this research (described in detail in Section

3), over 60% of non-participants claimed to have no interest whatsoever in adult education, and many expressed strong hostility to education in general. In the same surveys, negative school experience was the second most frequently stated reason (after lack of time) for non- engagement in learning.

Perceptions of education

Primary and secondary data both reveal that a disturbingly large proportion of the public has a stereotyped view of learning dating from school experience. Many believe that all forms of post-compulsory education are formal, inflexible and examination-oriented, and that participants will be judged on their ability to meet certain standards. This perception undoubtedly has a powerful deterrent effect. Feedback from former non-participants who have enrolled in special or targeted learning programmes invariably includes expressions of surprise at the scope, relevance and informal nature of some educational opportunities for adults.

Misconceptions, however, exist on both sides. There is evidence that some teaching staff, particularly in further and higher education institutions, have stereotyped views of mature learners, particularly groups such as the elderly, ethnic minorities and women. There is little doubt that the inaccurate view of education held by many members of the public and the inaccurate view of adult learners held by many teaching staff have contributed to keeping education and the majority of adults rigorously apart.

Inability to anticipate or control the future

Another powerful psychological barrier has been identified by Hedoux (1981): perceptions of powerlessness linked with the lack of a future perspective. Hedoux argues that decisions to participate in education and training are intimately connected with a person's ability to control his/her own life and anticipate the future. Among the groups he identified as "radical" non-participants, this ability is blocked, particularly in the case of elderly people and married women whose autonomy and freedom of movement are severely constrained by their partners.

Combination of deterrent factors

The evidence as a whole, therefore, suggests that dispositional factors – attitudes, perceptions, expectations – constitute perhaps the most powerful deterrents to participation among the groups investigated. When these are added to the numerous practical obstacles that prevent individuals from taking up educational opportunities – lack of time, money, transport, day-time facilities, and childcare – the immense difficulties faced by providers wishing to recruit non-participant sections of the community can be appreciated.

There are, then, multiple obstacles which prevent large sections of the public from seeking or taking up educational opportunities, and there is now a strong consensus that non-participation results from the combination and interaction of diverse factors, rather than one or two obstacles which would be relatively easy to overcome:

> *An individual decision not to participate in organized adult education is typically due to the combined or synergistic effects of multiple deterrents rather than just one or two in isolation (30).*

> *Deterrents to participation is a multidimensional concept ... Demographic variables such as sex, marital status, age, race are not by themselves deterrents to participation: more likely it is the social and psychological correlates of these vital attributes that function to hinder or impede participation in adult education ... Many of the situational variables related to non-participation such as one's job role or employment status probably exert their influence only by virtue of association with other more relevant situational or dispositional factors (31).*

> *It is easy to say that some groups don't want or need education. That is reducing to one all the many interlocking reasons why they don't participate" (32).*

Motivations

Why do people participate?

Much of the emphasis in participation research has been on what motivates people to learn. According to Beder and Valentine:

> *The concept of motivation ties together concepts of need, preference and demand so central in understanding why learners choose to exchange their scarce resources to engage in learning. Motivation is the force which balances the costs of attending (interpreted very widely). If motivation exceeds costs, participation is likely. If the reverse is true, participation is unlikely in a voluntary program (33).*

Research into motivation has often involved "factor analysis" – subdividing a number of item responses or variables into meaningful categories – and "cluster analysis" – grouping respondents into mutually exclusive clusters according to similarity. One of the pioneers of motivation research was Houle, who identified three categories of adult learner: goal-oriented (to fulfil conscious objectives); learning-oriented (pursuing knowledge for the love of it); and activity-oriented (participation for reasons unconnected to programme purpose or content). Despite a view that researchers have "clung perhaps a bit too lovingly to Houle's shirt-tails" (34), later studies have found these categories – particularly the first and second – to be generally accurate. A number of American researchers have categorised stated motives for voluntary learning and come up with largely similar clusters (Figure 1). These show that, although factor analysis has its critics, there is a certain consistency in survey findings.

Figure 1. Stated motives for participation in organised adult education

DESIRE FOR KNOWLEDGE
[Johnstone and Rivera (1965), Sheffield (1962), Morstain and Smart (1974), Ghazzali (1979), Beder and Valentine (1987)]
TO MEET PERSONAL/SELF-DEVELOPMENT GOALS
(Johnstone and Rivera; Sheffield; Ghazzali; Beder and Valentine)
TO MEET OCCUPATIONAL GOALS
(Johnstone and Rivera; Morstain and Smart; Beder and Valentine)
TO MEET SOCIAL/COMMUNITY GOALS
(Sheffield; Morstain and Smart; Ghazzali; Beder and Valentine)
TO COMPLY WITH EXTERNAL EXPECTATIONS/FORMAL REQUIREMENTS/URGING OF OTHERS
(Morstain and Smart; Ghazzali; Beder and Valentine)
TO FIND ACTIVITY, ESCAPE, DIVERSION, STIMULATION
(Sheffield; Morstain and Smart; Ghazzali; Beder and Valentine)
TO MEET ECONOMIC NEED
(Beder and Valentine)
TO FULFIL NEEDS TO DO WITH RELIGION OR CHURCH
(Morstain and Smart; Beder and Valentine)
TO FULFIL FAMILY RESPONSIBILITIES
(Beder and Valentine)
"LAUNCHING"/ROLE DEVELOPMENT
(Beder and Valentine)
(Note: the Beder and Valentine study was of basic education students.)

Instrumental and expressive motives

Beder and Valentine (1987) distinguish between the extrinsic (such as job advancement) and intrinsic (self-improvement) benefits of participation. Percy (35) adds a third dimension – social/affiliative. He points out that although motives for participation are often a mixture of the three categories, explicitly educational motives are rarely cited as the reason for attending learning activities in voluntary organisations: people engage in voluntary organisations for other than educational reasons and perceive their activities as "doing" rather than learning.

In most British and North American surveys, the majority of respondents have given instrumental (extrinsic) motives for participation in organised education. From her analysis of US research, Cross (1981) found that the major emphasis in adult learning was on the practical – obtaining skills – rather than on acquiring knowledge. She also found that non-participants put as much stress on the instrumental aims of education as participants, a trend reflected in the surveys conducted for this research.

Other evidence, however, implies that people who engage in voluntary learning have a greater range of motives than surveys sometimes suggest. Research into participation occasionally contradicts widely-held assumptions. Hedoux' survey in French mining communities disclosed that 90% of working-class adults participating in education in their leisure time were engaged in learning activities that were totally unrelated to their work or job-related concerns. In the UK, the Consett education scheme for redundant steel workers also confounded expectations: although participants generally cited retraining or the financial allowance as their motives for enrolment, many eschewed the purely vocational activities and became engaged in a whole range of general and more academically-demanding learning options (Holmes and Storrie, 1985). In a more recent survey of participation at six ILEA adult education institutes (Bird and Varlaam, 1987), 25% of students cited job-related reasons for participation, while the majority, many of them working-class, ethnic minority and educationally deprived, stated interest in a subject as the major reason for participating. In the Scottish survey (Munn and MacDonald, 1988), 41% of respondents also cited a personal interest or hobby as their main reason for participation. This confirms another of Cross's (1981) findings: that people are increasingly engaging in education for interest and personal development.

While stated motives obviously correspond to a large extent to the type of educational activities sought, it is possible that instrumental motives predominate in survey responses because of a limited view among the public of the scope of post-school education. It is also clear that some people express instrumental motives to justify participation to friends, relatives or co-workers. Male respondents in particular tend to cite instrumental motives. This may be due partly to an awareness of the link between employment and educational level, and partly to the need to conform to accepted male behavioural norms. In some sections of the community it is not regarded as normal behaviour for men to participate in education without a clear employment-related aim. When actually participating, however, many rapidly develop other interests and put more stress on personal self-development and recreational motives.

Patterns of motivation

Existing research shows that motivations vary according to age and gender: younger adults and men learn mostly for employment-related reasons, while older adults and women learn more for personal satisfaction, self-development, leisure purposes and family or role transitions (Aslanien and Bricknell, 1980). The evidence also suggests that there is some correlation between socio-economic circumstances and learning choice, with disadvantaged groups tending to be found on lower level, non-advanced courses.

Theories of Participation

The reasons for participation, according to Beder and Valentine (1987), are complex and multi-dimensional and often not reducible to a single motivation. Most explanations of participation involve the interaction of external (environmental, situational) and internal (dispositional) factors. There are a number of well-known theories. As most of these are described in detail elsewhere (e.g. Scanlan, 1986), the following is a brief and far from exhaustive summary of some of the best known.

Needs hierarchy theory

According to theorists such as Miller (1967), participation and non-participation depend on the extent to which an individual has been able to meet a range of primary and secondary needs and the influence of positive and negative forces. As one's socio-economic status improves, basic primary needs are met, higher level needs are activated, and the ratio of negative to positive forces declines. This leads to a situation conducive to engagement in educational or other activities.

Congruence model

Theorists such as Boshier (1971) have suggested that participation is more likely to result if there is some congruence between the learner's view of him/herself (self-concept) and the nature of the education programme and the educational environment.

Force-field theory

According to this theory, people who participate in adult learning believe they are capable of learning and value the outcomes of learning which they see as relevant to their personal needs. Rubenson (1977) proposed that motivation results from an interaction of "expectancy" and "valence". "Expectancy" refers to expectations of success in learning and its positive consequences; "valence" refers to the total sum of positive or negative values an individual assigns to learning activities. Both expectancy and valence are determined by an individual's previous experiences, social environment and personal needs.

Life transitions theory

A number of studies find that the decision to participate frequently coincides with changes in life circumstances. Aslanian and Bricknell (1980) found that over 80% of a large American sample were learning because their lives were changing in some way. British studies have also often found that the proportion of participants in organised education who have experienced life change, such as divorce or bereavement, is high in relation to their numbers in the general population.

Reference group theory

This theory maintains that individuals identify with the social and cultural group to which they belong – "normative" reference group (NRG) – or with another to which they aspire to belong – "comparative" reference group (CRG). Habitual participants usually belong to an NRG that is positively oriented to education. They are likely to have had parents, relations, neighbours or friends who have taken part in learning or who have positive attitudes to education. Several researchers refer to the same phenomenon using other terms, for example "learning press" (Darkenwald and Merriam, 1982).

Other people participate in education in order to achieve the perceived advantages of a group to which they do not belong. A comparative reference group presents a contrast to an individual's personal situation, creating what Gooderham (36) refers to as "a sense of relative deprivation". Individuals with upwardly mobile socio-economic aspirations use the values, standards and attitudes of a comparative reference group to evaluate or change their own socio-economic situation. CRGs may be provided by the mass media, the local neighbourhood or colleagues, but, according to Gooderham, the most potent example is marriage, with women in particular seeking education to keep up with better qualified partners.

According to reference group theory, elements within an adult's current social situation may be a more decisive determinant of participation than comparable elements located in pre-adult years. Anderson and Darkenwald (1979) also believe that an individual's *current* situation should be given more emphasis in attempts to explain participation behaviour. Their analysis of the American National Educational Statistics Database for 1975 revealed that, in contrast to most research findings, factors such as sex, race and initial schooling accounted for only about 10% of variance between participants and non-participants. In view of this, they suggest that participation needs to be explained according to "more sophisticated personal or situational variables".

Social participation

A number of other commentators maintain that participation in education should be explained with greater reference to social participation in general. Cookson (37) criticises participation theories for their restriction to a purely educational context; their "narrow psychological view of reality"; and lack of comprehensive, integrative theories or models. He argues that research should make greater reference to broader social behaviour, as does Courtney (38), who contends that, like most forms of social participation, educational participation is bound up with factors such as occupational status and income which define an individual's standing in the community. Although variables such as age, sex, marital status and place of residence play their part, educational participation is related to the "perceptions of power and self-worth mediated through the instrumentality of those variables".

Composite theories

There are a number of composite participation theories or models which integrate some of the theories mentioned above, and which purport to show how a variety of different factors in an individual's pre-adult and adult life interact to promote readiness to participate. Most of the models have some features in common.

"Chain of response" model. Cross's well-known "Chain of Response" model (Cross, 1981) incorporates elements from a number of theoretical frameworks in a seven-stage process which starts with the individual and ends with external influences. The seven stages are perceived as interacting links in a chain. The more positive the learner's experience at each stage, the more likely he or she is to reach the last stage – the decision to participate.

1. Learner's own self-evaluation.
2. Learner's attitude to education.
3. Motivation to learn (goals and the expectation that these will be met).
4. Life transitions.
5. Opportunities and barriers.
6. Information on educational opportunities.
7. The decision to participate.

Recruitment paradigm. Rubenson (1977) proposed a recruitment paradigm in which there are three sets of interacting variables, in the following order of importance:

☐ personal variables (prior experiences, personal attributes, current needs) and environmental factors (control over one's situation, reference groups, study possibilities)
☐ "active preparedness": perception and interpretation of the environment; the experience of individual needs
☐ the perceived value of an educational activity (valence) and the probability of being able to participate in and benefit from it (expectancy).

Psychosocial interaction model. Darkenwald and Merriam (1982) proposed a similar sequence of interacting variables which influence participation or non-participation:

☐ early individual and family characteristics
☐ preparatory education and socialisation
☐ socio-economic status
☐ "learning press" (the extent to which current social or working environment requires or encourages further learning)
☐ perceived value/utility of adult education
☐ readiness to participate
☐ specific stimuli
☐ barriers to participation.

Combination of favourable circumstances. French researchers have also come to the conclusion that participation is most likely when there is a combination and interaction of specifically favourable circumstances and conditions. De Montlibert (1973) contends that only people with a long initial schooling, advantageous professional status, and an entourage with a positive orientation towards education manage to break the "logic which leads to disparities in access to education". Hedoux (1981) adds two other favourable conditions: a "dynamic of upward social mobility" offering future change, and involvement in a range of social and community activities. But he argues that participation will only ensue if, in addition to these favourable circumstances, individuals:

☐ perceive a need for education/training in their social, professional or non-professional domains
☐ know that courses are provided which will respond to that need
☐ are ready and prepared to formulate a future learning project (which implies some degree of anticipation and control over the future)
☐ possess enough social and spatial autonomy and free time to participate

☐ possess sufficient basic skills in the area of education chosen to face a group learning situation.

Hedoux contends that the number of people likely to enrol diminishes with each of these conditions, and, in consequence, relatively few non-participants are potential participants. This gloomy prognosis is perhaps over-pessimistic. In this country, there are numerous examples of learning programmes which have succeeded in recruiting individuals from the identified non-participant categories. The methods used to attract them are explored in Section 2.

References

1. Courtney, S. The factors affecting participation in adult education: an analysis of some literature. *Studies in Adult Education,* 13,2, pp104–5, 1981.
2. Usher, R. & Bryant, I. *Adult Education as Theory, Practice and Research: The captive triangle.* Routledge, 1989, p106.
3. FEU *Marketing Adult Continuing Education.* FEU, 1987.
4. Munn, P. & MacDonald, C. *Adult Participation in Education and Training.* SCRE, 1988.
5. Woodley, A. *et al. Choosing to Learn: Adults in education.* SRHE/Open University Press, 1987, p85.
6. Advisory Council for Adult and Continuing Education *Adults: Their educational experience and needs.* ACACE, 1982, p58.
7. Alloway, J. & Nelson, P. *Advice and Guidance to Individuals.* SIACE/UDACE, 1987.
8. Woodley *et al., op. cit.,* p5.
9. Wiltshire, H. Quoted in *The WEA and the Black Communities.* WEA, 1987.
10. Advisory Council for Adult and Continuing Education *Continuing Education: From policies to practice.* ACACE, 1982, p22.
11. Hedoux, J. Des publics et des non-publics de la formation d'adultes: Sallaumines-Noyelles-sous-Lens des 1972. *Revue Francaise Sociologique,* Avril–Juin, pp253-274, 1982 (citations translated by researcher).
12. West, L. Challenging the WEA: crisis, learning and purpose. *Workers Education,* 1,2, Autumn–Winter, pp7–11, 1987.
13. Organisation for Economic Co-operation and Development *Learning Opportunities for Adults: Participation in adult education.* OECD, 1977.
14. Johnstone, J.W.C. & Rivera, R.J. *Volunteers for Learning: A study of the educational pursuits of American adults.* Aldine Publishing Co., 1965, p231.
15. Organisation for Economic Co-operation and Development *Learning Opportunities for Adults: The non-participation issue.* OECD, 1979, p111.

16. Hedoux, *op. cit.*; and Hedoux, J. Les non-publics de la formation collective. *Education Permanente,* 61, Decembre, pp89–105, 1981.

17. Osborn, M. Withnall, A. & Charnley, A.H. *Review of Existing Research in Adult and Continuing Education: Volume 3, The disadvantaged.* NIACE, 1980.

18. Rubenson, K. *Old and New Barriers for Participation. Occasional Papers of the Dutch Open University,* 1, p30, 1986.

19. Darkenwald G.G. *Comparison of Deterrents to Adult Education Participation in Britain and the United States.* SCUTREA, 1988.

20. Daines, J.B., Elsey, B. & Gibbs, M. *Changes in Student Participation in Adult Education.* University of Nottingham, 1982.

21. ALF *Report on Adult Education in Newcastle-upon-Tyne.* Adult Learning Federation, 1987; and Percy, K. *Post-initial Education in the North-west of England: A survey of provision.* ACACE, 1983.

22. Mee, G. & Wiltshire, H. *Structure and Performance in Adult Education.* Longman, 1978.

23. Van Enckevort, H. *From Old to New Barriers for Participation. Occasional Papers of the Dutch Open University,* 55, 1986.

24. O'Shea, J. & Corrigan, P. Surviving adult education. *Adult Education,* 52,4, p229, 1979.

25. *See* Jones, D. *Access to the Arts: Adult education and cultural development.* Routledge, 1988.

26. Woodley *et al., op. cit.,* p168.

27. Schuller, T. *Education Through Life.* Fabian Society, 1978, p25.

28. Lewis, L. An issue of support. *International Journal of Lifelong Education,* 4,2, pp163–176, 1988.

29. McDonald, J. *Education for Unemployed Adults.* DES. 1984.

30. Darkenwald, G.G. & Valentine, T. Factor structure of deterrents to public participation in adult education. *Adult Education Quarterly,* 35,4, Summer, 1985.

31. Scanlan, C.L. *Deterrents to Participation: An adult education dilemma.* National Center for Research in Vocational Education, Ohio State University, 1986, p23.

32. Hedoux, J. *op. cit.,* 1982.

33. Beder, H. & Valentine, T. *Iowa's Basic Education Students: Descriptive profiles based on motivation, cognitive ability and socio-demographic variables.* Department of Education, Iowa, 1987.

34. Cookson, P.S. The nature of the knowledge base of adult education: the example of participation. *Educational Considerations V,* XIV, 1987.

35. Percy, K. *et al. Learning in Voluntary Organisations.* UDACE, 1988, p58.

36. Gooderham, P. Reference group theory and adult education. *Adult Education Quarterly,* 37,3, Spring, pp140–151, 1987.

37. Cookson, P.S. *op. cit.*

38. Courtney, S. *op. cit.*

Section 2

Access for Non-Participant Groups: Stages, Issues and Approaches

This section utilises primary and secondary sources of information obtained through surveys, interviews, case studies and the literature search to investigate the different stages at which access to education might be improved for specific groups. It explores the views and experience of a range of education providers and some of the approaches which they have employed to attract a greater cross-section of the community.

Why Increase Participation?

The question is often posed: why try to increase participation among groups who ostensibly have little or no interest in engaging in any forms of organised education? A variety of arguments for widening adult access have been put forward. They can be summarised under the following headings.

Equity and social justice

☐ A system which benefits only a small section of the community is unjustifiable. Educational opportunities should be open to everybody who wants them.

☐ Many people are not achieving their full potential: education offers people the chance to improve their life-styles and life chances.

☐ Positive action is needed to compensate people for previous educational disadvantage.

☐ It is essential to end the "negative intergenerational cycle" whereby parents with negative perceptions of education and low levels of educational attainment pass on negative perceptions and attitudes to their children, who, in turn, become parents with low levels of education and pass negative attitudes on to their children.

Pragmatism/Expediency

☐ Changing demographic patterns require educational adjustments: we need to train older adults to fill labour shortages caused by dwindling numbers of younger workers; to fill places in further and higher education that would normally be taken by younger entrants; and to find fulfilling opportunities for the growing numbers of elderly people in the population who otherwise might be using up scarce health resources.

☐ Access to continuing education is necessary to help people adapt to rapidly changing work and life-style patterns:

> *Society is moving away from the "linear life-plan", in which education is for the young, work for the middle-aged and leisure for the elderly, to a "blended life- plan", in which education, work and leisure continue concurrently throughout life ... adults will need to focus on successful transitioning – transitions from school to work, work to leisure, on-the-job transitions, and transitions from work to no work and / or retraining (1).*

National self-interest

☐ We have far fewer people participating in education or training after school than other industrial countries and we may lose out to our overseas competitors because we have an under-educated, inadequately trained population.

☐ Investment in human capital can lead to an increase in productivity and material gains.

☐ Involving more people in education is preferable to paying out welfare benefits.

Not everyone is convinced by these arguments. It is often stated that education by itself can do little to solve the inequalities in society. Moreover, some adult and further education staff interviewed during the project argued that it is not worth trying to correct imbalances in participation since there is little evidence of demand from the non-participant groups. They maintained that it would be arrogant to "thrust" education at groups who regard it as irrelevant. Others expressed the view that since adult and further education opportunities are open to everyone, no special recruitment measures are necessary. Some people find the arguments to increase participation spurious, suspecting that the real motive behind them is to secure jobs and services.

> *Because participation in adult education is, in the main, voluntary then all those with an investment in the area are anxious about increasing it (2).*

Potential Participants

> *The population contains three aggregates of individuals: those*

*interested in learning and favorably disposed toward taking courses;
those interested in learning but not prepared to take courses; and those
uninterested in learning anything (3).*

According to surveys of public attitudes and perceptions, there is some
evidence of an untapped demand for education. According to the ACACE
survey (1982a), 61% of respondents expressed an interest in future
participation. The published report of the survey, *Adults: Their educational
experience and needs*, estimated that there was an appreciable latent demand
for educational activities among non-participants, and identified two specific
groups of potential participants: working-class individuals who want to
improve their employment prospects (IPA groups D and C2) and people in
groups A, B and C1 who wish to improve their general culture or follow
personal interests.

The more recent Scottish survey (1988) is less optimistic:

*Attracting back into education and training those who have not
previously participated in it will be difficult. Our data do not suggest
that there is a latent demand among non-returners (4).*

Although 25% of "non-returners" in the Scottish sample expressed an
interest in educational opportunities, only 8% were identified as "potential
returners" (people who had made enquiries about courses but not
participated). The majority of individuals in the Scottish potential returner
category have features in common with actual participants: that is, they tend
to be young (under 35), in social class AB, and motivated mainly by job-related
interests. Their major constraint is time.

Another survey, *Marketing Adult Continuing Education* (FEU, 1987),
found potential participants predominantly among the younger adult cohorts,
and two of the groups identified were part-time workers and unemployed
people. This survey found that the people least likely to be recruited are the
retired, the elderly, housewives, and people in social classes D and E: a
conclusion also reached by Hedoux (1982) during his research in France.
Hedoux assessed the recruitment potential of four "radical" non-participant
groups – older adults, unwaged married women, unskilled manual workers
and younger qualified or skilled workers. Since participation in voluntary
learning is related to the ability to anticipate and control one's own future,
Hedoux concluded that recruitment is unlikely for older, non-working
populations, for non-qualified workers, and for certain married women unless
"big changes take place in their working conditions or daily life". He concluded
that the fourth group – younger qualified or skilled workers – is the one most
likely to contain potential participants.

The groups identified as potential participants on the whole, and
unsurprisingly, share some of the **characteristics** of participants. However,

even these need special recruitment measures. Hedoux estimated that 13% of his potential participant sample might be persuaded to enrol, but only if new targeted programmes were developed or if there were some modification of existing courses. He warned that where the "radical" non-participant groups are concerned:

> The obstacles to access ... are usually too bound up with people's social situation and constraints in their daily life for pedagogical change alone to bring about enrolment.

As this implies, recruitment of non-participant groups requires substantial intervention by education providers.

The need for provider intervention

Outreach workers interviewed during the project argued that it is unrealistic to expect people with ambivalent attitudes to education and no post-school educational experience to articulate recognised learning needs. Moreover, as post-school educational opportunities are generally perceived to be for an affluent middle class, they will automatically be considered irrelevant or out-of-reach by large sections of the public. Some interviewees feared that economic realities might force this situation to continue. Their main worry was that the selective nature of adult education opportunities would be reinforced as services are increasingly required to cover costs or raise revenue: a situation which could lead to services for adults being taken over by entrepreneurial private providers with more interest in profit than questions of equity. This concern has also been expressed by practitioners in the US:

> If a broad social effort is not made to acknowledge the desirability of lifelong learning, and adult education is left to entrepreneurs, the tendency to cater to affluent well-educated adults will determine the kind of educational opportunities which will be available (5).

One provider propounded what he termed the "new realist" view: post-school educational opportunities will remain predominantly selective and the most practical approach might be to examine ways of making the existing system more relevant and appropriate for currently under-represented groups. The problem with this strategy is that it may only result in the recruitment of some well-motivated individuals. To attract the "radical" non-participants requires financial subsidies and significant intervention and changes in practice by education providers. Currently, however, the system operates largely from the assumption that all adults are self-directed and in possession of the attributes that lead to participation.

The Different Stages of Access

This leads to a question of definitions: does increasing access mean attracting new groups to existing programmes or developing new provision especially for them? The answer is both. Each of the non-participant populations is composed of several sub-groups with different educational experience and attitudes to learning:

A. Individuals without qualifications and post-school educational experience, who perceive education as totally irrelevant.

B. Individuals who would like to participate, but have not done anything about it or have not gone beyond making enquiries.

C. Individuals who have participated at some stage and would like further experience but are unsure which direction to take.

D. Individuals who have been involved in the same course repeatedly, year after year.

Group A contains the hardest-to-reach non-participants. Few individuals in this group take up existing opportunities. To attract this group, special programmes and recruitment measures need to be devised. Group B contains most of the "potential participants" discussed above. Some of these can be drawn into existing opportunities as the system becomes more flexible and more responsive to non-traditional adult learners, and the indications are that many of the programmes designed to attract Group A succeed primarily in recruiting members of this group. Groups C and D require specific intervention and support measures *within* the system, e.g. institutional strategies such as guidance to assist their progression to further learning opportunities.

Thus, depending on the group concerned, different measures to assist access are required at different stages. The fact that whole sections of the community do not participate suggests that particular efforts should be directed, as a priority, at members of Group A with particular attention to the first stages of access: targeting, contact in the community, consultation and negotiation.

Access stage 1: Targeting

The principle of market segmentation – dividing the population into relevant sub-groups – runs counter to the undifferentiated, single approach to recruitment traditionally operated by many educational institutions. However, special targeting is essential if opportunities are to be extended to those groups and individuals who are most educationally deprived and who experience a huge cultural divide between their norms and values and those reflected in the education system.

There are certain problems associated with targeting: it is more costly than responding to a known and available market; targeted initiatives often have to rely on external funding, with the result that they may be largely peripheral to mainstream education; special targeting may be at the expense of other equally deserving groups; some people may not wish to be identified and labelled as members of a certain group. However, there is considerable evidence that targeting is an effective and equitable way of improving access for some groups in the community and it is already an established feature of some adult education practice, as reflected in the growth, in the last two decades, of basic education and English as a Second Language programmes, courses for women and the unemployed, Second Chance to Learn and Access (to higher education) courses.

Analysis of sub-groups. Targeting requires a broad knowledge of the groups concerned based on analysis of their needs (overt and latent), motivating factors, constraints, attitudes, values and perceptions. Many providers now conduct surveys of local needs, but new programmes based on these are sometimes not enough to bring about large-scale recruitment of hard-core non-participants. Newly-created introductory programmes often chiefly benefit an "active minority": people who are already involved in the community, have a positive attitude to education and are materially able to participate. Thus recruitment strategies need to be based on a clear understanding of the diverse and interacting factors that act as deterrents to the majority. Many practitioners interviewed during this project were fully aware of the situational and institutional problems of access faced by different client groups, recognising that with sufficient flexibility and resources, some of these could be eliminated. But they have frequently found that removal of practical barriers does not automatically lead to enrolments. Cost, for example, is frequently identified as a major deterrent, which implies that reduction or elimination of fees will increase participation. The evidence does not always support this assumption. Many campaigns to recruit groups such as the unemployed to free learning activities have met with failure. The reason for this could be that cost is a readily-understood, face-saving reason for a lack of interest that really stems from a number of powerful dispositional constraints. Thus, although there are a whole range of practical measures that providers and institutions could implement to attract and support new clienteles, the real challenge is to address the mesh of inter-related attitudes, perceptions and misconceptions which prevent many people from considering education as an option.

Dealing with dispositional barriers. It has been observed (Scanlan, 1986) that the major dispositional factors that impede participation are negative and characterised by *absence* of something. This is borne out by the fact that non-participants frequently lack:

☐ confidence and self-esteem
☐ trust in the system
☐ perspectives on the future
☐ awareness of opportunities
☐ "educational preparedness" (communication skills, basic education skills, etc.).

This suggests that, in order to increase recruitment among the *radical* non-participants, education providers need to concentrate on supplying the missing elements *in addition* to addressing practical obstacles to access such as intimidating enrolment procedures, inappropriate timing, formal locations and costs. The difficulty is that attitudes and perceptions need to be tackled at the recruitment stage, and this requires very careful preparatory work in the community.

Access stage 2: Contact and communication

The experience of education organisers who have targeted programmes at specific groups (for example *Action Formation Collective* programmes in France and Second Chance programmes in England designed for people in working-class communities) is that they attract a minority of well-motivated individuals already active in other areas of life. To attract individuals from the majority requires addressing, at first contact stage, some of the ingrained attitudes and perceptions engendered by social and economic background and circumstances. Essentially this means persuading people to perceive education as something useful and relevant with benefits that justify expenditure of time, money and effort. Messages about learning opportunities, therefore, need simultaneously to convey positive images of learning and address negative attitudes: a dual aim that cannot be achieved through publicity alone. People who are suspicious of education and unaware of any personal learning needs will neither respond to promotional materials nor approach places and services connected with the education system: "One of the main reasons that groups are hard-to-reach is that they don't respond to the normal marketing strategies employed by continuing educators" (6).

Personal approaches are now widely held to be the most effective and perhaps only means of reaching non-participants and overcoming their resistance to education and anything associated with it.

Outreach. Work with non-participant groups therefore requires a fundamental shift away from what has been termed the "come and get it approach" towards outreach methods. Outreach now has a long and respectable pedigree, thanks to the innovative community education approach of people like Freire and Lovett. It has been defined as a process:

whereby people who would not normally use adult education are contacted in non-institutional settings and become involved in attending, and eventually in jointly planning and controlling activities, schemes and courses relative to their circumstances and needs (7).

There is ample evidence that direct personal approaches can result in enrolments from non-participant sections of the community. However, few outreach workers underestimate the difficulties involved. Larson (8) has identified the kinds of "interpersonal barriers" that may lead groups to reject attempts to persuade them to participate in learning:

☐ conflict in perceptions (people may not recognise or admit interests or needs)
☐ status discrepancy (older adults may find it threatening to accept information from younger ones; men from women; black from white, etc.)
☐ resistance to inappropriate language or dialect (outreach workers who use the wrong vocabulary and register will not be accepted).

As this implies, outreach workers need multiple attributes and skills: they need to share at least some of the characteristics of the target group (race, gender, cultural background) and speak the same language (dialect, register); they need considerable communication skills and should be good listeners as well as informants. They have to persuade individuals to see education as relevant to their circumstances, abilities and goals, without sounding patronising or giving the impression that groups are being offered what others think they need. Larson (1980) makes the point that acceptance of a (promotional) message depends on the extent to which it corresponds with one's own beliefs and values. The needs identified by education providers may not be those felt by targeted individuals and thus may have no motivational effect. The evidence generally supports this contention: in one example described to this project, a number of LEA courses organised in a shire county failed to attract take-up. In virtually all cases suggestions for these had emanated from providers and tutors. Programmes mounted after consultation on learning interests led to viable classes.

Networking and liaison. A primary role of outreach workers is to establish networks, liaise across agencies and to initiate or extend links between education providers and the community. The importance of this role is now widely recognised and many of the Local Authorities and education institutions contacted during the project had appointed community outreach or liaison workers. In one LEA with a community education policy, neighbourhood community workers are trained as facilitators whose principal task is: "to build up relationships in the community and to engage in a dialogue which will reveal expressed or perceived needs" (9). In some areas, a broad liaison role is being performed by guidance or special project workers whose aim is to bring together local education providers and people in the community. A REPLAN project leader interviewed in South Wales was acting as an effective intermediary – or communication channel – between specific groups of non-participant adults and a wide cross-section of local education providers: "People were able to discuss interests and needs with me but they wouldn't have requested things cold from providers."

Working with existing groups. A large proportion of people in the main non-participant categories "failed" in the school system. As a result, many have little confidence in their ability to learn and are reluctant to join activities as individuals. This was underlined in the surveys conducted for this project by the number of people, particularly older adults, who expressed a qualified interest in learning but said that they would not attend on their own. A typical comment was: "I would feel exposed".

Most of the outreach workers contacted during the research have found that non-participants are not easily recruited as individuals and it is considerably more effective (as well as less time-consuming) to approach groups, community centres and associations than to knock on doors. The Leeds Pioneer Work Project with the adult unemployed demonstrated that a community approach – working with existing neighbourhood or community groups and centres – can be very successful in attracting people not previously interested in education. Another advantage of consulting with existing groups, according to a community education tutor in South London, is that it often leads to viable programmes whereas responding to individual requests frequently does not: "The key to recruitment here is that people come as ready-made groups".

The powerful influence of peer and reference groups within certain sections of the community reinforces the argument for targeting groups rather than individuals. Attempts to attract ethnic minority groups, male industrial workers and working-class communities have often foundered because of reluctance to depart from established cultural and behavioural patterns. A survey conducted in Northamptonshire to investigate the attitudes and educational interests of people in manual and non-managerial occupations received "definite messages" about the influence of family and friends over the appropriateness or otherwise of attending education courses. Respondents would only envisage enrolling in education programmes when providers "had persuaded those who might prevent them from attending of the appropriateness of provision" (10). In such circumstances it is more practical to persuade groups, rather than individuals, of the relevance and advantages of attending learning activities. An experimental outreach programme in Sweden (FOVUX) demonstrated that far more people were recruited in the workplace where there was group targeting of a powerful reference group – male manual workers – than in private housing areas where recruitment was directed at individuals.

Many of the adult education providers contacted during the project employ a group recruitment strategy. At Northern College, for example, group or collective education is central to the college ethos. A team of short course organisers, working jointly with the institution and its supporting LEAs, negotiate special programmes with groups such as pensioners, women's groups and people from ethnic minorities. A large number of education-providing voluntary organisations also target groups. One of the voluntary groups contacted, Exploring Parenthood, which provides support and informal learning activities for parents, specifically aims much of its work at groups such as single parents and ethnic minorities.

Reaching the hard-to-reach non-participants. Many educationally disadvantaged individuals are isolated and not involved in community activities or groups. As a result, reaching them requires lengthy and patient groundwork involving approaches to other agencies and "key" individuals. It may be politically, as well as practically, impossible to bypass those people who are already in contact with the individuals concerned. Thus, reaching the radical non-participants often involves a "multiplier" effect as outreach workers develop ever-widening links in the community. This process was described by a REPLAN development worker in Wales:

> It's a question of using "influential" people in the community. I targeted an estate in a rural area. I spoke to community education staff, councillors, Open University staff, then community groups, church leaders, people in schools. It was a matter of "snowball" links reaching into communities – from senior managers down through community workers. It took me 10 to 20 days to reach the people we eventually did a course with.

Getting past the gatekeepers. The director of a voluntary organisation observed that liaising with key individuals requires more skills than the subsequent educational work which "any competent adult educator could do". The most important skill required is the ability to negotiate with the "gatekeepers":

> They can be group leaders, headteachers, school councillors. They have the power to let you in or not. They have views about themselves and others, what people do or don't do, what they want or don't want, and

this often has a lot to do with their own problems. They may feel their own status or position is threatened when outsiders come in. Sometimes they won't let us in and members of the groups have had to contact us secretly!

Similar experiences were reported by a number of interviewees. Attempts by LEA workers to set up learning programmes for elderly women in sheltered accommodation in Derbyshire had been thwarted by the warden:

If we went to speak to them direct we got protests from wardens. If we gave information to the wardens it didn't get distributed. It's not easy to break down these barriers. It's a power thing.

This view was confirmed by a community education worker in Coventry who related how efforts to organise learning activities collaboratively with local voluntary groups had been frustrated by community leaders: "Certain people may say they want to collaborate but in fact they put every obstacle in your way because they don't want to lose power".

ALBSU outreach workers targeting ethnic minority communities in Bedfordshire experienced similar problems negotiating with individuals who had their own ideas on what the community required:

On some occasions it was felt that the views expressed were personal to the community leader, e.g. "we don't need any adult education" ... On other occasions it was felt that a community leader was talking about what HE wanted members of the group to have in the way of provision ... without giving any evidence of consultation. Some community leaders didn't appear to consult their members at all, relying entirely on a small group of people forming some kind of executive committee (11).

Recruiting agents. There was also evidence, however, that once persuaded of the value of proposed learning activities, gatekeepers can become very effective recruiting agents. Some of the work with the elderly described to the project had been enthusiastically promoted by wardens and nursing staff in residential homes and day-care centres. Women's participation in first stage learning activities has often been encouraged by nursery head teachers, social services staff and health visitors.

The effectiveness of using community leaders as recruiting agents is well known. A national study of urban basic education programmes in the United States (Mezirow, Darkenwald and Knox, 1975) found that 40% of programmes had used local community personnel – social workers, teachers, religious leaders – as recruiters, a recruitment strategy which proved to be highly successful. Religious leaders are currently being used in the US as recruiting agents for literacy programmes, particularly in the black communities.

An even more effective strategy is to use members of the target groups themselves in recruitment campaigns. As a development worker in Yorkshire observed: "Members of existing groups possess what adult educators often lack – familiarity and credibility." This was confirmed by the experience of a community education worker in Birmingham:

> *The more motivated individuals in the community affect the behaviour of others. They are the people who respond to professionals but the others will be drawn in only by them.*

For this reason Larson (1980) recommends that adult education organisers identify the opinion leaders within target groups. These he describes as individuals who influence the establishment of norms and have greater freedom than others in violating norms. They reflect the basic orientation of their groups but are readier to accept new ideas and are more open and cosmopolitan in outlook. Larson proposes that such people should be invited to join advisory groups where they can contribute to decisions about programme goals and methods. They can then communicate this information to their families, friends and co-workers. However, Larson warns against identifying the wrong people. He points out that those chosen on the basis of their formal status in a group may lack the power to influence group opinion. The most innovative members of a group often have low status within it precisely because of their frequent departure from accepted norms (12).

Access stage 3: Consultation and negotiation

> *The missing link is development work ... educational needs and wants require stimulation and assessment through education awareness campaigns and a dialogue between educator and potential student (13).*

The extent to which the traditional adult education curriculum acts as an obstacle to greater participation is rarely investigated but it is clear that subjects associated with middle-class interests and life-styles (hostess cookery) or which seem over-specialised or intellectual (archaeology) will deter large sections of the community. A community education worker observed that staff in education institutions: "constantly underestimate the amount of work needed to get people to the point where they will voluntarily take up learning opportunities." To involve new groups in learning requires patient consultation and negotiation of *their* learning interests and requirements – a process which experienced development workers insist must take place on a basis of mutual equality. The aim of the Leeds Pioneer Work Project was not to offer people an existing package:

But to establish dialogue so that the project and people could jointly decide what contribution, if any, adult education could make to their situation. This process is sometimes referred to rather narrowly as "identifying learner needs" with the assumption that adult educators can then meet them ... Individuals and groups in the community already have much experience and expertise, and the need is to marry this up with whatever contribution adult education can make. This involves a more equal partnership than is implied by the phrase "identifying learner needs" (14).

The consensus among outreach workers interviewed during this research was that all aspects of the learning process should be negotiated in advance: not just the form and nature of provision but methods of delivery, styles of learning, modes of attendance and evaluation. Many stressed the importance of spelling out the anticipated outcomes and benefits of participation. An outreach worker with the unemployed reported that the men he had contacted were sceptical about the benefits of informal education, described by some as "just sitting round chatting". A survey of perceptions and attitudes among working people in Northamptonshire underlined this point: "People want definite outcomes from participation whether it be qualifications or more out of life. Activities must be purposeful and not titillation" (15). An American practitioner contends that providers who fail to address the "augmented element" of education (its meaning, worth and relevance) "may unknowingly be creating perceptions of questionable worth or relevance among prospective learners" (16).

Thus recruitment of non-participant individuals and groups depends, to a significant extent, on the way in which learning activities are initially presented. People with less than happy memories of compulsory schooling and who have ambivalent or hostile attitudes to education can be suspicious of the motives of those attempting to involve them in learning – especially if such attempts imply that they are intellectually or socially inferior or deficient. The language used in initial contacts is therefore of crucial importance. According to one community outreach worker: "You have to drop the word *education*. The moment you use it you get a resistance."

A REPLAN-funded initiative to develop informal learning opportunities in South Wales also avoided making direct references to education. The project worker sought instead to identify people's main interests and preoccupations. He discovered that the groups contacted – women with young children, people on isolated housing estates, long-term unemployed men – had a number of primary concerns. Informal discussion of these led, in many cases, to the recognition and articulation of learning needs and eventually to the negotiation of specially-tailored learning programmes:

I went to a working-class estate and befriended people, got them to talk about their worries and grievances. I discovered that they wanted to use their hands. This led to the setting up of a craft course and the identification of other potential learning groups. If we had advertised a craft course first, they wouldn't have come! I start with their concerns. I don't mention education or learning. It's a simplistic notion to go knocking on doors saying "I'm working for the education service; what do you want?" Get people to articulate their concerns before you decide what you offer. You need to get fundamental questions right first and get people to reach decisions for themselves through a programme of negotiation. We take real-life circumstances and mould education to them, then we come up with a specification sheet. In Monmouth I spoke a lot to people setting up a tenants' group. Eventually they articulated some needs – holding meetings, fund-raising, balancing books, understanding local government, etc. I enabled them to set up a course when and where they needed it. In Ebbw Vale there were older long-term unemployed. A field worker had 15 days to parachute in there to reach them and learn their ideas and concerns. A traditional activity for older men is allotments. He spoke to the chairman of the allotment society and encouraged him to bring his mates along for a chat. Their crisis was that the local Borough Council has relinquished responsibility for allotments and associated land and the men have been asked to form themselves into an Association and manage it themselves. They used the meeting with us to air their fears. They are horticulturalists but have no management skills. They identified the areas they needed help with so our involvement will be in that area we're negotiating to get a menu tailored for them in the community education centre. In Pontypool we negotiated with people on the Enterprise Allowance Scheme and this led to a series of one-day schools held locally on topics such as book-keeping.

This approach is very similar to the one employed in the Leeds Pioneer Work Project, where it was also found that, among the targeted groups:

No one was interested in "Adult Education" explicitly ... there was, however, much interest and detailed discussion about other major issues in the area which affected their lives – welfare rights, housing, the environment ... consultation with the local authority, organisational and group issues for tenants' associations (17).

Similarly, an LEA with a community education policy uses negotiation of primary concerns as the basis for programme development:

They may raise issues such as poverty and unemployment, lack of amenities, housing, transport, needs of the elderly, disabled or single parent families ... Learning opportunities emerge from the dialogue and may be supplied by informal adult education techniques (18).

Access stage 4: Programme development

The project confirmed the well-established principle that the starting point for outreach consultation is: "Working from where people are; using their environment, issues and concerns as a basis for development" (19). Thus the first step that takes someone from being non-participant to participant is often more to do with personal, social and economic needs than any recognised learning needs, and people may not want or expect an educational outcome. It is well known that many people engage in learning as a result of involvement in non-educational activities such as community action. Given the widespread tendency to come to learning by an indirect route, it is not surprising that informal learning in non-educational venues is frequently not recognised or acknowledged as learning. What *is* surprising, however, is the vehemence with which adults who have enrolled in explicitly educational programmes also refuse to view their activities as educational. A WEA worker who conducted a survey of participants in a range of development courses (see pages 53–59) reported that respondents used tortuous turns of phrase to avoid describing what they were doing as learning. The problem arose from their inability to reconcile activities which they were finding interesting and enjoyable with their notion of education as something formal, compulsory and not, on the whole, enjoyable. Once this semantic hurdle has been overcome – which can take some time – new participants are able to accept that education can have different forms and styles. Indeed, participation in negotiated learning activities can often change attitudes and perceptions of education far more effectively than anything else, as Fraser and Ward found in their work with the unemployed: "The course helped demystify and open up the idea of adult education in an area where traditional attitudes to education range from awe to apathy" (20).

Expressed interests. Among non-participant sections of the community, recognised and stated educational interests often reflect instrumental aims. Many surveys, including the ones conducted for this project, reveal a clear demand from three groups, the unskilled, the unemployed and ethnic minority groups, for practical programmes, vocational courses, English for speakers of another language and basic education courses. However, investigations of local learning needs sometimes yield confused and contradictory messages: some people express the interests they feel are appropriate or expected of them while others express limited interests because their experience and perceptions of education are limited. As a result, programmes developed in response to expressed interests sometimes have no take-up. A number of providers have also found a contradiction between individual demands and eventual learning choice: i.e. the courses requested are not those which are subsequently followed. Several interviewees have noticed that instrumental motives sometimes diminish in importance during participation. This can lead to apparent discrepancies between stated motivations and learning destinations, as found in a small informal survey conducted for the research in Essex where 70 first-time participants in a range of LEA programmes were asked about their reasons for attending. Responses were anonymous and no personal interviewing was involved which eliminated the risk of respondents' answering in a "socially acceptable" way. Although roughly half of the classes involved were qualification-based or specifically occupational (typing, shorthand, book-keeping, A-level courses), less than 25% of respondents actually cited instrumental or work-related aims, or 30% if one counts those wishing to gain qualifications or improve existing skills. However, 50% claimed to be involved for pleasure or out of interest in the subject.

The evidence as a whole indicates that the question of expressed learning interests is complex and, although a genuine demand for practical programmes exists, it would be unwise to consider programming in purely instrumental terms. Many LEA outreach staff stressed the need for diversity in first stage provision, although some felt this was precluded by funding arrangements. A guidance worker targeting groups which were not using existing provision expressed concern at the limited learning options available to people with low educational attainment and qualifications:

> *There's a lack of general education opportunities such as looking at society or modern history or the causes of unemployment. This is because a lot of short-term work has to be justified economically and, therefore, has an instrumental orientation.*

A concern expressed by several tutors in short, work-related programmes is that people enrol with high expectations that are frequently dashed: "One day a week for six weeks can't change the reality of bleak employment prospects." Moreover, it would grotesquely emasculate the role of education to present it solely as a means of helping people into jobs, although the general tendency of external funding agencies has been in that direction.

Several outreach workers maintained that the content of first stage learning programmes was less important than the process: "It doesn't really matter what we put on as long as we get them in and started on the learning process" (community education worker, Coventry). Most people working with non-traditional adult students also stressed the overwhelming importance of:

☐ acknowledging and using people's experience in learning programmes

☐ encouraging experiential learning: helping groups to learn through organising their own activities.

This view was allied to the notion of informal learning as a route not to acquisition of formal knowledge, but to personal or collective "empowerment".

Programme aims. Informal learning activities developed with the groups most alienated from education tend to have multiple goals, among which increasing personal or collective effectiveness is often considered the most important. Freire (1971) proposed that educators should raise self-awareness to the point where people will establish their own goals and devise means of obtaining them. Much of the outreach work initiated with non-participants aims to do this, first by encouraging people to take control of their own learning, second by helping them to explore the best available options for personal or collective progression. The new direction may not necessarily be educational:

> *Non-educational access is often equally if not more important for both the community and the individual. Involvement in community action or the establishment of some useful, relevant and enjoyable community activity, or the coming together of like minds over particular issues or concerns, are just as valid outcomes in educational terms as the conventional access ladder to a higher level formal educational setting (21).*

Informal first stage learning activities therefore differ significantly from formal education and training. Over and above dissemination of knowledge or training in skills, they aim to assist people to:

☐ develop a sense of self-worth
☐ value their own experience
☐ use individual experience to understand their situation and the world about them
☐ take more control of their own life
☐ make decisions and plan ahead
☐ be aware of available opportunities.

As these aims imply, there is a strong element of personal guidance and support in first stage learning which again differentiates it from conventional formal education. A tutor at Northern College referred to the "almost parental" counselling role staff adopt to support students who are learning for the first time as adults.

Access stage 5: Programme implementation

Certain conditions are now generally acknowledged as essential in work with people who have previously shunned formal education:

☐ flexibility of timing to suit those with family responsibilities
☐ informal learning environments in which people feel safe, comfortable and unthreatened
☐ programmes with low risk or threat levels
☐ sufficient time to master skills
☐ informal, participative and flexible learning methods
☐ support mechanisms (e.g. help with costs, childcare)
☐ tutors with a facilitating and enabling role.

Several tutors described the challenges they face in working with non-traditional learner groups. An outreach worker in Wales found that the composition of groups was in a state of constant flux: "There are groups within groups; we're not always dealing with the same people. New people are being brought along, others drop out." Tutors at a residential college have found their teaching abilities constantly stretched as group recruitment inevitably leads to mixed ability groups:

> When a group approaches us, such as ex-offenders, a rape crisis group, we can't separate out those with qualifications and those without. We get people who are illiterate and people who have done a lot of study in one group.

A community education tutor spoke of the difficulty of maintaining the right balance in groups between highly motivated people and the rest:

> It's like streaming where you get all low motivated ones together. You need more motivated members to raise general motivation. The balance is extremely important. If you get too many motivated ones the less motivated ones won't stay.

Several tutors have noticed how some groups maintain a lurking suspicion of their intentions and constantly put them and the providing institution to the test. At one residential college, for example, it has been found that students make great demands on tutors to prove the college's claim to be non-racist and non-sexist. However, it is generally found that new groups quickly make their mark on the educational environment. According to a tutor in an FE college with a traditionally male ethos: "This place has a different tone since we've had so many women coming in."

Many of the adult educators interviewed during the project testified to the rapid and positive changes that people undergo when they participate for the first time in informal group learning. As a short-course organiser in a residential college claimed: "They may be non-participants when they come but when they return to their communities they are participants in the broadest sense of the term."

Examples of First Stage Learning Opportunities

The research shows that initial opportunities for new adult learners are frequently, if not in the majority of cases, enabled by special project money and collaboration between a number of agencies. The European Social Fund (ESF) and the MSC (now Training Agency) have financed programmes for the unemployed and other adult groups under-represented in education. National programmes such as ALBSU and REPLAN have also encouraged the development and extension of learning opportunities for non-participant groups in many areas. In some cities, use of Urban Programme funds has had similar outcomes. During the time of the project, statutory and voluntary providers in the Bradford area were able to bid for finance from the Bradford Urban Programme Education and Training pool to mount short courses for disadvantaged groups and those not using existing provision. According to the fund administrator, this led to increased co-operation between sectors and education providers and the range of short-term opportunities for non-traditional adult students increased: "dramatically. Many developments would not have happened if the short-term money had not been available."

Example 1: Mobile services

Mobile units have proved a highly effective way of taking learning activities to people who cannot or will not take advantage of existing provision. They have been used to provide specific services for which a need has been identified (computer education, health education), or to supply groups such as the unemployed with general information and advice about education and training opportunities. In 1988, a variety of mobile units, supported by statutory and voluntary finance, were providing information, advice and educational activities to isolated or educationally disadvantaged groups: the Rock Community Bus in Birmingham, the "Need to Know" van and Dove Valley Community Bus in Derbyshire, the WHISE women's mobile service in Truro, "Columbus" in Fareham and Gosport, and a number of REPLAN-supported initiatives for unemployed people.

The Need to Know Project. The Need to Know project was a converted caravan providing information, homecraft and basic education skills in a number of urban and rural locations in Swadlincote. Originally funded as a pilot scheme by ALBSU and Derbyshire County Council, the project was eventually taken over by the County and, since the researcher's visit, has become a "Study Bus". The project's main aims were to provide a first point of contact and a basic education service for non-users of education services; to establish classes alongside mobile provision and to refer people to appropriate programmes elsewhere. With a seating area at one end, a children's play area at the other and a small kitchen for demonstrations in the middle, the van provided an informal and non-threatening environment in which people could learn and discuss problems. A stock of pamphlets and leaflets on a range of educational, social security and practical issues were always available for clients to take away with them.

Between 1985 and 1987 the van was visited by 334 people, mostly women aged 20-50, many of whom returned on a number of occasions and over 20% of whom joined education classes. The van was also used by elderly people who particularly wanted help with filling out forms. Motives for contacting the van fell into the following categories: cookery and homecraft skills/demonstrations, 50%; welfare rights, 20%; counselling 10%; social reasons, 10%; basic education, 10% (22).This suggests that the service was perceived primarily as a support to people in their everyday lives, providing further evidence of the importance of using everyday concerns as a starting point in outreach work.

The experience of Need to Know project workers illustrates the range of skills and flexibility required in reaching and providing a service for non-participant sections of the community. The main factors that have been identified as contributing to the project's effectiveness are:

INITIAL GROUNDWORK: "A contact period of six-seven months was required to build relationships to the point where people had sufficient trust to ask for things."

CONTACTS WITH LOCAL AGENCIES: "If people with *clout* don't know about you, life is much harder."

APPROPRIATE PARKING SITES: "Locations had to be reconsidered several times."

APPROPRIATE APPROACHES AND CONTACT POINTS IN EACH AREA.

NEUTRALITY: The van was not associated with any particular educational institution.

TIMING: The van was well used in the mornings but not afternoons, so times were adjusted accordingly.

CONTINUITY: The van was parked in shopping centres and other central venues for short periods during vacation times: "the more it was seen and used, the more people knew and passed the word on."

STAFF READINESS TO ABANDON PLANNED WORK: "Many roles have to be undertaken and at times we appeared to verge on that of teacher, counsellor, social worker, health visitor."

USE OF HOMECRAFT SKILLS TO ATTRACT WOMEN: "For many women with families these skills are the sole foundation on which their lives are built and are therefore a useful tool for identifying needs."

CARRYING A STOCK OF LIBRARY BOOKS: "This proved a useful point of contact and a good opener for conversation. Visitors coming to the van for this facility may not otherwise have called. Other information about the project was carried away and disseminated."

CONSTANT EVALUATION: "Experimentation and change has been the keystone. It would be easy to justify a repetitious pattern: the "just in case someone calls syndrome"."

MOVING ON TO "SPEARHEAD" IN ANOTHER AREA: "We only stay as long as we're needed otherwise we become a crutch."

THE PROJECT SUPPORT GROUP: raising morale and supplying advice and help.

GOOD WORKING RELATIONSHIPS WITH THE LOCAL DISTRICT COUNCIL WORKS DEPARTMENT: to help with breakdowns and maintenance.

The main problems identified by staff were (23):

TOWING AND REPAIR COSTS

CONSTRAINTS OF SIZE: making structured group teaching difficult.

INSUFFICIENT FINANCIAL FLEXIBILITY AND VIREMENT BETWEEN BUDGET HEADINGS.

LACK OF CONSTANT CONTACT POINTS

DIFFICULTIES WITH ATTRACTING MEN

CLIENTS' RELUCTANCE TO MAKE REGULAR COMMITMENTS

DIFFICULTY OF EXTENDING ACTIVITIES TO OTHER NEIGHBOURHOOD VENUES: "because we lost the secure atmosphere of the van."

DEPENDENCY: "If the caravan's not here we don't want anything."

Example 2: Group learning in the community – the OU–MSC Community Programme

In 1986 the Open University became a National Community Programme Agency, offering unemployed adults places in community education projects. The aim was to take educational opportunities to groups for whom access to education centres was difficult or impractical. Four hundred unemployed people were trained as group facilitators, their role being to encourage active participation in group learning, using distance-learning materials on topics related to everyday living.

The project led to the development of an impressive number of group learning schemes in different parts of the country, organised in collaboration with a variety of local voluntary and statutory agencies. The schemes involved taster and small group work with video, audio tapes and printed materials. Flexible learning methods were employed and volunteers were trained to help groups use materials flexibly and select an appropriate route through them to suit the interests and pace of individual groups. Target groups included unemployed adults, ethnic minorities, the elderly, ex-offenders, single parents, widows, mothers with young children and people working with the mentally handicapped:

> *In contrast to most adult "education" opportunities the project has been able to offer support to those who desire to learn informally, when and where is most convenient for them, in accordance with the ideals of "open learning"... In seeking not to teach but to draw on and respond to the experience and needs of participants we have found considerable local demand from those for whom traditional provision is either daunting ("like school"), expensive, or impractical. Many of these have been women with dependents, a substantial number have been elderly, housebound or in institutions and they are all further disadvantaged by lack of access to the educational facilities through which they can inform themselves and begin the process of change in their lives (24).*

Example 3: WEA development courses (25)

At the time of the project, the WEA in South East Scotland was developing learning programmes with groups such as the unemployed, the elderly, women, the mentally ill and ex-offenders. The geographical locations of the work – areas of very high unemployment – were decided by the Regional Council which funded half the WEA tutor-organiser post and most of the student hours. Activities included discussion groups, local history, reminiscence, photography and writing workshops and were held in local community venues. They were free of charge and some had creche support. Most were widely publicised, although some (such as courses for ex-offenders) recruited on a referral basis. The development officer stressed the necessity for personal outreach work in recruitment of new learner groups:

> *One of the main reasons for our success lies in the personal nature of our recruitment procedure. It even helps if you take your children along. I go round the area where we wish to start classes, visiting pubs, betting shops, schools, and so on talking to people to get around the mystique of education and give it a "human" quality. We have to break down a general mistrust and suspicion of education. Once a course has started we find people bring along their friends. Word-of-mouth's a very powerful recruiting agent for us.*

The organiser found that although the initial response was slow, it snowballed once people had tested the water.

Survey of participants. The tutor-organiser conducted a survey of participants (Appendix 2) for the research. The aim was to elicit from first-time attenders their reasons for participating, how they heard about the course, their views on the learning process and whether or not they intended to continue with learning. At the time of the survey, all the courses had succeeded in recruiting people from the target groups, in particular women and the elderly, the majority of whom had never participated in anything similar before. However, relatively few men had been recruited, because, according to the tutor: "In a macho society, self-improvement is something women do." All courses were negotiated with the groups who were encouraged to take control of the pace and content of programmes as soon as possible.

The following tables present the results of the survey according to each development programme.

(ASLA = Average School Leaving Age; WQ = Without Educational Qualifications)

CLASS 1: LOCAL HISTORY DISCUSSION GROUP
TARGET GROUP: older adults
NUMBER OF RESPONDENTS: 16
SEX: F:11; M:5
AGE: All but one over 60.
FAMILY STATUS/OCCUPATION: Most described themselves as retired or housewives.
ASLA: 14–15
WQ: 11
REASONS FOR ATTENDANCE:
Interest: 13
Time on hands: 3
INFORMATION SOURCE:
Word-of-mouth: 11
Meeting with WEA tutor: 3
Conventional publicity (local press, leaflets): 2
COMMENTS: Two participants claimed that attendance had increased their interest in the locality; one expressed enthusiasm about the "active participation" approach. Several felt they had been helped intellectually. Only three people said they intended to take another class.

CLASS 2: REMINISCENCE GROUP
TARGET GROUP: older adults
NUMBER: 10
SEX: F:9; M:1
AGE: all were over 60

FAMILY STATUS/OCCUPATION: all retired, 2 housewives, 7 widows
ASLA: 14–15
WQ: 10
REASONS FOR ATTENDANCE:
New interest: 7
To meet people: 3
INFORMATION SOURCE:
Word-of-mouth: 6
Local befriending scheme: 4
COMMENTS: Four said they felt "broadened" and had a new outlook; one appreciated the new stimulation and another now "realised the importance of education". Six said they would like to continue with similar courses.

CLASS 3: OLDER WOMEN'S DISCUSSION GROUP
TARGET GROUP: Older women
NUMBER: 15
AGE: all over 60
ASLA: 14
WQ: 14
FAMILY STATUS: Six described themselves as housewives, nine were widows
REASONS FOR ATTENDANCE:
New interest: 6
To meet people: 5
To get out: 2
Time on hands: 1
To recover from illness: 1
INFORMATION SOURCE:
Word-of-mouth: 12
WEA tutor: 2
Conventional publicity: 1
COMMENTS: Five people said the group had made them more tolerant of others and better mixers; one that she had a greater interest in everyday affairs and another that she had become "a more mature person". However, only one said she wished to continue learning.

CLASS 4: WRITERS' WORKSHOP
TARGET GROUP: all groups
NUMBER: 15
SEX: F:9; M:6
AGE:
under 20: 1
20–29: 2

30–39: 5
40–49: 5
50–59: 2
OCCUPATION: Eight described themselves as unemployed (five of the six men) and three as housewives. The remaining man was an electrical engineer while the three employed women included a social worker, a machinist and a companion/help.
ASLA: 15–16
WQ: 8
REASONS FOR ATTENDANCE: only six answered this question, four of whom cited interest in subject and two to meet people.
INFORMATION SOURCE:
Word-of-mouth: 8
Conventional publicity: 3
Contact with WEA tutor: 3
Doctor: 1
COMMENTS: Comments were unanimously appreciative of the informal approach: "I always thought it [learning] would be boring but since starting WEA classes have discovered differently." Several participants said they had started to write regularly as a result of participation. One was now "looking in other directions" and another had learned to express her own views.

CLASS 5: "WRITE NOW" (several groups)
TARGET GROUP: all groups
NUMBER: 34
SEX: F:25; M:9
AGE:
20–29: 6
30–39: 4
40–49: 7
50–59: 7
60+: 10
OCCUPATION: The majority of participants were in higher occupational categories A, B and C1. Nine described themselves as housewives, five as unemployed, and four as retired.
ASLA: 17
WQ: 14. (The courses attracted a more educated clientele. Twelve participants had higher education qualifications.)
REASONS FOR ATTENDANCE (not all answered this question):
Interest in subject: 17
Geographically convenient: 1
Inspired by others: 3
To meet others: 2

New stimulus: 2
"Badgered into it": 1
INFORMATION SOURCE:
Conventional publicity: 27
Word-of-mouth: 5
Contact with WEA tutor: 2
COMMENTS: Comments were unanimously favourable: "I just had no idea of the variety and scope of education. I had a very sheltered life and was ignorant of life outside." Twenty-one participants said they would like to continue with education, 18 specifying that they would like more of the same. The elderly participants requested "more general education, "anything to keep the mind going" and "more daytime classes".

CLASS 6: WOMEN'S DISCUSSION GROUP
TARGET GROUP: young mothers
NUMBER: 7
AGE: all were aged between 20 and 29
CHILDREN: 4 had more than 1 child
OCCUPATION:
Unemployed: 3
Housewives: 1
Part-time employed: 3
ASLA: 16
WQ: 5
REASONS FOR ATTENDANCE: In every case the women had responded to a suggestion by the nursery head teacher who had arranged a meeting of interested parties.
COMMENTS: There was unanimous enthusiasm. All respondents said that, as a result of participation, they felt "broader", more aware, and more tolerant of others' views. They also enjoyed the informal learning experience: "I found this an easier and better way to learn as learning before has always bored me". Five said they would like to continue learning citing a range of subjects.

CLASS 7: WOMEN'S DISCUSSION GROUPS (2)
TARGET GROUP: all women
NUMBER: 15
AGE:
Under 20: 1
20–29: 10
30–39: 2
40–49: 2
FAMILY STATUS:

Married with dependent children: 9
Single parents: 5
Single: 1
OCCUPATION:
Housewife: 10
Shop assistant: 2
Typist: 1
Usherette: 1
Self-employed: 1
ASLA: 16
WQ: 10
REASONS FOR ATTENDANCE:
To meet others: 11
Suggestion by community worker: 4
New interest: 2
INFORMATION SOURCE:
Word-of-mouth: 5
Contact with WEA tutor: 5
Information from community worker: 4
Conventional publicity: 1
COMMENTS: Five respondents said the group had enabled them to "open up and speak freely", and six that they had developed more open and tolerant attitudes. One found it a welcome relief from isolation. Participants were particularly appreciative of the informality of the group.
All declared an interest in continuing in the group or pursuing other targeted activities organised by the WEA.

CLASS 8: PHOTOGRAPHY
TARGET GROUP: all groups
NUMBER: 6
SEX: M: 5; F:1
AGE: Participants were between 20 and 34
OCCUPATION:
Unemployed: 3
Housewife: 1
Employed: 2 (chef, butcher)
ASLA: 16
WQ: 4
REASONS FOR ATTENDANCE: all cited interest in subject
SOURCE OF INFORMATION:
Conventional publicity: 4
Word-of-mouth: 1
Contact with WEA: 1

COMMENTS: Participants unanimously expressed enthusiasm. All wanted to continue with photography or other learning activities. Four commented on how much they enjoyed the informal learning methods.

Summary of findings. The more educated clientele (at the writers' workshop) was the only one that found out about the course mainly from formal publicity (local press, library, leaflets, exhibition in town hall). The majority of non-participants in the other groups had heard about activities from other people. Activities with end products (photography and writing courses) were the only ones to attract a relatively high proportion of male participants. It is also interesting to note that 50% of participants in the Write Now courses were over 50.

One of the most striking findings was the unanimous enthusiasm of participants, particularly regarding the informal approach. Most found the activities relevant and enjoyable although, according to the tutor conducting the survey, they refused to associate what they were doing with learning:

The question on outcomes really flummoxed them because of the use of the word "learning". They didn't equate what they were doing with learning. I explored this in some detail with the writers' and photographers' groups, to find out why they found the word "learning" so difficult. While they don't appear to view what they do as a hobby or practical activity, they wouldn't apply the word "learning" or even "education" to it either, because of the formal implications and associations of those words.

This reaction was common among many groups engaged in informal first stage learning activities. It underlines the importance of how activities are presented in recruitment campaigns. The responses suggest that it was primarily the personal outreach approach that attracted non-participants to these courses and the informality and participatory style that kept them there. Interest in subject was the most important reason for participation among all groups except younger women who participated mainly for social reasons and to "get out of the house". Younger adults were particularly enthusiastic about the courses. The majority wished to continue participating either in a similar course or in other learning activities. Older adults, in spite of expressed satisfaction and enjoyment, were less likely to be considering future learning activities.

Development work issues. The WEA tutor stressed that development work with first-time participants is likely to have a slow initial response and providers may have to be prepared to allow small groups to run in the early stages. This is important in view of the fact that much adult education work is dependent on minimum numbers. Another issue highlighted in the interview with the tutor-organiser was the conflict between a tutor's need to establish new groups and his/her reluctance to abandon existing ones which may not have achieved sufficient confidence or momentum to continue without support: "It's difficult to maintain and support existing groups while breaking new ground and establishing new ones."

Although some autonomous single parent and mental health groups emerged as a result of the Scottish development work ("the educational element provided the catalyst"), other groups did not feel able to continue. This raises questions about the long-term value of short education programmes which may not leave groups with the confidence or resources to move on. As development work implies progression, this was something which worried the tutor and many other outreach workers interviewed during the project.

Access stage 6: Progression

Progression from first stage informal learning to other forms and levels of learning appeared, from this research, to be one of the most crucial stages of access for adult students but one that is often neglected by education institutions. Although educational progression is not necessarily the primary goal of first stage learning activities for non-participant groups, one of the aims should be to make people aware of other opportunities and to help them move on to other forms and levels of learning if they wish to do so. It is often found that informal learning acts as an appetiser by giving people a first, enjoyable taste of adult learning and the confidence to move on to formal education. In many areas, however, there are no mechanisms to assist this transition.

Short-term opportunities. Much of the introductory work initiated with new adult clienteles is financed by special funding. The value of pump-priming finance in spearheading innovation is widely acknowledged. The general idea behind special funding is that the good practice it supports should provide models for mainstream providers to take over or replicate. While this has happened in some cases, in others, initiatives have disappeared without trace once funding has ceased, either because outside funding has been taken up purely for reasons of expediency, or because the providers concerned genuinely believe that short introductory courses are all that is needed to encourage the participation of new groups. Thus short-term opportunities can turn out to be the be-all and end-all of work with new clienteles. This was one of the greatest concerns of the outreach and development workers interviewed during the project:

How much will remain after me? Nothing we set up lasted. Now I

*wonder, is it worth setting up something that's going to fold? [ESG
Development worker, Coventry]*

*I refused to set something up which had no long-term future.
[REPLAN project organiser, Liverpool]*

*One of the problems is the provision of incredibly short-term
opportunities. It's like a pack of cards. You pull one out and the whole
lot collapses. [Guidance worker, Bradford]*

An LEA adult education organiser questioned the "replicability" of
special-funded provision. He argued that short-term models may be ignored
by mainstream providers precisely because they are short-term and better
resourced than is possible within mainstream budgets. He cited the example
of a course for women presented to LEAs as a model of good practice:

*By trying to do everything well it became non-replicable within normal
budgets, and along with rejection for budget reasons went rejection of
the lessons to be learned about outreach, etc. There are examples of
effective work going on with non-traditional audiences but no one has
time to document them. To assess and write up what is already being
done within normal regulations, finances, and staffing is more likely
to lead to replication than the promotion of specially-funded and
selected models operating under certain conditions.*

Lack of progression routes. It was clear from the research that a large
proportion of introductory learning programmes have no natural progression
routes. This was another matter causing concern to the development workers
contacted during the research and several identified it as the greatest problem
associated with short introductory programmes:

*I'm really worried about short introductory or taster courses – access
courses with a small "a": access to what? There may be nothing for
people to progress to. You're creating two tiers of provision. This is
nowhere more apparent than with ESL people taking short-term
funded courses. We get clients in here who have done had a dozen of
such courses and they just can't get any further. [Guidance worker,
Bradford]*

A short-course organiser in Yorkshire commented that it is easy to provide
appropriate courses for beginners but much harder to provide "somewhere for
students who want to progress further to move on to", a sentiment echoed by
an outreach worker working with ethnic minority groups in Bristol. He
referred to the "desperate need" to develop progression routes and curriculum

links to enable his students to gain access to higher level courses and qualifications.

Bridging courses. Courses of the Return to Learn, Fresh Start and Second Chance variety ostensibly provide a curricular link to formal learning. They attract potential returners who have had a gap since their formal education and people who have participated in community or basic education activities and wish to progress further. Such courses aim to develop abilities and confidence, critical thinking skills and study skills. Return to Learn courses often recruit from basic education programmes and some are specially targeted, e.g. at women, parents of young children, ethnic minority groups, people with mental problems, working-class individuals. However, one tutor investigating the scope of such programmes had observed signs that staff and resources for them were gradually being cut. Another pointed out that few Return to Learn courses offer bilingual support, which creates a barrier for some ethnic minority groups. Moreover, research reports suggest that people who complete Second Chance or Return to Learn courses experience just as much difficulty in progressing as people who have been on less advanced courses:

> It's a horrible anticlimax when you finish with Second Chance ... all these career people coming, they really make you believe that you can go on out there and do more things. I really felt like ringing somebody up and saying "look, where are all these classes?" They're just not available (26).

This highlights the disturbing lack of connection and continuity between the different forms and levels of post-school education – a problem which is beginning to be recognised and which education guidance services and open college federations and networks are working hard to overcome.

Issitt and Spence (27) argue persuasively for the development of formal and informal learning links between local communities and education institutions, pointing out that this would require significant changes in the way resources are allocated and different criteria of efficiency. Some providers are already trying to move in this direction: in Erdington, an area of Birmingham, the adult education service provides *learning extensions* from existing community and informal groups, a process described by the adult education organiser as "a key step" in their approach to access. When groups are identified as ready to take the next step, pilot bridging courses are arranged "to draw on the educational benefits of community involvement and extend them in a more structured way". Some further education and community colleges now provide special preparation or bridging courses with built-in guidance support for new mature student groups: skills profiling, study skills, pre-Access courses, English-language and mother-tongue courses, women-only science and technology courses at Bradford and Ilkley Community College, Newham Community College, Handsworth Technical College and Sandown College in Liverpool. Like many first stage learning opportunities, bridging programmes for mature learners are frequently developed with short-term funding support. One example – a REPLAN-supported project – has been designed to create better progression routes for Afro-Caribbean adults in London.

Problems experienced in the transition from informal to formal learning. A common problem reported by tutors of first stage learning activities is dependency. Initial learning experiences for new groups are usually flexible, student-centred and take place in a supportive and non-threatening environment. As a result, tutors often find that new learners prefer to repeat the experience rather than move into an unfamiliar and intimidating formal education institution:

> There are immense difficulties about people leaving here and moving into what they perceive as alien territory. Although the college is only a mile and a half away, they say "it's not for us". It's a psychological rather than a geographical separation. [Organiser of introductory training courses for ethnic minority groups]

> It may be too cosy and sheltered: most of our students keep coming back and one of the problems is developing or changing the group. [Tutor running a group for older adults]

The sharp contrast between formal and informal learning environments prompts Issett and Spence to ask:

> What happens when adults move on from a part-time neighbourhood-based course to full-time study in an institution? Does the experience follow naturally and consolidate community education or Second Chance experience? How do non-traditional groups fare in a system geared to white middle-class, able-bodied students without family responsibilities? (28)

The answer appears to be: not well. People who do succeed in moving from community-based learning schemes to formal education institutions often experience shock and disorientation. The main problem is lack of support. "Non-traditional" students commonly find that few efforts are made to accommodate their needs. A review of former Second Chance students showed that 31% had dropped out of further education courses for reasons such as the level of work (too advanced, too theoretical); lack of childcare; and uncongenial teaching methods (29).

Some of the problems which different groups encounter when they return to learning are explored in Section 3.

References

1. Mullarney, P. & Lewis, L. *Resolving the Dilemma: Where do we go from here?* School of Education, University of Connecticut, 1984.
2. Courtney, S. *op. cit.,* p98.
3. Johnstone, J.W.C. & Rivera, R.J. *op. cit.*
4. Munn, P. & MacDonald, C. *op. cit.,* p43.
5. Mullarney, P. & Lewis, L. op. cit., 1984.
6. Darkenwald, G.G. & Larson, G.A. What we know about reaching hard-to-reach adults. *New Directions for Continuing Education,* 8,18, p90, 1980.
7. Ward, K. (ed.) *REPLAN Review,* 1, 1986.
8. Larson, G.A. Overcoming barriers to communication. *New Directions for Continuing Education,* 8,18, p36, 1980.
9. Derbyshire LEA. *Community Education in Derbyshire.* Derbyshire LEA, 1988, pp12–13.
10. McPherson, J. *Development of Co-ordinated Adult Education and Training Provision in a Rural Area (RP 278).* FEU, 1986.
11. *Bedfordshire Project, Interim Report.* ALBSU, 1987, p21.
12. Larson, G.A. *op. cit.*
13. McIlroy, J. & Spencer, B. *University Adult Education in Crisis.* University of Leeds, 1988, p153.
14. Fraser, L. & Ward, K. *Education from Everyday Living: An assessment of community-based courses with unemployed people.* NIACE/REPLAN, 1988, p98.
15. Dobbs, C.R. Educational Opportunities for Adults Provided by Northamptonshire LEA. Unpublished MEd dissertation, Huddersfield Polytechnic, 1986, p66.
16. Beder, H. Reaching the hard-to-reach adult through effective marketing. *New Directions for Continuing Education,* 8, p46, 1980.
17. Fraser, L. & Ward, K. *op. cit.,* p98.
18. Derbyshire LEA *op. cit.,* pp12–13.
19. Ward, K. *op. cit.,* 1986, p1.
20. Fraser, L. & Ward, K. *op. cit.,* p98.
21. *Ibid.,* p94.
22. Information provided from interviews with project workers; and White, J. *Need to Know Project: Final report.* ALBSU, 1987.
23. *Ibid.*
24. Gray, E. *First Year Report of the Open University National Community*

Programme, Feb 1986–Feb 1987. Open University National Community Programme Agency, 1988, p11.

25. Information supplied during telephone interviews and correspondence with the tutor-organiser, Faith Mann, who also conducted the survey on behalf of this project.

26. Kearney, P. *Second Chance to Learn: Final report.* WEA Berks, Bucks and Oxon, 1987, p25.

27. Issitt, M. & Spence, J. An exploration of the relationship between community education and higher education. *Journal of Community Education,* 6,4a, pp14–17, 1988.

28. *Ibid.*

29. *Review of Second Chance to Learn Courses.* FEU, 1988.

Section 3

The Non-Participant Groups

This section is in two parts: the first presents the results of interviews conducted with individuals in the non-participant categories chosen as the main focus of the research; the second explores specific issues affecting access, programme development and progression for each group.

Surveys of Non-Participants

Surveys were carried out in three different locations: rural (South Yorkshire), central urban (Bristol) and suburban (Erdington, Birmingham). In each area, structured interviews (Appendix 3) were conducted with small samples of the following groups:

GROUP 1. Unskilled/semi-skilled manual workers.
GROUP 2. Unemployed people.
GROUP 3. Women with dependent children.
GROUP 4. Older adults (aged 50-plus).
GROUP 5. Ethnic minority groups.

The aims were:

☐ to see whether the results confirmed or contradicted other research
☐ to identify the experience of, and attitudes to, education of different groups
☐ to identify perceived obstacles to participation within each group
☐ to see whether these deterrents vary according to geographical location
☐ to assess awareness of local educational opportunities
☐ to see whether adults who disclaim any interest in learning are actually involved in informal learning activities which are not perceived as such.

The interviews

Three hundred interviews were conducted altogether. The overall number of non-participants interviewed was 200, 240 in groups 1–4, but only 40 in group 5, as it turned out that there were few ethnic minority residents in the rural area. Twenty respondents from groups 1–4 who were participating in learning activities were used as a control group.

THE URBAN AREA: interviews were conducted within the Bristol city area. Local adult education provision in this area is provided by South Bristol College, which has a good community base. There are some WEA courses in the area, and courses and programmes for adults are also provided at the University and the Folk House Adult Education Centre about two miles away. Contact with interviewees was made through local community centres, cafes and working places.

THE RURAL AREA: interviews were conducted in the centre of Dinnington, nine miles from Rotherham in South Yorkshire, an area of high unemployment. The majority of programmes for adults are provided at two main centres in Dinnington – a comprehensive school and a Further Education college, both of which serve a very large rural area. Other educational activities are available at four sub-centres, all within a four-mile radius. The interviews were carried out at a local community centre and a local club.

THE SUBURBAN AREA: interviews took place in Erdington, about four miles from the centre of Birmingham, a mixed environment containing areas of multiple deprivation and areas of relative affluence. Learning opportunities in the area are provided at a number of locations: two adult education centres, one providing evening and the other daytime and evening courses; two daytime community centres; a recreational leisure centre with evening adult education programmes; two private fitness/recreation centres; and four churches which also offer adult learning opportunities. The majority of interviewees were approached in the street.

Survey results

According to the interviewer in the urban area, women were generally more forthcoming than men and unskilled manual workers were the most difficult to interview. The urban interviewer found the local Asian community difficult to contact and reached them through a community worker. In the suburban area, interviews with members of the Asian communities were conducted in the mother tongue with the help of a bilingual community worker. Where the schedule of questions was concerned, interviewees experienced the greatest difficulty in articulating reasons for non-participation. There were few major differences between geographical areas. The results for all three areas have therefore been combined, with any significant differences in detail noted.

GROUP 1: UNSKILLED WORKERS

Number: 60

Sex: M: 43; F: 17

Age:
20–29: 21
30–39: 24
40–49: 13
50–59: 2

Marital status:
Married: 30
Single: 19
Divorced/separated: 11

School leaving age (SLA):
16 or under: 58
17: 1
18: 1

Educational qualifications:
Some: 10
None: 50

Educational activities since leaving school:
Skills training: Some: 14; None: 46
Other organised learning activities: Some: 6; None: 54

Current involvement in organised community, leisure or sports activities: Some: 15; None: 45

Knowledge of local learning opportunities for adults: Some: 39; None: 21

Interest in learning opportunities: Some: 22; None: 38

Perceived deterrents to participation:
Lack of time: 23 mentions
School experience: 13
No perception of need: 5
Lack of information: 5
Lack of confidence: 4

Perceived learning requirements: Vocational and practical courses: 12 mentions

Compared with the other groups in the survey, members of Group 1 participate least in education/training programmes and other organised group activities. Over a third of respondents had no knowledge of local learning opportunities and a large number claimed to have no interest whatever in educational activities. Some members of this group were overtly hostile to education, particularly in the rural area, where 19 out of 20 respondents claimed to have absolutely no interest in taking up any learning opportunities, citing school experiences as one of the main reasons. Nineteen rural respondents had received no education or training since leaving school, although 4 had been engaged in other group learning activities. The unskilled rural respondents were much more likely to be participating in community and leisure activities than their counterparts in the suburban and urban areas. Members of Group 1 cited lack of time as an obstacle to participation more often than any other group. The urban interviewees mentioned the greatest number of deterrents, including lack of confidence and no perception of need. The urban and suburban respondents expressed a need for more practical or vocational courses.

GROUP 2: UNEMPLOYED ADULTS
Number: 60

Sex: M: 39; F: 21

Age:
20–29: 32
30–39: 18
40–49: 8
50–59: 2

Marital status:
Married: 19
Single: 30
Divorced/separated: 11

SLA:
16 and under: 55
18: 5

Educational qualifications: Some: 34; None: 26

Educational activities since leaving school:
Skills training: Some: 26; None: 34
Other learning activities: Some: 11; None: 49

Current involvement in organised community, leisure or sports activities: Some: 14; None: 46

Knowledge of local learning opportunities for adults: Some: 41; None: 19

Expressed interest in learning opportunities:
Some: 28; None: 32

Perceived deterrents to participation:
Lack of money: 16
School experience: 15
Lack of confidence: 6
Lack of relevance: 6
Lack of time: 4
Lack of childcare: 3
Dislike of going out in evenings: 3
Distance to opportunities: 3
Potential loss of welfare benefits: 1

Perceived learning requirements: Vocational or practical courses: 17

This was the only group to perceive lack of money as a major obstacle (mainly the urban respondents). School experience again emerged as a strong deterrent factor, affecting mainly the rural respondents. Most respondents without skills training were in the suburban area. In the urban area, sixteen respondents had received some training, mainly on the YTS and Community Programme schemes. Respondents tended to dismiss learning programmes which were not related to employment, and their perception was that education does little to help people find jobs. Several viewed adult education as something exclusively concerned with hobbies. One man referred to it as time-wasting frivolities and another as something mainly for women. Other members of this group perceived all education as formal, academic and elitist and a number expressed great bitterness towards the school system which, in their view, reflects the power and vested interests of the establishment. There was some confusion between government training schemes and other forms of adult education. No one expressed interest in retraining schemes: "once bitten, twice shy". Expressed learning interests included: specific job-related courses; electrical skills; motor mechanics; office skills; driving; French; photography and film-making; fitness and beautician courses.

Among respondents under 30, peer group influence emerged as an important factor in decisions to participate or not participate:

My friends persuaded me not to join classes.

I don't think I'd get on with the types who do evening classes. I'm not a "book type".

Some respondents said they might participate if their friends did.

GROUP 3: WOMEN WITH DEPENDENT CHILDREN
Number: 60

Age:
20–29: 40
30–39: 16
40–49: 4

Marital status:
Married: 41
Single: 7
Divorced/separated: 12

SLA:
16 and under: 46
18: 14

Occupational status:
Employed: 22
Unemployed: 10
Housewives: 28

Educational qualifications: Some: 42; None: 18

Educational activities since leaving school:
Skills training: Some: 16; None: 44
Other adult learning activities: Some: 13; None: 47

Current involvement in organised community, leisure or sports activities: Some: 48; None: 12

Knowledge of local learning opportunities for adults: Some: 46; None: 14

Expressed interest in learning opportunities: Some: 12; None: 48

Perceived deterrents to participation:

Lack of time: 19
Lack of childcare facilities: 18
Lack of money: 9
Distance to learning opportunities: 9
School experiences: 7
Lack of daytime opportunities: 8
Lack of confidence: 5

Learning requirements:
Childcare: 18
Practical and vocational courses: 10
Daytime facilities: 8
Social contacts: 3
Women-only courses: 3
Local courses: 3

Together with older adults, this group mentioned the greatest number of practical deterrents to participation, particularly lack of time, childcare facilities and neighbourhood opportunities. Over a third of respondents were in employment as well as caring for their families, therefore time constraints figured largely as a reason for non-participation. The greatest number of obstacles were mentioned by respondents in the urban area. Time constraints were mentioned most often by rural women, and "dispositional" deterrents – negative school experiences and lack of confidence – mostly by rural and suburban respondents. Rural respondents were the least disposed to participate.

Members of Group 3 were involved far more than respondents in the previous two (male-dominated) groups in local community, social and leisure activities. They were also more aware than other groups of local educational opportunities, although they manifested a generally low level of interest in learning. This could be to do with the multiple practical difficulties of access which they face. Some said that they might consider attending activities when the children were older, and there was a general preference for joining as a group rather than as individuals. The learning requirements expressed by this group focused more on practical arrangements – programme delivery, provision of childcare – than on the type and content of programmes.

GROUP 4: OLDER ADULTS
Number: 60

Sex: M: 26; F: 34

Age:
50–59: 11

60–69: 30
70+: 19

Marital status:
Married: 37
Widowed: 20
Divorced/separated: 2
Single: 1

SLA:
14 and under: 55
15: 3
16: 2

Occupational status:
Employed: 7
Retired: 29
Housewives: 24

Educational qualifications: Some: 3; None: 57

Educational activities since leaving school:
Skills training: Some: 6; None: 54
Other adult learning: Some: 9; None: 51

Current involvement in organised community, leisure or sports activities: Some: 48; None: 12

Knowledge of local learning opportunities: Some: 37; None: 23

Expressed interest in learning opportunities: Some: 20; None: 40

Perceived deterrents to participation:
Lack of time: 17
Distance to learning opportunities: 11
Dislike of night-time travel: 11
Physical disabilities: 7
Lack of money: 7
Lack of information: 6
School experiences: 5
Lack of confidence: 4
No perception of need: 4

Perceived learning requirements:
Daytime courses: 5

This group emerged as the most educationally deprived of the five. It has the largest proportion of people who left school at an early age and the largest number without any educational qualifications at all. They are also among the least likely to have engaged in organised educational activity since leaving school. A large number, second only to the women's sample, declared that they had no interest in adult learning activities, although some respondents were in fact engaged in independent learning projects at home: learning crafts and skills from books, etc. This reluctance to identify informal learning as learning or education reflects a phenomenon found throughout this research, especially among people engaged in learning outside educational environments.

Some members of this group confused adult education with higher education and expressed fears about examinations and formal approaches. Others considered education to be irrelevant and of little value to adults. A number declared themselves "too old" to learn. However, several respondents stated that though they would not participate in activities as individuals, they might join as a group. Rural interviewees had the least time and were most disinclined to go out at night. Distance to opportunities and lack of money were deterrents cited exclusively by the urban respondents.

Although over 50% of respondents were retired, lack of time was the most frequently stated reason for non-participation. This could be explained by the fact that the older respondents were more involved than any of the other groups in a whole range of hobbies, leisure and community activities. Several respondents were caring for other relatives, which affected their ability to participate in outside activities.

GROUP 5: ETHNIC MINORITY ADULTS
Number: 40

Ethnic group:
Asian: Punjabi: 14; Urdu: 11
Afro-Caribbean: 12
Iranian: 3

Sex: M: 13; F: 27

Age:
20–29: 17
30–39: 9
40–49: 8
50–59: 5
70+ : 1

Marital status:
Married: 25

Widowed: 4
Single: 9
Divorced/separated: 2
19 of the women (including 4 Afro-Caribbean) had dependent children

SLA:
Age 14 and under: Punjabi: 5; Afro-Caribbean: 5
Age 15: Afro-Caribbean: 3
Age 16/17: Urdu: 9; Punjabi: 7; Afro-Caribbean: 3; Iranian: 2
Age 18: Urdu 2; Punjabi: 1; Afro-Caribbean: 1; Iranian 1
No school: Punjabi 1

Educational qualifications:
Urdu: Some: 8 (school certificates; CSEs and O-levels); None: 3
Punjabi: Some: 5 (CSEs and O-levels); None: 9
Afro-Caribbean: Some: 5 (CSEs and O-levels); None: 7
Iranian: Some: 3 (diplomas and university)

Occupational status:
Employed: 13
Unemployed: 7
Housewives: 20

Educational activities since leaving school:
Skills training: Some: 4; None: 36
Other learning activities: Some: 11; None: 29

Current involvement in organised community, leisure or sports activities: Some: 15; None: 25

Knowledge of local learning opportunities: Some 25; None: 15

Expressed interest in learning opportunities: Some: 14; None: 26

Perceived deterrents to participation:
Lack of confidence: 15 (mostly Punjabi women)
Lack of time: 10 (all races but predominantly working women)
Negative attitudes to education and no perception of need : 13 (mostly male, Afro-Caribbean)
No appropriate courses: 8 (all races)
Distance to college: 7 (all Urdu women); Language problems: 7 (Urdu and Punjabi women)
Problems from male family members: 6 (Punjabi women)
Lack of money: 3 (mainly Afro-Caribbean)
Perceptions of being too old: 3 (Asian and Afro-Caribbean women)

Problems in English groups: 2 (Afro-Caribbean women)

Perceived learning requirements:
Courses in English for everyday living: 14
Childcare facilities: 8
Courses to help children at school: 5
Daytime courses: 5
Basic maths: 3
Asian-only courses: 5
Courses leading to jobs: 2
Practical/business courses: 2

The Urdu and Iranian respondents were interviewed in the urban location, the Punjabis in the suburban, and the West Indian group in both. All the Afro-Caribbean and Iranian males in the sample were unemployed. Among the women, nine Urdu, seven Punjabi and four Afro-Caribbean respondents described themselves as housewives. Three Punjabi women were employed – in a shop, a factory and an office. Two Afro-Caribbean women were nurses and one worked in a shop. The Asian males included two shopkeepers, a bus driver and one on a Community Programme scheme.

The Urdu sample were generally aware of educational opportunities provided at the local further education college and the community centre as well as those available at their own centres and mosque. (Most of the Urdu males were or had been involved in English classes organised through the mosque.) In contrast, only five of the Punjabi group were able to name centres offering learning activities. The majority of the Punjabi women were not involved in any group activities, and several considered participation in learning would be inappropriate for them:

> *It would be untraditional for women to participate in learning activities.*

> *These activities are not for us villagers.*

Three Afro-Caribbean males had received no education or training since leaving school. Two expressed an interest in skills training and job-oriented learning. Five of the Afro-Caribbean women had been involved in some group learning and community activities and most knew about local opportunities.

The ethnic minority sample was the most forthcoming of the five groups in articulating specific learning requirements. The strongest demand was for vocational and practical programmes and English courses to help with everyday living. Monocultural learning groups were preferred, particularly by Asian respondents.

GROUP 6: CONTROL GROUP ("accidentals" – interviewees who were participating in organised learning activities)
Number: 20

Sex: M: 8; F: 12

Age:
20–29: 7
30–39: 5
40–49: 5
50–59: 2
60+: 1

Marital status:
Married: 14
Widowed: 1
Divorced/separated: 2
Single: 3

SLA:
14: 1
15: 7
16+: 11
18: 1

Occupational status:
Employed: 14
Unemployed: 1
Housewives: 5

Educational qualifications: Some: 11 (O and A-levels; CSEs); None: 9

Educational activities since leaving school:
All were engaged in some adult education or training and had participated in a number of organised learning activities since leaving school.

Current involvement in organised community, leisure or sports activities: Some: 12; None: 8

Members of the control group had some of the characteristics of typical participants, confirming a common finding that individuals in non-participant categories who do take up education or training opportunities tend to be those with some qualifications and in paid employment. Most respondents had been engaged in a variety of learning activities since leaving school, ranging across the spectrum of adult and further education. This suggests that once people have embarked on voluntary learning it becomes a habit. The choice of learning activities also reflected the findings of other research: the men had been involved mainly in practical, vocational and qualifying courses (car maintenance, painting, welding, woodwork, management training, mechanical engineering, Start Your Own Business, food hygiene, GCSE and A-level courses) while the women had enrolled in a wide range of leisure and self-development courses as well as vocational and certificated programmes: painting, pottery, crafts, sports, flower-arranging, cookery, yoga, dancing, dressmaking, tailoring, GCSE, A-levels, CQSW, RSA typing and shorthand.

Points Emerging from the Surveys

The surveys confirmed a number of the findings of available research, in particular, the widespread lack of interest in education among members of non-participant groups, a common view being that learning is for "others" – the "ruling classes", "younger people", "older people", an "academic elite". However, statements of lack of interest were contradicted, in some cases, by subsequent suggestions of the types of learning in which respondents might engage.

The least interest in learning was expressed by women with dependent children and older adults. These two groups, however, were the most involved in group activities in the community. Unskilled manual workers and the unemployed, the only male-dominated groups in the survey, were the least involved in group or community activities. The unskilled were the group with least educational experience since leaving school. The unemployed and unskilled groups were generally hostile to education, and only considered learning of value if it assisted in obtaining employment or promotion.

Nearly a third of all non-participants questioned did not know about local educational opportunities. Those least likely to know what was available were older adults, unskilled and unemployed people. Overall, the survey revealed a striking lack of awareness of the difference between school and other types of learning. There was also confusion between training and other kinds of education for adults.

Most frequently mentioned deterrents

The perceived deterrents to participation correspond closely to those identified elsewhere, and are generally what one would expect (in order of frequency of mention):

1. Lack of time was cited most frequently as the main obstacle, particularly by unskilled workers and young mothers.
2. School experience seems to have had a particularly negative effect on the unemployed and unskilled.
3. Lack of money affects particularly unemployed people, but women and older people also perceive this as a substantial deterrent.
4. Lack of confidence appears to be a considerable obstacle for black groups.
5. Distance from facilities deters mainly the elderly, women with dependent children and ethnic minority groups (particularly Asian women) in the urban area surveyed.
6. Not surprisingly, lack of childcare was mentioned most by the mothers with dependent children, followed by the ethnic minority groups. Some unemployed men with working spouses also referred to this as a problem.
7. Lack of daytime opportunities was mentioned mainly by women and older adults.
8. The perception of education as an irrelevance: this view was held chiefly by unskilled people.
9. Lack of transport and the cost of transport were mentioned most by mothers with dependent children, older adults and ethnic minority women.
10. Reluctance to go out at night was mentioned by women and the elderly.

Difference between areas

Given the diversity of locations and the facilities they offer, as well as the variations in people's individual circumstances, the differences between the three areas revealed by the survey are probably of little generalisable value.

Rural respondents were the least likely to have had any skills training and expressed the least interest in education. The groups living in the suburban area, particularly the unemployed, appeared to be least involved in community or leisure activities and the least likely to have participated in any learning activities since school. Urban respondents appeared to have a greater knowledge of local learning opportunities than their rural and suburban counterparts, but they were by far the majority to cite the practical constraints on participation – lack of time, money, childcare, geographically accessible facilities and daytime courses.

Pointers for recruitment

Some respondents had tried post-school education but had been disappointed and disillusioned, particularly with the *level* of courses: "too low", "too advanced", "too theoretical". Such comments indicate that many people join classes with insufficient knowledge of what they will entail. This highlights the need for better information and publicity services. Several respondents had also lacked the basic skills necessary to undertake the courses they had started, and it would undoubtedly have been beneficial to student and provider if this had this been recognised at an early stage. This emphasises the need for accessible guidance and referral services, as well as support programmes such as English, mathematics, and Return to Study.

The requirements most frequently mentioned in all groups were:

☐ practical programmes relevant to everyday circumstances and employment acquisition

☐ avoidance of formality in enrolment procedures and teaching styles

☐ group recruitment and group activities. Reluctance to enrol on one's own was expressed by some respondents in all groups. This is an important point for recruiters, particularly in view of the evidence of strong reference group influence within non-participant sections of the community.

The Non-Participant Groups: Access Approaches and Issues

The surveys, interviews and review of existing research led to identification of the major obstacles faced by different non-participant groups and provided examples of measures and approaches that have been effective in assisting their access to educational opportunities. These have been set out in the following brief overview. (N.B. In discussion of such large sections of society, broad generalisations are unavoidable.)

Group 1: Unskilled and Semi-Skilled Manual Workers

The evidence consistently shows that manual workers, particularly males, are the most difficult to recruit to educational activities. This appears to be due to a powerful combination of dispositional and situational barriers.

OBSTACLES TO RECRUITMENT

☐ Time constraints, especially for those doing part-time or shift work at unsociable hours. Women part-time workers have the least free time.

☐ Low educational achievement. A high proportion of unskilled and semi-skilled manual workers left school at the earliest age without educational qualifications.

☐ Lack of confidence in ability to learn.

☐ Lack of awareness of learning needs.

☐ Low perceived value of education. This group is the least favourably disposed towards post-school education.

☐ Education not considered as part of reference group norms: "It's not what people like us do."

☐ Education perceived as incompatible with traditional male bread-winning role and inappropriate for women.
☐ Fear that return to learning would be degrading and involve loss of face.
☐ Low expectations. The majority of low-paid manual workers have few prospects of change or promotion.
☐ Resistance to influence by other social groups.
☐ Place of residence.

The last of these factors is rarely given attention but may be a significant factor in non-participation. A survey conducted in two areas of Skipton – a private housing area and a council housing area – demonstrated that the physical lay-out and amenities of the private housing estate offered lots of opportunities to socialise, join in group activities and share information. In contrast, the geography of the council estates – isolated from the rest of town, with no centre and few collective meeting places – discouraged socialising, and residents were less likely to be involved in a network of relationships which could introduce them to educational opportunities and sustain their attendance (1).

Recruitment strategies

Two points which have a strong bearing on recruitment strategies for this group are:
☐ Many people in working-class occupations are hostile to the education "system" hence to education in general.
☐ Reference group attitudes and norms exert a powerful influence over attitudes and behaviour within this group.

These factors suggest that resistance to voluntary learning will be strong and that group recruitment and activities organised in the community or workplace may be the most effective approaches with unskilled workers. Outreach workers have also found that an approach which emphasises practical concerns and outcomes and avoids jargon and explicit references to "education" is more likely to be effective with this group than conventional publicity.

Workplace recruitment. Recruitment of male manual workers has been achieved through the involvement of Trades Unions and the workplace. The widespread participation in adult education in Sweden, for example, has been attributed to the involvement of the unions and use of the workplace as an educational setting. In Britain, however, opportunities for paid educational leave are rarely given to unskilled workers and when workers do attempt to take time off, paid or unpaid, for learning purposes, they face enormous problems. A report on Second Chance programmes in Liverpool (2) gives a graphic account of the many and varied difficulties encountered at work by low-paid staff, particularly women, who have requested or taken leave to attend courses. There have, however, been some innovative work-based learning schemes, such as the *Take Ten* scheme in Sheffield targeted at City Council employees and the *Workbase* scheme for manual staff in London (3). These received both managerial and trade union support and – crucially – incurred no loss of income or free time for those involved.

Work-based learning schemes demand care in setting up. Information can get lost or removed from noticeboards and may only reach the active and more educated workers. Moreover, workers sometimes view attempts to engage them in learning activities as a managerial plot to prepare them for redundancy. This emerged during a basic education project in Sheffield, where, in a general climate of cutbacks and redundancies, learning programmes organised in the workplace were regarded with suspicion. Participants in the *Take Ten* scheme also feared that ulterior motives were behind attempts to recruit them to the scheme:

> *We were suspicious of the leaflets inviting us to take a day off a week for 10 weeks ... What was it all about? What was the Gaffer's angle – giving us time off with no obvious advantage to him? ... No one ever gave us 'owt (4).*

The same reaction was observed during this research when the non-participant survey was piloted in a factory with a male manual workforce of 200. The workers were asked to respond to questions (Appendix 4) on their experience of post-school education/training and educational interests. It was emphasised that the survey was nothing to do with management; that it was completely voluntary, confidential (no names were required), and that the aim was to identify learning experience and interests. With the consent of management, explanatory posters and a box containing the questionnaires were placed next to the clocking-in point. Most were picked up although witnesses observed some unease and bemusement in people's reactions. In spite of several reminders, only a handful – six in all – were eventually returned, all from skilled workers with some experience of post-school training. The worker who distributed and collected the questionnaires found it hard to allay fears that the survey was in some way connected with management. Moreover, from overheard remarks, most of the men considered education of little relevance or interest.

Another problem associated with workplace learning has been identified as the fear among low-paid workers, especially men, that participants may be stigmatised and labelled as "stupid". Attempts to negotiate programmes with manual staff at Goldsmiths' College highlighted:

> *The reticence of male workers in voicing any positive interest which could lead to a commitment, let alone expressing any "needs" likely to reveal vulnerable or weak points in their education. Even the women*

who were interested expressed a fear of being viewed as "a bunch of dumbo cleaners" (5).

Thus workplace recruitment needs long, careful and sensitive preparation. It took six months of meetings and consultations at Goldsmiths' College before any courses could be initiated.

Word-of-mouth. Recruitment to any scheme for manual workers is most successfully achieved through peer group recommendation. People from the same background who have similar views and doubts have credibility: they are able to put across factual information and persuade their peers more effectively than formal publicity. There is substantial evidence to support this. During the adult literacy campaign in the 1970s, it was found that personal contacts from people already receiving help with literacy were more effective in recruiting than regular peak-time TV publicity (6). The Liverpool Second Chance to Learn programme for working-class people recruits most successfully through its own ex-students, and more than half of the participants in the scheme for ex-steel workers in Consett obtained information from ex-colleagues who knew about the course or were already on it.

Programme development

The learning programmes that have recruited manual workers have generally been informal, student-centred, flexible and democratically run. Examples are the Second Chance programmes in Liverpool and the programmes initiated during the Leeds Pioneer Work Project. Outreach staff working with this group stress that these can be attracted to learning activities if they are seen as relevant and related to everyday circumstances and concerns: a factor now widely considered to be essential in programme development with people from working-class backgrounds. Some adult educators, however, fear that the educational element in informal schemes for working-class groups may be disguised and secondary to the achievement of other objectives, such as the reinforcement of existing roles or social positions (7). Another view is that informal schemes sell people short by concentrating on "life adjustment skills and diminished cognitive content" (8). Organisers of Second Chance programmes in Liverpool maintain that providers generally underestimate working-class individuals' capacity and enthusiasm for study. They have found that their experience challenges popular assumptions about this group of students:

Students demonstrate a keen interest in education rooted in the real world, based on information and debate and will go to some lengths to pursue relevant education, even when it does not lead to material gains such as qualifications or improved job prospects.

The course's relaxed, informal style ... attracted students yet, at the same time, they wanted the challenge of a course which made intellectual demands. More than half expressed the need for mental stimulation. They were driven crazy by jobs which offered no opportunity for initiative, choice or even thought (9).

In instances where manual workers have been fully consulted on their learning interests and requirements, the programmes negotiated have turned out to be broad and varied. One example, a programme developed for manual workers at Goldsmiths' College, was preceded by a long period of careful consultation with porters and cleaners. Negotiation resulted in a wide-ranging general education course which included discussion, reading, writing, interviewing, media studies, study skills and investigation of a variety of topics. The programme was organised in the early morning (before normal office hours) and was attended mainly by women cleaners (10).

Surveys consistently reveal that the expressed learning interests of male manual workers are oriented exclusively towards practical and vocational skills. Although this suggests a predominantly instrumental view of education, some practitioners have found evidence of wider educational interests among this group. The REPLAN Creative Arts project in Liverpool attracted many unskilled and semi-skilled men in their thirties. During the Consett scheme for redundant steel workers, participants, once involved, engaged in a wide range of non-work-related options. However, the first stage work reviewed during this research suggests that the non-work-related programmes that are most effective in reaching male manual workers are practical (rather than discussion-based) and have an end-product: photography, writing, video, etc. Linked skills programmes involving both basic and practical (including creative) skills can be particularly effective in attracting male manual workers.

Conflicting styles. A factor to be taken into consideration in planning and programme development for this group is the contrast between informal, student-centred learning and the more regulated working conditions to which manual workers are accustomed. The report of a linked building and basic skills project in London highlighted an essential incompatibility between industrial styles of working and the participatory, interactive and non-authoritarian approach at the adult education centre:

There was a conflict and a tension between the relationships encouraged within the centre and those typically experienced in a building site, both between worker and task and worker and management. Traditionally these relationships are hierarchical, rigid

and authoritarian with little room for initiative ... the training on
which this work pattern is based is inflexible (11).

Various problems emerged during the project: the men, used to working for profit-oriented bosses, had difficulty adjusting to a non-commercial project devoted to community interests, and were initially suspicious of a democratic "management" which treated them on equal terms. The site supervisor felt that his authority was being eroded and perceived those who attended class regularly as "skivers". As this suggests, the provision of linked skill learning schemes for manual workers requires a patient and diplomatic approach in order to bring two very different worlds together.

Support

Many unskilled and unqualified people who are recruited to informal learning programmes participate because there are no formal entry or assessment criteria and they receive help with study skills and guidance from tutors. Those who subsequently move from informal to formal education face a number of problems. The experience of community-based education does not prepare them for the reality of middle-class-dominated education institutions. This emerged in a project targeted at male industrial workers, which aimed to reduce the "physical and cultural distance separating adult education from the lives of working people" (12). The informal learning activities developed during the project were constructed around working-class networks and although this helped people take the first few steps towards social mobility, "the bridging of the difference between working-class culture and education never fully occurred." As a result, the students who progressed to formal education encountered severe culture shock and found themselves in a kind of limbo – a class apart – neither accepted by their working-class peers nor fully assimilated into the college population. In some cases this resulted in "severed relationships, disrupted families and political ambivalence" – costs which only those with motivation of "heroic proportions" would be prepared to face. O'Shea and Corrigan (1979), who reported on this project, castigate education institutions for perceiving this as the students' problem rather than their own:

> *Our institutions must adapt in some way to facilitate a process of*
> *wider involvement and co-operation ... If we really want the working*
> *class to come to our institutions, we must be prepared to transform*
> *fundamentally the form of our institutions.*

People from working-class backgrounds and occupations who move into education institutions require, at the very least, some mechanisms for personal support, such as access to personal guidance and counselling from people with an understanding of their circumstances and problems.

Group 2: Unemployed Adults

Unemployed non-participants share many of the attributes of the unskilled group.

OBSTACLES TO RECRUITMENT
- ☐ General distrust of education and education institutions.
- ☐ Psychological effects of unemployment: depression, despair, lack of confidence, guilt, shame, fear of stigma.
- ☐ Social deprivation (particularly lack of money).
- ☐ Fear of losing state benefits (exacerbated by the "availability for work" condition being applied more tightly).
- ☐ Isolation: they are often invisible and not collectively involved in community and group activities, therefore difficult for recruiters to reach.
- ☐ Education is generally considered a low priority.
- ☐ Low awareness of existing educational opportunities.
- ☐ Perceptions of age barriers.

According to many education organisers and outreach workers contacted during the project, recruitment of unemployed men is especially difficult, and many carefully thought-out and well-publicised schemes have failed. Apart from Skillcentre programmes, special programmes for unemployed people, including short courses funded by the former MSC, have tended to recruit a majority of women. The national Employment Training scheme (ET) has not achieved its target recruitment number, and various changes have been introduced to make it more attractive to unemployed adults, particularly in the inner cities. Some local initiatives have also had limited results. A free six week course for unemployed men in Milton Keynes, for example, attracted a maximum of four participants after an intensive publicity campaign. Group recruitment has also proved ineffective as, in many areas, unemployed people do not congregate together and many may not wish to be identified as unemployed. A project in Yorkshire which attempted to recruit the long-term unemployed through the Working Men's Club – the "most popular social club in the area" – failed to attract more than a handful of potential participants.

Various reasons for the recruitment problem have been suggested: men do not generally perceive education as "fitting in" with their male role; older men tend to consider themselves too old for education or retraining and younger ones often lack motivation and a sense of direction. Another reason suggested by education staff was reaction against perceived pressure to join schemes, for example from RESTART or JobCentre personnel. A tutor on an MSC Work Preparation scheme in Croydon attributed the non-attendance of some referrals to this pressure.

Recruitment strategies

Publicity. The most urgent requirement of unemployed people is not education but paid work. Because of this, conventional publicity about education and training opportunities may not catch their attention. To circumvent this problem, the co-ordinator of a centre for the unemployed in Croydon placed a "carefully worded" advertisement in the Situations Vacant column of the local paper inviting anyone unemployed and interested in education and training to contact the centre. In the following week, 69 people visited the centre asking for advice and a considerable number made telephone enquiries then and during subsequent weeks:

> This has given us the opportunity not only to fill all our courses, but also to provide advice and collate information on other opportunities in Croydon. In fact the demand for educational guidance was so great that I have now been given a room at the college with access to the Careers Office.

The co-ordinator found that the bulk of enquiries came, as usual, from women. He warned that providers need to be able to respond to the overwhelming interest that can be generated by this kind of publicity: "The main problem we have had is keeping up with demand."

Personal approaches. As with most non-participant sections of the community, personal contacts have been effective in recruiting unemployed men from unskilled or semi-skilled occupational backgrounds. Male participants in a REPLAN-supported Creative Arts Project in Liverpool were all recruited through personal contacts after long and painstaking outreach work in the community. It took three to four months for the project worker to gain their trust and prove that she was "credible" and had the right politics: "I had to be acceptable and identify with them."

Mobile units. There is considerable evidence that unemployed men have scant knowledge and information about local educational opportunities. One solution to this can be mobile information and guidance units, particularly in scattered rural areas. Several units of this kind have been initiated with help from agencies such as the Training Agency and the REPLAN programme. In Wales, a custom-built vehicle housing six Nimbus computers was used by Community Task Force (an ET Training Manager) to help people with literacy, numeracy and job-search. In Harrow, a REPLAN bus staffed by people from REPLAN, the Careers service and further and higher education, has taken education and training videos and computers into shopping centres and council estates to provide an information and guidance service for the unemployed.

Non-educational activities. In many areas unemployed men have become involved in learning as a result of non-educational activities. According to a REPLAN worker:

> *Many successes within this target group occurred when men had become involved in some form of voluntary work or campaigning group and needed further education to make the group more effective.*

In drop-in centres which provide a range of social, recreational and educational activities for the unemployed, it is commonly found that people come for one thing and stay for another. This process leads people to become adult students without realising it. In one example reported to the project, 25–30% of visitors at an LEA and voluntary initiative for unemployed people in Essex become involved in learning activities after coming for sports and coffee.

Programme development

If asked about educational interests, unemployed people usually (and understandably) state a strong preference for vocational programmes. According to surveys, many members of this group perceive activities without job-related aims as having little value.

Work-related programmes. The Employment Training scheme (ET) aims to provide training and work experience for two priority groups – younger adults unemployed for between six and twelve months, and older long-term unemployed. In March 1989, new initiatives were announced to assist the inner city unemployed to train in labour shortage areas. Some additional categories can participate in the scheme on a part-time basis if they can meet certain criteria – labour market returners, unregistered unemployed, and lone parents with school-age children. Participants in the programme receive their normal state benefit plus 10 weekly.

As the new scheme started when the research was more than half-way completed, it was not possible to get a clear impression of how it was working. Some tutors previously involved in MSC programmes considered Employment Training less attractive because of the lack of training allowances:

> *There is an important psychological benefit of having a training allowance rather than benefit. Although the overall amount isn't significantly different, it's different psychologically. The allowance gave people a different relationship with the world. The new set-up is*

just a continuation of benefit: people may not come just for that. [Tutor working with unemployed from ethnic minority groups]

Some tutors in the early stages of the scheme had the impression that the really long-term unemployed were not being accepted on schemes which contradicted one of its principal aims. A literacy tutor in a suburban area also felt that the scheme was not benefiting the most educationally disadvantaged people. She complained that a local scheme had no literacy or English as a Second Language support: "It's too expensive; so a lot of people get turned away as unsuitable." She also referred to a lack of awareness of different cultural needs, citing the example of a Bangladeshi woman being interviewed on her own by men. Given the local structure and nature of the scheme, however, it must be assumed that it varies very widely from area to area.

Skill preparation and short courses. Specific skills training, such as that supplied in Skillcentres, can have a strong male ethos which deters other groups. An outreach worker complained: "They won't look at anyone out there as being in any way different from a 35-year-old, redundant white man." Unemployed women particularly feel out of place in Skillcentres which do not take account of their specific needs. Women with dependent children require specially-timed programmes and childcare – support which is often only available in short-term projects and women's training centres.

Short work preparation courses of the type formerly provided by MSC have attracted people anxious to improve their employment prospects; but staff contacted during 1988 claimed that participants were experiencing problems with the regulations governing availability for work and benefit entitlement. As a result, providers were finding people increasingly reluctant to join temporary schemes. According to a tutor engaged in teaching on an MSC work preparation course in Bristol:

People are unwilling to renegotiate benefits as there are frequent delays when you sign on again. If you're on a very low income this is a frightening prospect which deters many. The view is once you've got benefit sorted out, DON'T TOUCH IT, especially if the course is only for a few weeks.

This situation, coupled with strict eligibility conditions, resulted in low recruitment to the course concerned. However, the tutor complained that the bureaucratic problems faced by unemployed adults are not generally recognised, even within the college. The Principal and other staff members attributed the low numbers to bad marketing or inappropriate course content.

Another problem mentioned by tutors was that people tend to enrol on short work preparation courses with unrealistically high expectations, although in most cases, participation can do little to improve their bleak employment prospects. As observed in a research report: "It is asking a great deal to provide students with a marketable skill in just 12 weeks" (13).

The problem of limited employment prospects is particularly acute for ethnic minority unemployed. A review of RESTART programmes in the Midlands found that provision of education and training did nothing to change the racism and stereotyping black people encountered in the labour market – a fact which was confirmed by the organiser of an ET scheme in Bristol to train black people as YTS supervisors. Here the major difficulty was getting managing agents in employer-led schemes to take on black people for work placements. A tutor running short skills programmes for the ethnic minority unemployed also reported that one of the greatest problems was limited employment possibilities:

> *Under 10 % actually go into the trade or further related courses. Very few become builders or electricians. A lot go into areas not connected with skills – the check-out at Tesco's. It's a job but it's not progress; jobs without a future.*

Wider education programmes. Work-preparation programmes are irrelevant to many older long-term unemployed whose experience of looking for work has been one of constant rejection. Thus a widely-held view among adult educators is that there should be a shift towards providing broader general programmes for this group. Significantly, some of the programmes most successful in recruiting the unemployed have been non-work-related. In one REPLAN project in Yorkshire, unemployed students enrolled predominantly in subject or interest courses, demonstrating: "a major unmet need for education that is additional to vocationally-oriented and qualification-based courses" (14). The REPLAN Creative Arts programme in Liverpool grew out of the recognition that vocationally-specific training is of limited immediate value in an area with few jobs even for those already skilled. Another arts project targeted at unemployed adults was the Arts Workshop programme in Hereford which provided drama, music, photography and batik workshops with support such as childcare and cheap meals. The photography workshops were particularly successful in recruiting men and younger adults (15). *Class*, a free programme for unemployed adults funded by South Bristol College and the WEA, aims to provide an alternative experience to job training. According to the tutor, participants "have already been down the qualification route and what then?" The programme operates like a club with about 15 members of both sexes and all ages involved in a wide range of student-negotiated activities: local history, trades union studies, calligraphy and photography. At the time of the researcher's visit, participants had conducted local surveys, produced displays, and collectively researched, written and printed a book on local miners. In a group interview, individuals claimed that attendance had transformed their lives in a number of ways.

Targeted provision. Since there are numerous sub-groups among the unemployed, the most effective programming approach is often based on specific targeting. In Newcastle, a neighbourhood education programme was devised for young unemployed males – a group which had rejected most forms of education. The programme was organised in their time and territory and participants had substantial influence on and control over activities which were based on their way of life, culture and local environment. They included legal rights sessions with a community lawyer, job search and acquisition, informal discussion, video and photography. Once motivated to learn, participants "happily took advantage of provision outside their own territory" (16).

In some cases, specific group work has become a major source of support for particularly vulnerable groups. In London, an impressive range of arts and general education programmes was negotiated by staff at Goldsmiths' College with a groups of unemployed and homeless men, a client-group with a vast number of problems:

> *Joint creation of a curriculum was the key to this project. We were reaching people with little or no other support systems. In a sense the activity of the group masked its real purpose, which was to provide social contact and a link with "the community" (17).*

These few examples suggest that a purely vocational response to unemployed adults may be unnecessarily limiting and may in some cases deter rather than increase participation. The readiness of unemployed adults to participate in any educational programmes may, however, diminish as pressure on them to prove they are looking for work increases. Tutors on Return to Learn programmes in London reported that unemployed participants were being "harassed" at social security offices and some were dropping out in consequence.

Support

Unemployed people experience greater financial barriers than other groups and many non-participants automatically expect costs to be beyond their reach. Not all LEAs or individual institutions have concessionary fee policies, and charges vary enormously between areas and institutions. It causes confusion and bewilderment that fees are payable for some classes but not others. In one LEA with no fee concession policy, a pilot scheme was initiated in the adult and community college allowing unemployed people and others on state benefits to purchase a 5 voucher. This entitled them to join as many classes as they wished for one term. The scheme had an overwhelming response, 40% from first-time enrolees. Part of its attraction for the unemployed was that it involved unthreatening enrolment procedures: the vouchers showed that students had paid and no further documentation was needed. This freed people from the stigma of regularly producing proof of benefit in order to be let off payment (18).

On-course support. Once engaged in learning, unemployed individuals and groups need a lot of psychological and practical support, particularly to boost their self-confidence and belief in their own abilities. In the Goldsmiths' project for the homeless, the development worker was available for consultation and counselling, and students had their own study room. Students planned and in many cases ran their own activities (19). In some colleges which have targeted unemployed people, a baseroom has been made available and staff have been appointed expressly to assist and guide this group.

Group 3: Women with Dependent Children

OBSTACLES TO RECRUITMENT
This group, particularly working-class women and single parents, experiences a combination of powerful constraints:

- ☐ SITUATIONAL: lack of time, money, transport, childcare.
- ☐ INSTITUTIONAL: limited curricula; education institutions with a strong male ethos.
- ☐ DISPOSITIONAL: cultural pressures to conform to traditional gender roles and resulting lack of social or spatial autonomy; low self-confidence; low expectations.

Recruitment strategies

Recruitment of women has been achieved through the adoption of practical measures such as: adjustment of timing; women-only provision; local venues; low fees and provision of low cost, good quality childcare. The right formula was found in the organisation of Women's Health Days in Coventry, for which free transport and childcare, low cost food and access for the disabled were "central, not marginal" issues. These events "reached and engaged women who had never been involved in this kind of activity" (20).

The range of "dispositional" factors arising largely from cultural pressures which inhibit women's participation are far more difficult to overcome, particularly when they are combined with social and economic deprivation.

Befriending schemes. Some women with dependent children are in such difficult circumstances that their situation precludes participation in any organised activities. For them certain basic needs have to be met before involvement in group learning is a possibility. A voluntary scheme, NEWPIN, was started in a deprived area of south London as a response to the multiple social, economic and personal problems experienced by young mothers in the area. The young women referred to the scheme by doctors, health visitors and social workers suffer from a combination of poverty, poor housing, single parenthood, bad family relationships, isolation, depression, anxiety and difficulties with parenting. Most exist on social security benefits. NEWPIN trains local volunteers – young mothers from the same background – to pair with referrals in order to befriend, support and draw them into activities at the NEWPIN drop-in centre. The centre offers social and educational activities, facilities for making group meals and facilities for children. The scheme offers opportunities for sharing problems, informal counselling, help with parenting, and informal education activities. Evaluation of NEWPIN has demonstrated that the personal and group support offered to referrals enables them to conquer depression and powerlessness and progress in a number of directions. Some referrals have subsequently trained as volunteers and, in many cases, the scheme has stimulated participation in other educational activities: "An unusually high proportion, by local standards, of women become involved in adult education and other community activities, suggesting that NEWPIN is for some at least the preparatory stage in a process of self-development that their earlier disadvantage had prevented" (21).

Informal community activities. As many women with young children are confined for long periods to their immediate environment, introductory learning schemes need to be located in the local community. It is often found that involvement in local organisations such as mother and toddler groups can lead to participation in informal learning activities. There are many examples of this. Activities organised for women on Nottingham council estates and run as social groups rather than classes resulted in enrolments at the local further education college (22). A similar process has occurred at Castle Vale, a large estate on the outskirts of Birmingham visited by the researcher during the course of this project. Here, a wide range of activities for women have been organised at the drop-in community centre which has a creche, playgroup facilities and a coffee bar. The Community Education Development Officer explained that educational programmes developed after an open morning was organised in 1979. This allowed women to try out a range of activities – craft, keep fit, talks, discussion groups, use of typewriters and sewing machines – while their children were looked after free of charge. The event was so successful that it was repeated on a regular basis and resulted in the development of informal learning groups. At the start of this process, the community education tutor was careful to avoid any association with formal education and to keep a balance between social and learning activities:

We started bringing local people in, often with small children themselves, to share their skills, who can identify with people at the centre and don't have a stereotype "teacher" or perfectionist approach. The people themselves run it as a community group not an adult education class, on a very informal basis, financed from fund-raising and a small admission fee. I built in a social time with coffee breaks. This has to be done to encourage access to learning for people who wouldn't respond to formal education. If it's purely educational, you'll lose the less motivated ones.

The informal learning activities at the centre led to the introduction of more formal education programmes: group learning using Open University Community courses; examination courses (GCSE English, Maths and Psychology) and Introduction to Computers. Some participants subsequently joined courses provided elsewhere in the locality: Access and New Opportunities for Women courses and a range of other formal education programmes.

The tutor stressed that increasing working-class women's involvement is a slow and painstaking process. Women undergo a number of changes in their role, and participation can come about at different life-stages: informal activities suit women with small children whose lives are largely taken up with parenting, whereas participation in more formal learning tends to coincide with a later stage in a woman's life. The tutor's approach is to provide support when that moment arrives:

Some mothers are totally in the world of children for a while and not looking outwards. The centre provided a break and something to do NOW. It's when their children start going to nursery or school that the women start looking out and thinking in terms of the future. Many have gone through a number of children before they participate but along the way they've picked up the notion that the centre has things to offer. Anything of interest in adult education outside, I put in front of them, and eventually there's an awareness and a confidence that leads to greater participation in more formal education. This sometimes coincides with changes in personal life.

Mobile schemes. Mobile services have been effective in reaching and attracting women in rural locations and those who are unwilling or unable to take advantage of existing provision. Examples which have been particularly successful at reaching non-participant women are the *Need to Know* project in south Derbyshire; WHISE (Women's Health Welfare and Information Service) in Cornwall; the Rock Community Bus in Saltley, Birmingham (which has been particularly effective in attracting women from ethnic minority groups); and a New Technology project for women in south Wales.

These initiatives have usually been collaborative, supported by joint statutory and voluntary funding.

Programme development

Conventional adult provision has been criticised for having a limiting effect on women's participation. It is claimed that women with children are restricted in what they can attend not only for family and job reasons but because of the limited range of opportunities available to them. According to one tutor the practical barriers to access for women are well known, but the constraints of a stereotyped curriculum are not generally acknowledged:

> *There is little point in overcoming the practical barriers to access if the subjects on offer remain only the traditional ones which reinforce a woman's role as carer and homemaker. The argument that women "choose" these subjects is a red herring: they can only select from the range of options available to them and as long as sex-stereotyping and sexist knowledge bases permeate education systems, no individual woman can be said to have a free "choice" (23).*

Several other tutors also expressed the view that women are short-changed by providers who assume that all they need is an endless supply of cookery, dressmaking and flower-arranging. Some felt that the educational element in informal programmes for women is often undefined and there can be a hidden agenda to reinforce their parental and domestic role. However, there is a dilemma for providers who wish to recruit women in non-participant categories. The experience of some tutors and organisers contacted during the project has been that many will only join informal group learning activities if they are not presented or perceived as educational. Moreover, they have found that those women who do enroll in explicitly educational programmes often confine themselves, in the first instance, to safe and familiar subjects. During an outreach project in the North East, for example, a group of single parents were prepared to enrol at the local college but only in familiar domestic subjects. A project worker organising activities for "non-users" at the Factory Community Centre in London reported that although she was reluctant to put on classes that reinforced gender roles, women students "needed to begin with something familiar" (24). Thus, in cases where providers want to develop programmes for women, familiar domestic subjects are sometimes used as a bridge to other educational activities. The *Need to Know* project, for example, used homecraft skills as a carrot to attract women to basic education and other classes.

The tendency of many women with young children to stick to safe and familiar topics undoubtedly arises from lack of confidence, but it is also probably related to the fact that women are motivated by different concerns at different stages: those with small children may need the stimulus of other company and activities but may be still primarily home- or child-oriented. Older women who are seeking a change in their lives will be looking for broader and more stimulating educational activities that will move them on from exclusively domestic concerns. Thus it is found that many participants in Second Chance courses attend out of a general and undefined need to change direction which is frequently related to life transitions. Women who joined a 30-week Springboard for Women course in Cornwall were all "at a crisis point in their lives: they had been frustrated in the past with endless cake-decorating and embroidery classes when they were actually seeking major life changes through education" (25). The problem is that in traditional adult education such subjects tend to remain the staple and, in some cases, only provision specifically for women.

Practical and vocational skills. There are numerous examples of practical and vocational programmes that have been developed specifically for women with families: courses in non-traditional skills at women's training centres; painting and decorating and computing courses for parents at Willesden College of Technology; carpentry and joinery for women at Bradford and Ilkley Community College.

However, a community education worker at a women's project in the North East questioned the practicality of offering purely job-related courses in areas of high unemployment. Among the problems she identified were:

☐ training does not increase the number of jobs; it only increases competition for existing ones
☐ it does not examine reasons for unemployment or consider local alternatives
☐ women who do not get jobs at the end of the course may feel they have failed (26).

This tutor urged provision of more broadly-based courses for women with both training and self-development elements, a mixture which is now common in the projects and training centres which are run by women for women.

Support

Financial support and costs. One problem that was frequently identified was that at many training centres and projects for women – in particular those specialising in non-traditional (i.e. male-dominated) skills – have been externally financed and have no guarantee of future funding. Similarly, short courses for women in education institutions are often short-term and funded by outside agencies such as the ESF, the Urban Programme and REPLAN. As a result, there is a danger that special funding may be viewed as the only means of providing programmes for women:

We should ask ourselves whether accepting short-term funding is still a useful strategy on the path towards real equality of access. Or are we merely assisting in "papering over the cracks" in a grossly discriminatory system (27)?

Cost is a strong deterrent for many women, particularly single parents and those in low-paid, part-time jobs. For reasons related to family and gender roles, women most often participate in general, recreational or non-vocational education programmes. As these are generally regarded as leisure-oriented, self-developmental activities, they are frequently required to be self-supporting, and fees are often high. Unwaged married women are not encouraged to sign on as unemployed, and as a result, many may not be eligible for fee concessions.

Childcare. Although provision of good childcare is generally considered essential by providers of women's education, services are still few and extremely inadequate. In many centres, organisations and institutions there are no facilities for childcare; in others creches are attached to certain courses only, which skews women's attendance towards those courses rather than others in which they may be more interested. A recent investigation uncovered evidence of a "marked struggle to get any childcare facilities or better childcare facilities" in further and higher education institutions (28). Of two very large colleges contacted during the project, both with sizeable numbers of mature students and an avowed policy to attract more women, one had a creche with places for seventeen children and the other a creche with places for twelve. This illustrates the extent of the problem. As there are often difficulties to do with space and insurance, some colleges are currently experimenting with child-minding arrangements off the premises.

Women-only provision. Initial women-only programmes (taught by women) are considered by many tutors as essential for women who have been away from learning for a long period. The problems women experience in mixed courses have been well documented. The greatest difficulties faced by women students appear to be when they join male-dominated groups taught by male tutors. At one residential college visited during the research, students complained of the attitudes of male students (the majority), who frequently used derogatory comments and terms in relation to women. One student had dropped out because of this and though the problem was recognised by individual tutors, they seemed unable to bring about changes in male students' attitudes. According to one member of staff, discussion of the problem had failed to eliminate it: "Working-class men cannot perceive any discrimination other than that of class."

Siting and timing of learning. It is now widely accepted that the siting and timing of first stage learning activities is of crucial importance to women.

Further and higher education institutions and centres for the unemployed are intimidating as most have a strong male ethos. Unthreatening local venues where there are other women are the most likely to attract them – community centres, village halls, primary and community schools.

Provision of daytime courses also increases the participation of women. A number of providers reported that evening programmes targeting non-participant groups did not attract many women. However, the proportion of women students on a microcomputer course for parents provided by the University of Nottingham increased when daytime courses were introduced. A review of research (29) has argued that the demand for education for women is not met precisely because institutions do not take into account the existence of family/student role conflicts.

Personal support. Research has found that girls and women need more support and encouragement during learning than their male counterparts and that girls tend to be more responsive to outside influences and react more to the attitudes and expectations of "significant others" (30). Providers consistently find that many women experience discouragement, and sometimes hostility, towards their participation from male partners, employers, friends and other family members. Several women students interviewed at a residential college described how they had encountered hostile and derisive reactions to their participation from male relatives and employers. A survey of women returning to education in the Bradford area reported that 50% had faced a negative response from family, friends and especially husbands for deviating from their accepted role or social position:

> Most of the problems were not with combining childcare with education but with husbands. The hub is men's unwillingness to accommodate themselves to a situation in which their partner's domestic role had become of secondary importance (31).

A paper on women students in residential colleges gives a graphic description of the difficulties they face, citing examples of women being prevented from attending by male partners:

> If four years of work has shown us where and how to begin to recruit women, then I fear that the main problem inherent in the process after that remains the same ... husbands ... the fact of a residential course, even just for two days ... will mean a crisis at home for many women. With some groups we would spend weeks in resolving this before a course could be planned (32).

One of the main achievements of women students identified in this paper is the mere fact of getting away from home, sometimes for the first time on their own in 20 years.

Given this situation, many women drop out of courses and the reasons most often identified are to do with health, family and personal crises. The difficulties many women experience in gaining support outside for their participation in education emphasises how important it is for them to receive support *inside* the learning environment. Personal guidance and counselling are essential to ensure retention of women students in organised education:

> *Courses and institutions which have a policy of attracting mature students need to be aware that the difficulties they have may be far more complex and sapping of energy and confidence than the essentially practical problems of finance and childcare ... Not every individual is willing to endure a war of nerves within their family (33).*

Group 4: Older Adults

As this group covers a wide age range, the following is mainly applicable to cohorts aged over 60, the section of the population which is least represented in adult education enrolments. It is estimated that only about 2% of people over 60 participate in education, and participation figures overall indicate that people tend to stop participating when they reach retirement age.

OBSTACLES TO RECRUITMENT
☐ Ill health and physical disabilities.
☐ Social and economic deprivation: many elderly people suffer problems arising from poverty, isolation, lack of transport and poor housing.
☐ Limited educational experience: older adults have received less schooling than the population as a whole.
☐ Blocked future perspectives (inhibiting anticipation or planning).
☐ Dislike of travel, going out at night and in bad weather.
☐ Negative self-perceptions (as being too old to learn).
☐ Negative perceptions of old age by others.

Providers referred to the last of these barriers as one that is often underestimated:

> *The problem is not their perception of themselves. It's the perception younger people have of them. A woman rang me up about her mother and said she shouldn't be tap-dancing. I said if she feels she can tap*

*dance, she can. She'll know when she's puffed! [Promoter of activities
for the elderly in Norwich]*

Recruitment strategies

Recruitment strategies for this group need to be targeted: approaches to the
frail elderly, for example, will, of necessity, be substantially different from
those aimed at younger and more active cohorts. In recognition of this, one
LEA has employed a three-pronged recruitment approach:

□ conventional publicity to attract the active elderly
□ links with social services to reach frail elderly in residential homes and
  day-care centres
□ links with agencies such as Age Concern.

The surveys conducted for the research indicate that older people are often
more likely to join activities as a group than as individuals. A variety of group
recruitment approaches have been used in different parts of the country, some
of which are listed here.

Learning clubs. In Colchester, the area Community Education Officer
initiated a club for older adults, the Grey Friars Guild, as a way of providing
specifically for that group and filling the adult centre on Friday afternoons.
Classes in various subjects are negotiated by members in consultation with
adult education staff. In 1988, the club had 90 members, with 60–70 on a
waiting list.

Luncheon club (for isolated elderly). In Walsall, a luncheon club scheme,
funded by the Health Authority by way of joint finance with Social Services
Department, was directed at isolated and semi-isolated elderly people in the
community. Based in local schools, community and youth centres, the scheme
catered for about 100 people a week, all of whom were referred by the Social
Services. All participants received prior visits from volunteers, accompanied
by persons known to them, to acquaint them with the scheme and discuss
their wishes. Those wishing to participate were collected by minibus on the
appointed days and taken to their local centre, where they were offered a meal
and the opportunity to join in a range of recreational and learning activities.
Although most of the people involved had never previously been engaged in
adult learning, a large number participated enthusiastically in activities such
as crafts.

Self-help groups using of peer tutors and counsellors. The use of older
people themselves as tutors and instructors has been found an effective way
of recruiting older adults and dispelling myths about the capacity of older
people to learn and participate in active pursuits. A number of national and

local self-help initiatives have been launched to improve the range and scope of opportunities available to older adults. National examples include the work of FREE (Forum on the Rights of Elderly People to Education); the University of the Third Age; the Pre-retirement Association and the "Age-Well Campaign". The latter, supported by the Health Education Authority, Age Concern and a variety of national organisations, has disseminated a pack containing case studies and support materials to encourage the formation of new groups and new activities for older people. The Beth Johnson Foundation and the Centre for Health and Retirement Education (CHRE) have piloted a scheme in which a group of 12 volunteers have been trained as health counsellors. Local initiatives include one organised through Age Concern in Yorkshire, which has free classes for elderly people tutored on a voluntary basis by retired experts and lecturers.

Programme development

Some LEA programmes for older adults have been criticised for having an underlying agenda of "disengagement" and reinforcing older adults' self-concept of being too old to engage in certain activities. According to Midwinter, "The major challenge to educationists is to persuade older people to reverse their view of themselves". He urges providers to develop learning opportunities which will help older adults rethink and redefine their role and lead to self-mobilisation, thus breaking away from the perception of older adults as people in need of assistance: "The only criterion for content is whether or not the activity is life-enhancing (34)."

Cooper and Bornat contend that the capacities of older adults are generally underestimated by educators. They recommend a shift from a passive to an active learner model and cite the example of a pensioner group in Hackney which, having identified health as an interest, did not merely listen to lectures on diet and exercise, but made visits to local agencies, cross-examined local health and Social Service officials, and expressed and recorded their views. Cooper and Bornat argue that programmes for older adults should be creative, intellectually demanding and stimulating, and seek to build on older individuals' experience and abilities:

> In mainstream some of the most exciting developments have taken place because tutors have seized opportunities to broaden subject area, e.g. by introducing reminiscence to a clothes-making class; in another, clothes-making led to fashion-printing and design (35).

Tutors contacted during the research who were working with frail elderly individuals and groups in day centres and residential homes were unanimous in their view that older adults require a range of mentally and physically stimulating activities. In Norfolk, Local Authority-funded activities in residential homes and day centres have included a wide range of traditional skills, reminiscence, discussion, writing, poetry, music, movement to music, drama, outings, growing flowers, painting, printing and clay modelling. A similar range of courses has been organised in centres and residential homes in Erdington, "often for people for whom nothing similar has ever been arranged". Some of these activities have had very positive outcomes. An art and craft class for 17 confused elderly people "stimulated memory, movement and mobility and sense of colour" and led to the production of very professional items.

Activity programmes: New Opportunities for Older Adults. New Opportunities courses for the elderly have been developed in some areas with the aim of encouraging older adults to explore a variety of interests and options. Three community-based New Opportunities courses for older adults set up during the Leeds University Pioneer Work Project offered a mixture of study skills, visits to local institutions, and advice on starting various voluntary and educational activities. A good proportion of participants – mostly women in their sixties – subsequently became involved in other informal and formal educational activities (36).

Some active learning schemes for older adults aim not only to enhance the lives of individuals but to utilise their skills and experience for the benefit of the community. A series of day schools for pensioner-activists organised by a welfare rights project and the WEA in the North East engaged participants in community-oriented skills: discussion of local topics and practice in writing business and campaigning letters and running public meetings.

Programmes that encourage coping skills. In later life, people experience decreasing family commitments, possible adjustment to the single state and various degrees of loss: of health, income, partner, relatives and friends. In some areas activities have been developed to help elderly people develop resources to cope with such changes. An oral history project in Coventry helped people come to terms with painful episodes and forge closer bonds with other residents. It also made them feel that "their lives and experiences had been validated in a major way" (37).

In Erdington, a number of practical courses have been designed to help specific groups of older adults. One group suffering from dementia participated in a domestic skills programme which included a six-week vegetarian cooking course. According to the tutor, this led to improved memory, organisation and co-ordination skills. A basic cookery course for elderly widowers succeeded in familiarising participants with modern kitchen equipment and technology. An additional spin-off in this case was that centre staff became more health conscious and more aware of clients' lack of domestic skills. Another targeted course was assisting elderly people to operate more independently in the community by helping them to make more effective use of local transport, education and sports facilities. As participants gained skills and confidence they were phased out and new participants were brought in. People leaving the course were supported by trained volunteers.

The importance of encouraging greater physical independence among the frail elderly was stressed by the co-ordinator of activities for the elderly in Norwich:

> *It's most important to start with activity-based things to show people they can do it. One woman was able to brush her hair for the first time in three years as a result of chair exercises. Often these physical-based things lead on to other activities, such as painting and creative writing.*

Support

Collaboration with other agencies. Most of the providers contacted who had developed educational opportunities for older adults had, of necessity, liaised with a range of statutory and voluntary agencies. In Erdington, the adult education co-ordinator reported that close links had been established with Social Services, the Health Service, libraries and voluntary organisations such as Age Concern in setting up learning activities for the frail elderly in residential homes and day centres. A one-year course, designed to assist the frail elderly and people with special needs to make better use of education opportunities and other community facilities and resources, had been initiated with the support of several Health and Local Authority Departments. This type of collaborative working had become an increasing feature of educational provision for adults in the Erdington area:

> *A strong development has been the increase in the number of agencies we now collaborate with on a constituency area basis. This reflects the idea that there is a total "adults learning" picture which is wider than formal adult education classes. It also reflects the strong inter-departmental and inter-agency basis of much of our developing work (38).*

The introduction of learning activities in centres for the frail elderly also requires the co-operation of the people in daily contact with them. Involving individuals such as wardens and nursing staff has been found to have benefits both for the elderly and for the staff themselves:

> *We negotiate carefully the aims and type of activity envisaged for the group. In all of our courses we work alongside care staff. In this way*

they get more insight into the capabilities of participants and themselves get "trained". [Tutor in Erdington]

The warden was able to promote enthusiasm for the course even before it began (39).

Changing negative perceptions of old age. There is evidence that the sight of older adults actively involved in a range of pursuits can effectively transform negative perceptions of old age. One of the case studies described in the *Age Well Pack* (1988) is a self-help scheme in south Northamptonshire involving a wide range of activities and classes for people between the ages of 50 and 86. According to the case study, the scheme had a very positive impact on the community by:

Serving to increase the self-image of older people and decrease the "bad" image of ageing frequently held by younger people, some of whom are now quite impressed by what the group is doing. This may well help them to age better when their turn comes (40).

Similarly, a small survey of education practitioners conducted a few years ago found that, although tutors working with older adults had encountered initial resistance from colleagues, the actual presence of old people acted as a "powerful solvent" of stereotyped negative expectations (41).

Practitioners have found that older participants tend to become dependent on a particular course or group and some return to the same activities year after year. At one of the ILEA adult education institutes, many daytime classes have a majority of older participants:

Some of whom have been coming for 20 years or more. They get "hooked". It can be a problem to stop them monopolising certain classes. [ILEA tutor]

Some educators believe that this tendency is not sufficiently discouraged by teaching staff. Cooper and Bornat observe (42) that tutors of the elderly often have an over-protective, pastoral emphasis that arises from narrow, stereotyped views of old age, and this discourages independence, choice and risk-taking. They argue that tutors need to be trained to help older adults to become more self-reliant, independent and resourceful.

Material support. As a long interval may have elapsed since an elderly person's last contact with education, tutors stressed the importance of introductory sessions at which the aims, content and expected outcomes of programmes can be carefully discussed. Those developing programmes for people over 60 stressed the need for attention to practical details such as location and its proximity to public transport; venues and positions of rooms (long flights of stairs can be a real obstacle); furniture, lighting, acoustics and visual aids.

Group 5: Ethnic Minority Groups

Generalisations about this group are difficult because of the number and variety of ethnic minority communities in the United Kingdom. The black communities are not cohesive, homogeneous groups: "In this area there are 157 different language groupings alone" (LEA officer, West London). There are, however, some common factors which can be taken into account in access strategies.

OBSTACLES TO RECRUITMENT
☐ Cultural differences, such as different perceptions of gender roles.
☐ Incompatibility of education systems resulting in different expectations.
☐ Alienation from the British education system arising from school experience; conscious or unconscious racism; stereotyping; lack of ethnic minority individuals in teaching and in other "authority" positions (43).
☐ Lack of English-speaking skills among some immigrant groups.
☐ Low expectations.
☐ Low confidence.
☐ Poverty and unemployment: compared with their white counterparts, members of the black communities are more likely to lack educational qualifications and to be in unskilled jobs; twice as likely to be unemployed and to face problems of discrimination and rejection in the labour market (44).

Recruitment strategies

Publicity in different languages is now common practice in areas with large ethnic minority populations, although with the hardest-to-reach groups, publicity needs to be combined with a range of other methods, such as personal contacts, in order to achieve maximum success.

Bilingual outreach workers. It is now widely accepted that the most effective recruitment strategy is for initial contacts to be made by outreach workers from the same cultural background as targeted groups, particularly when these have limited English. The appointment of a multi-lingual guidance worker in Bradford enabled Asian people on housing estates to be reached by LEA education providers for the first time. As a result of this modest initiative, the Asian residents began to view the education service as one for the whole community, which led to increased enquiries and requests from minority communities. In some areas of Birmingham, LEA bilingual interpreters are now available on a part-time basis to assist communication between providers and members of local communities. In Manchester, the success of one scheme – TUBE (Trades Union Basic Education programme) – in negotiating learning programmes with the black communities was attributed by a WEA worker to the use of a team of black workers known and respected in the black communities.

Outreach and the Asian communities. Making contact with some ethnic minority groups can be difficult, even for bilingual development workers. ALBSU development workers in Bedfordshire found reaching members of some Asian communities a time-consuming and challenging process. According to one, telephone contacts brought no results and correspondence was ignored: "They think you're trying to force people into education. They're terrified". Individual door-knocking proved time-consuming and arranged meetings were frequently missed or delayed: "It's very labour-intensive because the barriers are so strong. People may not open the door. They always look through the window first, but when they see I'm Asian, they'll come down."

One of the greatest obstacles the project workers had to surmount was general ignorance about the education system. Most of the individuals contacted did not know there was any difference between adult education and school: "Our big problem was explaining that it isn't coercive, but responsive."

Outreach workers in other parts of the country have also found that with isolated groups such as Asian women, their task is far more complex than simply raising awareness of local educational opportunities. A part-time bilingual WEA tutor in Leicester claimed that her work entailed a social and cultural as well as educational role: "I'm dealing with social and personal problems; making links between Asian groups; counselling; stimulating group formation; helping to preserve culture and traditions."

Enlisting members of the targeted community. A problem which has come to light with industrial decline is that some groups who came to the UK to work in specific industries and subsequently remained, still have very limited English. In Bedfordshire, for example, it has been discovered that a high proportion of Bangladeshi car workers speak very little English even after 30 years' residence, and some are illiterate in their own language. To alleviate this problem requires the development of specific bilingual language programmes, organised with the active assistance of the community concerned. In Sheffield, where a similar problem has been identified with redundant steel-workers from the Yemen, a Council literacy scheme has been launched in which 12 young Yemenis are being trained as literacy assistants to help older members of the community.

Programme development

A particular constraint on ethnic minority participation was identified by some tutors interviewed during the research as the ethnocentric curriculum. One commented: "People will not come to classes which are clearly designed by white people for white people". Some (white) staff working with the black communities argued that the curriculum should validate black experience by incorporating black perspectives and references to other cultures. However, a (black) co-ordinator of a targeted Access course suggested that this well-meaning strategy sometimes goes too far: in her opinion there had been some "over-compensation" in course development, with multicultural perspectives often being grafted, awkwardly and artificially, onto existing content. As a result, she claimed that black students were sceptical of the value of such courses.

Consultation with ethnic community groups. The surveys conducted for this project indicated that ethnic minority groups have a clear idea of the educational services they require. However, contacts with providers and visits to deprived urban areas made during the research revealed a widespread tendency among education staff and referral agencies to consider ethnic minority learning needs exclusively in terms of English for speakers of other languages or low level basic education programmes. In one area of London, it was reported that JobCentres automatically referred all black clients, irrespective of experience and qualifications, to ESL courses in the local college where there was no guidance or self-assessment service. Thus little or no account was taken of individual ability and experience. In other areas, however, adult educators have consulted fully with local ethnic groups and developed courses in response to identified and stated needs. In Tower Hamlets, for instance, there has been liaison between the Adult Education Institute, local industry and the Asian communities to help ethnic minority groups move into employment areas where skill shortages have been identified and into occupations where they have been under-represented. Among the results of this collaboration have been an Access to Childcare course for Bangladeshi women and courses in industrial garment making and leather work.

Schemes which have resulted in enhanced provision for the black communities have usually involved consultation and negotiation with the targeted groups. The TUBE scheme in Manchester operated a "demand response model" involving careful consultation with groups before any educational activities were organised. The ALBSU project in Bedfordshire (45) involved ethnic minority groups in the planning, design, delivery and evaluation of basic education and ESL programmes. This led to the identification of group learning requirements and the development of a range of taster linked-skills programmes.

Other examples of successful demand response models are the

UDACE-supported Luton Black Opportunities Project where a consumer-negotiated curriculum included tasters in word-processing, computing, wood trades and Starting your Own Business; Bangladeshi Fresh Start in Camden, launched after wide consultation with the target group; and the Croydon Language Scheme where over 600 people are regularly involved in a wide range of negotiated classes and activities.

Expressed interests and needs. Many members of ethnic minority groups are unemployed and the evidence received during the project overwhelmingly suggests that they are more interested in practical or vocational programmes leading to qualifications or jobs than in activities that are leisure or self-development-oriented. At an outreach centre in Bristol, the co-ordinator quickly discovered that members of the ethnic communities were not interested in courses in social and communication skills: "They wanted useful and practical training." FEU surveys have found that courses without instrumental aims are viewed as "diversionary luxuries" by ethnic minority groups (46). A survey of Asian women in the London Borough of Ealing revealed learning requirements which appear to be fairly representative of a number of minority communities:

☐ skill-based courses with language support
☐ technology training, particularly information technology
☐ care-based courses (related to health and children)
☐ English language courses and help with understanding the British system (issues to do with local community, schools, racism and personal safety)
☐ programmes to do with preserving indigenous culture and communicating it to the next generation
☐ certificated courses
☐ educational guidance
☐ help in achieving recognition of existing qualifications (47).

The overwhelmingly instrumental view of education held by many black people was confirmed in interviews with the researcher. A mature student who had attended a conference on Access to Higher Education found it impossible to relate to the more varied aims and objectives being discussed: "Black people only go into education for job training, not for the joy of it but to increase their career potential." Although other black students expressed the fear of being restricted to a "ghetto" of practical courses, on the whole this was a minority view. The evidence as a whole suggests that the programmes that are most successful in attracting ethnic minority communities are those which provide useful, practical and certificated skills and, where possible, routes into employment.

Support

Some ethnic minority groups prefer to join activities which are restricted to members of their own culture. This was clear in Asian responses to the surveys conducted for this research. Although some black students have an understandable fear that targeted courses might become a form of segregation, there are a number of good reasons for providing them, at least at the initial stages of adult learning: some ethnic minority individuals avoid courses where the majority of students are white; some have restricted English skills and need language classes and bilingual support; women in some Asian communities lead very sheltered lives and will not attend classes open to both sexes and all races. For this reason, it is necessary to provide separate programmes in the first instance. The Asian Women's Project in Newham provides a sheltered environment where women can meet socially in a supportive atmosphere, learn English and a range of vocational skills, and gain knowledge of the local community. This initial experience gives many participants the confidence to move on to courses at Newham College.

Bridging the culture gap. The surveys revealed a strong demand from the Asian communities for programmes that would help them understand the British education system and enable them to assist in their children's education. In some areas courses have been specially designed to involve more ethnic minority people in local schools: e.g. pilot school governors' training schemes for ethnic minority groups in Newham and Ealing. Elsewhere this interest has been effectively used as a springboard to participation in other educational activities. In Leicester, a WEA worker initiated a course specifically to help Asian mothers become involved in the educational progress of their children. The course recruited about 30 women and as participants started to discover other learning needs, swiftly led to the development of a range of other courses.

Preserving traditional culture. As well as learning more about the host culture, many ethnic minority groups are anxious to preserve their own traditions and to pass them down to British-born generations. To meet this need, the WEA worker in Leicester initiated programmes in traditional Asian culture and skills: traditional crafts, Asian dancing, Gujerati drama, Indian history, Indian culture and mother tongue languages. She also pioneered a course to help white teachers communicate better with Asian children.

Guidance and language support. Guidance services are urgently required for ethnic minority groups so that individual learning needs can be properly assessed and people referred to the appropriate levels. Some ethnic minority individuals are already highly qualified but cannot use their qualifications or get them validated in this country. Such people are often judged more on their ability to speak English than on their existing qualifications and abilities, and many are automatically referred to English as a Second Language classes which sometimes carry a low level stigma. A particular barrier for second language speakers is that they need a certain level of proficiency in English language in order to be eligible for certain forms of education and training. Thus without language support, the range of education opportunities open to many ethnic minority individuals is severely limited. This highlights the need for bilingual support in education institutions. Lack of bilingual support and bilingual teaching staff was identified throughout the research as a major reason for the low participation of ethnic minority individuals in many theoretically open courses.

Psychological support. To counteract the low confidence and expectations of ethnic minority individuals, particularly those who are unemployed, some providers have tried to convey a "positive achiever", rather than a "deficiency" message in their recruitment methods, programming and curricula. One community school has tried to emphasise an achiever model by putting posters and pictures around the walls featuring nationally and internationally known black achievers. Black students also need encouragement to take up educational opportunities at all levels. Part of Croydon's 1988 in-service training programme was a course on counselling bilingual students about education opportunities. The general aim was to enable ESL teachers to refer and encourage bilingual students to participate in a wider range of courses. However, the lack of black teaching staff, at all educational levels, may undermine such initiatives. It undoubtedly contributes to ethnic minority non-participation in, and alienation from, post-school education:

> *The failure of institutions to recruit black staff and to be seen effectively to be challenging the racism of individuals and curricula, itself conveys the message to black people that further and higher education is not intended for them (48).*

Teaching staff. The research highlighted a widespread need for staff development to help white staff understand and respond sympathetically to ethnic minority cultural expectations. One of the problems that arises from having predominantly white teaching staff is that they may be unfamiliar with the traditions of different ethnic groups. Some tutors contacted during the research had unknowingly scheduled activities for Asian groups during their religious events and festivals which led to non-attendance. Others had organised mixed classes, with disastrous results: "Our worst problem last year was that we had Muslim Imams and women in the same group. Since respect is due to the Imams, the women wouldn't contribute at all." This indicates the importance of preliminary research and consultation in ethnic minority group targeting. Staff recruiting Asian women to short residential courses found it took a year of painstaking discussion and negotiation. Consultation over practical arrangements was essential: "It was essential to let Asian women know the exact times of starting and finishing activities, and the mixed washing facilities at the college had to be changed."

Some groups, particularly more recent immigrants, have experiences and expectations of education which make it difficult for them to accept the informal methods commonly used in first stage adult learning. An Afro-Caribbean student complained to the researcher about informal, discussion-based types of learning: "I find it difficult to adapt to this new style. I'm used to people lecturing to me and I listen if I want to. Many of us aren't prepared for these new ways of learning." Such attitudes create difficulties for tutors accustomed to encouraging a more participatory style of learning. A tutor in Bradford reported that recent immigrants in her classes expect to learn books off by heart: "They are used to the old instructional model and as a result we have to do a lot of preparatory work on the nature and value of discussion."

Progression to more advanced levels of education. The evidence as a whole suggests that black students who wish to take more advanced courses often experience acute problems. There appears to be a general lack of provision to help black people move from ESL and basic education classes to other levels of education. FEU surveys (49) have found that black students generally do not gain access to courses leading to clear job opportunities, to higher status vocational training or to higher education. According to the authors of these reports, this is often due to stereotyping, prejudice about ability range, insensitivity and misconceptions.

One initiative visited during the research provided a good example of the problems faced by black people wishing to progress from introductory short courses to more advanced college courses. Ludlow Annexe in the St Paul's area of Bristol was at that time providing MSC-funded, City and Guilds-accredited short courses in electrical skills and painting and decorating. Recruitment to the courses was no problem: "We get people of all ages, all races and nationalities. They bring their brothers, sisters, even mothers and fathers sometimes. Eighty per cent are Afro-Caribbean." The major problems identified by the outreach worker were to do with progression to the main college, notably:

☐ The preliminary courses were too short and too basic to lead smoothly to further training in the areas covered.
☐ There were no clear progression routes to more advanced courses at the college. (Here a vicious circle was in evidence: to enrol on the short courses people had to be unemployed, but College provision was weighted towards those in employment and on part-time release.)
☐ Some college courses were oversubscribed and others had inflexible entry criteria.
☐ Individuals who did get into college courses experienced intense problems

of alienation in a white, middle-class institution with no support mechanisms.

Recognition of these kinds of problems has led to attempts, in some areas, to provide better progression routes. In London a collaborative initiative by REPLAN, OCSL (Open College of South London), local councils and black community groups has aimed to develop trade and craft courses for Afro-Caribbean adults which are linked with existing certificated provision and therefore have clear progression routes.

Progression to employment. Several of the tutors interviewed pointed out that participation in education and training cannot alter or eliminate the enormous problems ethnic minority groups face in competing for jobs in the labour market. One outreach worker was particularly worried about presenting training or study as a solution to the employment difficulties experienced by black groups. He referred to the growing sense of despair he had noticed in the local community:

> *I sense now a mood of almost resignation among residents about not being able to progress. People aren't trying any more. Just to take individuals onto courses isn't enough. ... In reality people can't get jobs so can't get employer support for training courses, and can't get grants. The problems of racism and stereotyping should be tackled ... There's lots of work going on but it's piecemeal. It needs to be tackled everywhere and at all levels.*

This concern was echoed by several tutors who foresaw even greater difficulties for jobless black individuals with the more stringent application of the "actively seeking work" provision at benefit offices.

Additional Non-Participant Categories

People with basic education needs

A survey carried out by Lancaster University for ALBSU and MSC (November 1987) suggested that at least six million adults in this country have problems with reading, writing or numeracy. The survey found that three-quarters of the people reporting difficulties were from manual working-class backgrounds, in particular poor or unemployed people in deprived areas and single parents. Members of this group, therefore, tend to be on low incomes and in low socio-economic groups.

OBSTACLES TO RECRUITMENT
As well as problems relating to unemployment, poverty and poor housing,

many members of this group have a number of *dispositional attributes* which inhibit their participation in education:
- [ ] insecurity
- [ ] distrust
- [ ] low aspirations
- [ ] limited time perspectives
- [ ] dependency
- [ ] negative attitudes to education
- [ ] shame at low educational level (50).

Recruitment strategies

Targeting. Research conducted in Iowa (51) identified six main sub-groups of people in basic education programmes. All had different motives for participation which indicated the nature of recruitment approaches which might be directed at each group.

1. Women homemakers. Many of these had left school early because of marriage or pregnancy. This group was the easiest to recruit. Family and domestic responsibilities were cited as the main reasons for enrolment.

2. People on the lowest incomes (mostly unemployed males). Their motives for involvement were literacy development, self-improvement, economic need and educational advancement:

> *ABE could be an economic end for this group and program linkages to job training agencies and job placement organizations might facilitate both recruitment and more effective instruction.*

3. Older adults. Members of this group had left school early to start work and were characterised by low incomes and the highest incidence of welfare entitlement. Described by Beder and Valentine (1987) as "the urged", these participants were mainly motivated by the support and influence of others: "Gentle and warm urging from ABE student, friends and relatives or employers might be an effective form of informal recruitment."

4. Young adults. These were mostly unemployed and motivation to learn was generally low. Beder and Valentine suggest that recruitment would be best achieved by emphasising the "launching" elements in learning: those which promote transition from youth to adult roles: "They need to be convinced that education leads to gaining respect and adult prerogatives."

5. "Climbers" (older skilled adults). This group had the highest number of skilled and black members and the highest incidence of separation, divorce and widowhood. Incomes were relatively higher than in most of the other groups and participants were generally motivated by socio-economic aspirations. The researchers suggest that recruitment for this group should be targeted at urban areas and promotional materials should emphasise the relation between education and socio-economic advancement.

6. *"Low ability strivers."* This was the smallest group, consisting predominantly of single, unskilled males. According to the researchers, this group, motivated exclusively by job advancement, presented the greatest challenge to recruiters because of a general lack of interest in education.

Raising self-concept. Many people with literacy problems do not attend literacy courses. Basic education tutors and organisers have found that some are too ashamed to reveal their lack of education:

> *There is little doubt that there is still considerable stigma attached to the problems associated with literacy. Words like embarrassment, shyness, self-consciousness accounted for over 50% of reasons for people not seeking help in this area (52).*

To deal with this problem, Beder and Valentine urge the use of positive promotional strategies which raise the self-concept of individuals, rather than negative ones which imply that students in need of basic education are "deficient". This requires careful and tactful use of language in initial publicity.

Integration with other activities. Outreach project workers in Sheffield found that an effective recruitment strategy was to present basic education not in isolation but in the context of other activities and topics:

> *Quite a lot of enthusiasm was generated by adults testing themselves out in a group even when it had been brought together for a completely different purpose. Another effective approach was to provide basic education courses immediately after popular and familiar classes such as Keep Fit. Once people came to things they'd heard of and didn't find threatening, they were often prepared to have a go at basic maths and English. This method of recruitment worked best when the basic education class followed shortly after the "popular" class. It was then really easy to encourage adults to stay on (53).*

People in rural areas

OBSTACLES TO RECRUITMENT
- ☐ Lack of learning opportunities.
- ☐ Lack of transport.
- ☐ Declining public services.

☐ Small populations.

Many rural areas are now suffering from a cycle of decline: reduction of agricultural employment, lower birth rates, loss of primary schools, closure of local services (sub-post offices, food shops, doctors' surgeries), loss of transport services and housing development. According to one report (54) approximately 25% of rural households are on or below the poverty line. Unemployment, though small in comparison to urban areas, can have a more devastating effect: "Although the numbers may not be great, its effect on the fabric of society may be greater than in urban areas" (55).

Educational opportunities for adults in rural areas are either non-existent or severely limited and, as a result, the problems of access are often worse than in urban areas. The inadequacy of public transport systems in rural areas are well known, and this deters particularly women and the elderly from seeking opportunities outside their place of residence. A tutor in Cornwall outlined some of the problems that inhibit the participation of rural women. As rural communities are generally more conservative and traditional, it is very difficult for women to acknowledge dissatisfaction with their lives. There is a general lack of employment opportunities, which reduces a major motivation. Moreover, activities and facilities for women "which have been commonplace in big cities for 10 years are still at a pioneering stage in rural areas and viewed with some suspicion (56)".

Recruitment strategies

In small communities personal contacts are especially important as a way of disseminating information. An ALBSU project discovered that 90.9% of rural respondents in one area claimed to have no knowledge of the literacy help available in spite of intensive publicity including information attached to milk bottle collars and a series of public announcement on television. The project workers concluded that personal contacts by people known and trusted in the community were essential to recruitment:

> *Without doubt the most effective way of reaching these people is through personal contact and establishing trusting relationships. This is only likely to be achieved by having local persons acting as contacts, the wrong selection of whom would almost certainly alienate potential students (57).*

Programme development

One of the problems with developing LEA courses in rural areas is that enrolment numbers are linked to funding, and allowances are not always made for the small size of rural populations. Several adult education organisers suggested that LEAs should contemplate developing more outreach learning in rural areas and permit small classes to run, or that they should provide seed funding to help rural residents start small self-help study groups with tutorial support, using open learning materials such as those developed by the Open University.

Some innovative rural learning programmes have been developed by the WEA and other voluntary organisations with pump-priming finance from rural charities or national agencies such as REPLAN. Examples are WEA/REPLAN Arts workshops in Herefordshire and rural Second Chance programmes organised by the WEA, West Mercia District. These have been organised in full recognition of the practical constraints which impede participation. Rural Second Chance, for example, provided "Community Wheels" – a taxi service for the equivalent of bus fares, cheap meals and a creche which was "massively used."

This brief overview of the sub-groups who make least use of existing education opportunities highlights not only their problems of access but the extent to which measures to increase their participation have been supported by special, usually short-term funding. Although there are some LEAs and institutions with a "whole community" outlook, the research suggests that a large proportion of targeted provision and support measures for people from non-participant groups are, as described by one LEA officer, "add-ons" and often the first to be cut at times of economic pressure. The extent to which different providers have been able, or willing, to provide for under-represented groups of mature students is explored in Section 4.

References

1. Hothersall, G. Education and social growth in contrasting neighbourhoods: a study in Skipton. *Adult Education*, 45,1, 1972.
2. Edwards, J. *In* Mace, J. & Yarnit, M. (eds) *Time Off To Learn: Paid educational leave and low-paid workers*. Methuen, 1987, pp122–34.
3. Described in Mace, J. & Yarnit, M. (eds) *op. cit.*
4. Burke, C. *et al*. Take Ten. *In* Mace, J. & Yarnit, M. (eds) *op. cit.*, p108.
5. Mace, J. *A Time and a Place. A study of education and manual work at Goldsmiths' College, 1983–84*. Goldsmiths' College, London, 1985, p26.
6. Jones, H. & Charnley, A.H. *Adult Literacy: A study of its impact*. NIAE, 1978, p75.
7. see Barr, J. Keeping a low profile: adult education in Scotland. *Adult Education*, 59,4, 1987.
8. Alexander, D. & Stewart, T. An educational perspective on community education in Scotland. *Scotttish Journal of Adult Education*, 5,3, 1974.
9. Edwards, J. *Working Class Education in Liverpool: A radical*

*approach.*Centre for Adult and Higher Education, University of Manchester, 1986, p74; and in Mace, J. & Yarnit, M. (eds) *op. cit.*, p133.

10. Mace, J. *op. cit.*, 1985.

11. Challis, J. *Building and Communication: Report on MSC-sponsored linked-skills project at the Lee Centre 1981–82.* The Lee Centre, 1982.

12. O'Shea, J. & Corrigan, P. *op. cit.*

13. Bridger, S. *op. cit.*, p49.

14. Fraser, L. & Ward, K. *op. cit.*, p89.

15. Shimmin, P. *Arts Workshops for the Unemployed.* Hereford WEA, Hereford Arts and REPLAN, 1988.

16. Kitchen, P. Non-formal adult education: the role it could play in the inner cities. *In Adult Education in the Inner City Areas: The practice, the policy and allocation of resources.* Adult Learning Federation, 1981.

17. Rogers, D. *Life Chances: A working report on community education with single, homeless people.* The Lee Centre, 1985, pp31, 44.

18. Adlington, E. *Educational Vouchers for Unemployed Adults.* NIACE/REPLAN, 1988.

19. Goldsmiths' College. *Something to Teach and Something to Learn: An initial research report on an outreach project.* Goldsmiths' College, 1986.

20. Issitt, M. Organising women's health days: a feminist approach to community education in Coventry. *Journal of Community Education,* 6,4, pp8–10, 1988.

21. Pound, A., Mills, M. & Cox, T. *A Pilot Evaluation of NEWPIN: A home visiting and befriending scheme in south London.* NEWPIN, 1987.

22. Drysdale, D.H. A joint experiment to combat social deprivation. *Adult Education,* 46, 1973.

23. Hutchins, S. Women's education in Cornwall. 1988.

24. Colwell, D. *Report on the Factory Project.* ALFA, 1988.

25. Hutchins, S., in correspondence with researcher, 1988.

26. Mills, J. *The Bridge Project: Training for women in Washington.* Washington Tyne and Wear Bridge Project, 1986.

27. Mills, J. Funding for women's courses. *Working with Women Bulletin, 2.* REPLAN, 1988.

28. Coats, M. *Childcare Provision in Institutions of Higher Education: A survey.* NIACE/REPLAN, 1989.

29. Osborn, M. *et al., op. cit.,* p96.

30. Finn, J.D. & Dulberg, R. Sex differences in educational attainment: the process. *Comparative Education Review,* 24,2, 1980.

31. Bridger, S. *op. cit.,* pp69–70.

32. Browning, D. Women and Northern College. A paper presented at a conference at Fircroft College, 1982.

33. Bridger, S. *op. cit.,* p83.

34. Midwinter, E. *Age is Opportunity: Education and older people.* Centre for Policy on Ageing, 1982, pp62, 66.

35. Cooper, M. & Bornat, J. Equal opportunity or special need: combatting

the woolly bunny. An assessment of the work at the ILEA Education Resource Unit for Older People. *Journal of Educational Gerontology,* 3,1, p35, 1988.

36. Liddington, J. What do you do after a "New Opportunities" course? *Adult Education,* 61,1, pp36–40, 1988.

37. Castle, E. Then and now: a course for old people. *Adult Education,* 60,2, p125, 1987.

38. Bateson, G. *Erdington Area AE Report.* Erdington Area Adult Education Office, 1989.

39. Castle, E. *op cit.*

40. *Age Well Pack.* Ideas Sheet 8, p43. Health Education Authority, 1987.

41. Groombridge, B. Older students: the perceptions of education providers in Great Britain. *Journal of Educational Gerontology,* 2,1, pp19–30, 1987.

42. Cooper, M. & Bornat, J. *op. cit.*

43. According to a CRE survey in 1988, 2% of teachers in schools and less than 20 head teachers are black.

44. Department of Employment statistics, March 1988.

45. Adult Literacy and Basic Skills Unit. *Bedfordshire Project: Interim report.* ALBSU, 1988.

46. Further Education Unit *FE in Black and White.* FEU/Longman, 1987; and FEU Project 396, Bulletin 2, 1988.

47. Report by the Ealing Economic Development Unit, outlined in a talk by Mrs Charangit Singh to the NIACE Women's Education Sub-Committee in 1988.

48. Bridger, S. *op. cit.,* pp122–3.

49. FEU *op. cit.,* 1987 and 1988.

50. *See* Irish, G.L. Reaching the least educated adult. *New Directions for Continuing Education,* 8, 1980.

51. Beder, H. & Valentine, T. *op. cit.*

52. Geraint Evans, J. *Adult Basic Education in Powys, 1983–85. ALBSU Development Project Final Report.* ALBSU, 1986.

53. Adult Literacy and Basic Skills Unit *Report of the Sheffield Outreach Project.* ALBSU, 1986.

54. Packman, J. Paper presented to Norfolk Rural Council, 1988.

55. *Rural Needs Bulletin,* 1. NIACE/REPLAN, 1987.

56. Hutchins, S. Women's education in Cornwall. 1988.

57. Geraint Evans, J. *op. cit.*

Section 4

Education Providers: Policy, Practice and Institutional Innovation

This section provides an overview of the main publicly-funded education providers, based on contacts and interviews with education staff and a review of relevant documentation. The section is divided into two parts: the first discusses access opportunities offered by providers of first stage (non-advanced) learning, in particular the Local Education Authorities; the second explores non-traditional student access to further and higher education.

Providers of First Stage Learning Activities

The main providers of informal, introductory learning opportunities for adults are Local Education Authorities (LEAs); the Workers' Educational Association (WEA); further education colleges; residential colleges; some universities and polytechnics; and voluntary organisations.

It is not an overstatement to say that, during the time this project was conducted, the education system was in a state of ferment. A variety of changes in structures and funding arrangements were taking place or anticipated and it is not possible to say with any degree of certainty how these will eventually affect the extent and nature of learning opportunities for adults, especially non-traditional learners. Many of the people interviewed were uncertain about the future of existing services, particularly work with new clienteles – an anxiety which in some cases turned out to be well-founded.

The extent to which the practitioners interviewed were providing a service for non-traditional learners depended on a combination of factors: organisational policy and lines of accountability; traditional practice; local socio-economic factors; local government priorities; the personalities, attitudes and views of senior staff and (in the case of Local Authority provision), elected members; and, crucially, the amount of finance and special funding available. For many providers of education for adults, economic survival was the key factor determining what was or was not provided: "What we're most concerned with these days is just keeping the show on the road" (LEA adult education organiser). This kind of comment was frequently made during the research.

The Workers' Educational Association

Like other educational organisations, the WEA has suffered financial problems in recent years, notably due to cuts in grant allocations from central and local government. Although provision varies greatly from district to district, the WEA has been one of the most effective organisations in taking learning activities to non-traditional learners. Some areas have an excellent record of providing outreach activities for specific groups such as women, older adults, ethnic minority groups and the mentally handicapped, often in collaboration with other providers. In some areas, however, there were signs that WEA provision was becoming polarised. Some tension was reported between staff involved in development work with "disadvantaged"groups and voluntary branches concerned more with maintaining traditional general and liberal arts courses for a more established clientele. One district organiser identified this as a growing problem:

> Work with disadvantaged groups generally depends on traditional popular courses for finance, but the new work upsets and threatens traditional work with established groups who are used to certain types of provision and social mix. This can lead to a resistance that can effectively stymie development work.

In Scotland, where the WEA operates under different funding arrangements, the extent to which individual districts provide for special groups depends largely on local conditions and local government priorities. In the south-east, courses for targeted groups had been initiated and supported by the local council; in another district, however, a tutor-organiser described how, at a time of acute financial constraint, her role was becoming increasingly one of fund-raiser:

> Adult education is at the bottom of the pecking order these days. We're now having to get funding from a variety of sources. There was no growth in the budget this year, so more and more of my time is spent chasing extra funds to help us keep the ball rolling.

In this case the tutor-organiser was being forced to work in an entirely opportunistic way: "Planned educational development is out of the window. We have to keep developing new programmes and trying to sell them."

The Universities

Similar constraints have been experienced in university continuing education and extra-mural departments, although universities such as Leeds, Nottingham and Southampton continue to provide a wide range of courses for their local communities. The results of cuts in resources, changes in funding and the current stress on cost-effectiveness have steered a number of continuing education departments into income-generating activities such as professional training, Post-Experience Vocational Education (PEVE), or the search for foreign earnings. These trends have aroused fears that university continuing education will lose the incentive to provide for educationally disadvantaged groups and will increasingly reflect the "elitism" of the parent body:

> *The updating conception and the bent towards the professional leads at least initially to more education for the already educated ... These trends will interact with the impact of the cuts and the fee increases which are already excluding the less well-qualified potential students who tend to come from the working class, to intensify the elite nature of British universities (1).*

Residential Colleges

Although traditionally concerned with providing full-time programmes of study and Trades Union courses, particularly for men from working-class backgrounds, several residential colleges now also provide a range of short residential programmes for local community groups. At one residential institution – Northern College – group education is central to the college ethos. A team of short course organisers, working jointly with neighbouring LEAs, negotiates short courses with local groups such as pensioners, women's groups and people from ethnic minorities. The approach involves three stages: contact and negotiation with groups, a half-day visit to the college (with transport provided), and implementation of the negotiated programme. The main problem, according to staff, is one of meeting demand, as there are constraints on bed space and the numbers of children that can be accommodated in creche provision.

Fircroft College in Birmingham also has a short course programme of weekend and two-to-three day events, negotiated with the local community and co-ordinated with other providers. In this case, the main problem identified by staff was finance: "Short courses don't earn and we have to subsidise them from money made from conferences. We try to make them as cheap as possible for participants but they're very expensive to run."

All the staff interviewed commented on the extraordinary growth in confidence and self-esteem that people with no previous post-school educational experience gain from a short experience of residential learning. Several tutors argued that residential institutions should shift more towards providing short residential courses rather than "pushing people into higher education", which seems to have become their principal role.

This is what the colleges should be doing. This is what they're good at and this is what no other institutions can do as well. A couple of days here can achieve more change in people than any number of part-time courses.

Local Education Authorities

Local Education Authorities have long been one of the main providers of educational opportunities for adults. Over two million adult students in England and Wales took more than 100,000 LEA courses in 1985–86 (2). There are, however, marked variations between authorities. Large city LEAs tend to provide more programmes and courses for educationally or economically disadvantaged groups than the shires, which cater predominantly for an affluent middle class. The ILEA in particular has operated a policy of targeting opportunities at groups usually under-represented in organised education. A survey conducted in six of the ILEA adult education institutes during the 1980s revealed that, compared with the 1960s, a much larger proportion of students were in educationally disadvantaged categories. Almost 50% were from ethnic minority communities – a group strikingly under-represented in most LEA provision. This change was attributed partly to economic and demographic factors, but mainly to the ILEA's policies on equal opportunities, fee concessions, changes in curricula and the allocation and redirection of resources by the institutes to meet particular needs (3).

By contrast, a large neighbouring shire authority with a mixed population has, according to an LEA officer interviewed during this project, "no development workers attached to centres, no outreach budget, only a tiny amount for publicity and no real publicity mechanisms." The obstacles to change which she identified were lack of awareness, complacency and a willingness to continue providing a service for an established and self-perpetuating clientele:

In the shires there's a danger of not recognising the different social groupings until someone prompts you. We need to reach out to new people. I feel our service is servicing only those who are traditionally joiners.

These examples represent two extremes of the service. Not all shires have been as slow to change as this one and not all inner city authorities have been as conscientious as the ILEA in providing a service for a real cross-section of the community.

Characteristics of LEA provision

In spite of geographical variations, LEA adult provision has largely retained its traditional image and ethos. HMI reports over a four-year period during the 1980s revealed the following characteristics:

☐ over 90% of provision is course-based
☐ centre programmes are remarkably similar
☐ classes are mainly delivered in the evenings
☐ the same students tend to return year after year
☐ most courses are subject to rules about minimum enrolment numbers
☐ classes are discrete and there is little activity to bring students together in centres
☐ there is generally little or no student participation in decision-making
☐ there is limited provision for special needs
☐ there is little correlation between programmes and community needs
☐ there is limited experimentation with new initiatives and exploitation of external funds and resources (4).

In spite of this somewhat depressing picture, there is evidence that LEA adult education provision has been evolving in some areas, albeit slowly, to meet the requirements of new learners. While continuing to meet demand from their established clienteles, many authorities have also initiated some programmes for specific groups and adopted measures to facilitate their access, such as fee concession policies and outreach and guidance services. In addition, community education policies have been adopted in various forms by an estimated 50% of authorities. Although there are a variety of definitions and models of community education, it is generally accepted that one of its guiding principles is to reach those sections of the community traditionally neglected or excluded by education providers.

The usual mix now offered by the majority of LEAs is a combination of general education, interest, leisure and qualification-based courses, with some initiatives for specific groups – the unemployed, women, older adults – often financed from external sources. Some authorities have gone a stage further by introducing special "innovation" budgets, new learning units and mobile services particularly to provide for hitherto unreached groups in the community.

Factors Important in Attracting New Clienteles

Venues and approaches

Adult education venues vary enormously in style and ethos, and, consequently, in the nature of their clienteles. Some centres visited during the project had a "whole community" approach and participants from all sections of the community; others had a more formal, middle-class ambience and clients to match. The differences depended to a large degree on the views and attitudes of individual centre heads, who undoubtedly stamp their personality on a place and the way it works. A newly-appointed principal in a rural area described to the project how, on taking up her appointment, she had immediately set about changing the centre's image in the community:

> When I arrived here there was a tutor-led philosophy. I've tried to introduce a new style. I made myself visible in the locality, sent letters home to school children, asked people to get in touch with me. We've changed the telephone manner and style of courses and generally become more user-friendly.

All members of the public are welcome at this centre, and cards inviting people to free tea and biscuits during the evenings of enrolment week have been incorporated into publicity material.

The principal of another rural centre in Derbyshire also had strong views on the centre's role as a focal point in the community where people can meet socially and for community purposes. He encourages users to feel that it is "their place" by inviting them to plan, publicise and run activities:

> The biggest step is getting people through that door and any step I can take to help that process I'll take. Most of the things that go on here that aren't classes are free of charge. It's really a community centre for all local groups. It operates as a community resource and focal social area. There are people in the coffee bar the whole time. We let groups use workshops, use rooms, borrow equipment. A group of young mums meet in the coffee bar every morning, they have become an autonomous group. It works like a big co-operative. We do all our own publicity and distribution is all done free of charge. We sent leaflets round the villages asking what people needed and they rolled in. We ask people for their suggestions and these are passed to teachers who collect them and we put a programme together.

As a result of this open-door policy, about 2000 people a week use the centre, some travelling a large distance to get there. They represent a wide cross-section of the community:

> People come here because of the ethos, atmosphere, liveliness; there are no social barriers. A lot of elderly people and young mothers use the centre during the day and 20% of users are unemployed. We did a survey in 1982 and it showed a large number of people are from groups D and E. We have millionaires who come as well! The mentally

*handicapped come for various things and we have physically
handicapped who come to everything, although there are special things
like cookery for people with visual impairment.*

The researcher visited a number of other centres and community schools
which operate according to the same community philosophy. A centre in
central London which, until recently, was open seven days a week, was
providing organised activities and educational programmes for a number of
community groups, as well as legal and financial advice services. According
to a staff member: "We're lively, small-scale and have an 'open-house'
atmosphere: people look after you here."

Publicity

Tutors at a popular and well-used community education project in London
had rented local market stalls and distributed free balloons and leaflets at
the local station and in shopping centres. However, many LEA staff
interviewed during the research were generally sceptical about the
effectiveness of conventional publicity in attracting non-users: "The trouble
with leaflets through doors is that you're competing with double glazing and
all the other rubbish. It all goes in the bin." One centre head was critical of
the style of conventional publicity distributed by LEA centres: "Look at the
first pages of this brochure, they're full of administration. It's ideal for us but
is it right for people in the High Street?" Several LEA officers also questioned
the value of using a single form of publicity, such as brochures, as such
publications usually attract only the traditional joiners. The consensus was
that publicity needs to be specially targeted at different clienteles, and that
publicity targeted at non-participants should aim to change perceptions of
"education" and stimulate an interest in what it can offer. It should contain
clear information on incentives and outcomes, and should avoid educational
jargon and patronising wording.

During the time the research was conducted, a number of local authorities
and individual centres were beginning to attach greater importance to
publicity and marketing. One ILEA institute had appointed a marketing
director to promote its role in the community. A needs questionnaire,
circulated to community groups and decision-makers, was intended to
"transform" local perceptions of the centre and of the nature and accessibility
of adult education.

Tasters and promotional events

An adult education centre in Croydon found that an effective way of attracting
non-users was to organise special activities and events during the summer
months. These included free "taster" courses, a family day, open days, sports

afternoons for the disabled and recreational activities, all of which had spin-offs for other classes once people were in the building.

Enrolment procedures

The research as a whole indicates that the nature of first contacts with an institution can strongly influence decisions to participate. Many centres hold informal open days when people can talk to staff and current students and see what happens on the premises. In some cases, however, any good impressions made may be undermined by the subsequent experience of enrolling on courses. Some of the staff in adult education centres were extremely critical of formal enrolment procedures. One principal had visited centres "where people are kept waiting for hours." Her informal research had left her "staggered by the poor quality of information, the difficulty of getting through by phone, and the enormous gap between what a centre does and what administrative workers THINK that it does."

Another centre head suggested that this problem arises because "administration gets in the way of access. There's money changing hands and administration takes over education. The tail wags the dog!" Several principals claimed that postal enrolments eliminate queuing and lead to a quick filling of places. However, this enrolment method favours people who already know the system and leads to self-perpetuating groups – a phenomenon which a number of staff identified as a considerable obstacle to the recruitment of new student groups. To solve this problem, some centres persuade established groups to become clubs; others have adopted enrolment procedures that favour new students. At the time of the research, one ILEA institute was operating a ticket system giving priority to new students who could try out courses during the first week with payment deferred until the second or third. A tutor in another part of London considered this scheme infinitely preferable to traditional practice: "We package our provision in paper bags and people don't see or experience it before they're committed."

Some LEAs have adopted special enrolment times and procedures for specific groups. In Erdington, for example, special enrolment sessions have been organised for ABE students enabling them to meet new tutors for coffee and informal discussion.

Fees

Most LEAs now offer reductions for second and subsequent courses and some fee waivers or reductions for certain categories of student: pensioners, the unemployed, people with disabilities, basic education students, full-time further or higher education students, and people on low incomes or state benefits. However, fee reductions vary widely between authorities, as do the standard fees charged (5), and in high fee charging authorities, even a 20%

reduction can still deter people in economically disadvantaged categories. Among the LEA staff interviewed, there was no general consensus on the extent to which fee levels deter non-user groups, since experience varied so widely. Some LEA staff have found that fee concessions do not necessarily lead to an increase in non-traditional enrolments. An interviewee in Birmingham reported that a reduced fee for basic education courses had not led to the expected "massive" increase in enrolments. In a rural area, however, concessionary fees had been instrumental in attracting a number of non-participant groups. Sixty per cent of enrolees at a large adult education centre in Derbyshire were in concessionary fee categories, with some people spending every day there "because it's cheaper than staying at home!"

The surveys and interviews conducted for the project show that fee levels have a differential effect on the participation of different groups. The financial cost of participation is clearly a barrier for the unemployed and some groups of women, whereas other groups are deterred more by other factors related to personal circumstances, family, work and patterns of living (6).

Opinions differed on the impact of methods of payment on participation. Community education staff in one rural area have found that a pay-as-you-learn system encourages enrolments: "When it was introduced, it increased enrolments by up to 70–80%." Staff in another rural area, however, claimed that reduced fees and a pay-as-you-learn system had lowered commitment and regular attendance. Such conflicting evidence suggests that there might usefully be a closer investigation of the link between LEA fee levels, methods of payment and participation.

Curriculum change

In some LEAs the recruitment of new groups has involved development of new programmes. In many cases, these have been made possible by outside funding from agencies such as ALBSU, MSC or REPLAN, although some authorities such as the ILEA and individual centres with a commitment to the local community have, as a matter of policy, created special programmes and progression routes for specific client groups. One urban provider – Erdington – was, in 1988, offering a range of new courses for community groups as part of an impetus to widen educational access. They included taster sessions for newcomers to education; women's education programmes; workshops on ethnic minority learning needs; English and maths workshops; special courses with the unemployed and the elderly; and "learning extensions" to assist groups to progress to formal education. The area co-ordinator claimed that the service as a whole was shifting towards greater responsiveness to the needs of the whole community:

> *The programme has shifted noticeably in certain directions. Over the year we have developed more basic education work, more work specifically with the elderly, more daytime provision ... More has been*

done to work with community groups and residents of specific areas to enable them to determine the kind of learning they want, where and when they want it (7).

Guidance services

There was evidence throughout the research of the urgent need for accessible advice and guidance systems for people who have little post-school educational experience. The importance of guidance in helping new adult learners choose and benefit from appropriate learning opportunities was emphasised by the majority of LEA tutors contacted. A UDACE publication has underlined the problems that can arise if people enrol on the wrong course or at the wrong level:

Every time a student fails to receive appropriate guidance and enrols for an inappropriate course, teaching resources and the student's time are wasted ... the message is tacitly conveyed that he or she cannot benefit from learning ... the effect ... repeated many times is to produce an adult population lacking in confidence and motivation to learn (8).

Several people made the point that centralised guidance systems do not attract people who would not normally engage in structured learning. More effective are locally-based services, outreach services such as EASA (Education Advice Service for Adults) in Bradford, MEASA in Manchester and CEGSA in Cambridge, and mobile services such as mobile TAPs and mobile information and guidance units funded by agencies such as REPLAN.

The value of guidance to clients and providers is now widely recognised. One guidance worker referred to it as "a catalyst for educational and social change". A head of centre in a shire county reported that all the courses and subjects requested through the guidance service in 1987–88 had got off the ground, whereas a number of those suggested by providers did not lead to viable classes. Nonetheless, some guidance services described to the project were extremely precarious. In one authority, an LEA officer claimed that the service "only operates due to the goodwill and commitment of workers involved who are often not paid for all the hours they work." In Yorkshire a guidance worker described her unit as "clinging on at the edges of the LEA rather than being something central. Every year we have to bid for refunding."

Although Education Support Grants were being made available by the Department of Education and Science for the development of guidance services, it appears that some have subsequently been withdrawn to provide extra funds for the National Curriculum.

Factors that have particularly favoured access for non-traditional learners in LEAs

The research showed that the following factors had particularly contributed to improved access for under-represented groups in LEAs.

Local Authority policy: a commitment to recruiting under-represented groups and strong community education policies.

Combination of access support measures. The education centres and projects that appeared most successful in recruiting people in non-participant categories were those where there was a combination of favourable conditions and support structures. A community education project visited in south London had succeeded in recruiting a majority of first-time learners including single parents and a large number of Afro-Caribbean and other ethnic minority groups. This was attributed by staff to the centre's proximity to a large housing estate and public transport; to ILEA's low fee policy; the low-cost creche; and the fact that classes were allowed to run with small numbers (a minimum of six).

Special LEA budgets to increase participation. In response to political pressures and recognition of community learning needs, some LEAs have created special budgets for innovative work with new groups. The aim is to redistribute resources to areas of need and explore new approaches with people unwilling or unable to use existing facilities.

Special or pump-priming funding (from ALBSU for people with literacy problems; the former MSC and REPLAN for unemployed people; Urban Programme for urban and inner city groups; Section XI for ethnic minorities; ESF for a variety of groups).

Development workers. Specially-funded development workers have acted as effective change agents in some authorities. According to one report, ESG REPLAN development workers whose role was to improve and enhance education provision for the adult unemployed "acted as a focus for identification of changes and also a means of demonstrating ways of responding" (9). The effectiveness of development workers in bringing about such changes depends on where they are located in the education system and the extent of their access to decision-makers. The ESG REPLAN initiatives judged most effective were those with:

> *Active support, access to resources and staff with sufficient seniority to deliver change. Without these factors it is clear that the potential for*

moving from localised good practice to a wider strategic role is severely constrained (10).

Creation of special posts. The appointment of outreach workers, bilingual workers and staff with a specific remit to improve access for certain groups.

The commitment of senior staff. Individual centres which were attracting a wide cross-section of the community were usually headed by principals with a strong commitment to providing a service for the whole community.

Staff bringing ideas from outside. An LEA head of centre in a shire authority claimed that her activities outside the county – going to conferences, keeping abreast of national initiatives – had exerted a strong influence on the nature of the adult service:

It's people like me who go outside and bring back new ideas that influence what goes on. Before me there were no attempts to do anything about non-participants. A year or two ago if you'd said "equal opportunities" they wouldn't have known what you were talking about!

Local pressure groups. Changing policy means persuading policy-makers and local politicians. In one city, a specially-formed adult learning federation became an active pressure group whose campaigns succeeded in preventing centre closures, securing LEA assurances on funding and acquiring resources for outreach, neighbourhood learning projects and renovation of centres.

Factors which have impeded wider access in LEAs

Lack of real commitment. Although a number of LEAs have equal opportunities policies, these tend to be restricted to employees and do not necessarily affect client groups. Moreover, the gap between policy and practice can be wide. In one metropolitan authority an adult education users' group identified a "massive discrepancy" between policy commitments and allocation of resources.

The nature of LEA adult education. LEA adult provision is constrained by regulations about minimum numbers, enrolment procedures and fee levels and this results in a certain amount of inflexibility. Moreover, LEA adult education is often isolated or disconnected from the rest of the education system. Some free-standing centres have little or no links with other educational institutions, resulting in lack of progression routes for students. This reinforces the service's image as something marginal and leisure-oriented for a small section of the community.

Lack of co-operation with other agencies and services. Liaison with other agencies and local government departments is necessary in work with people in the most disadvantaged categories. However, the adult education service often operates in relative isolation from other local authority services, and mechanisms for such liaison appear to be generally lacking. In some LEAs this situation has led to duplication and territorial disputes. In one area visited, the role of the LEA in providing opportunities for specific groups had been "usurped" by another (non-educational) local government department. This had led to duplication and friction. The LEA service was viewed as expensive and inflexible by staff in the other department, and LEA staff were annoyed at incursions into their territory.

Elsewhere, lack of mechanisms for liaison had obliged adult educators to work in a hasty, unprepared and ad hoc manner. Education staff in south London complained that, as a result of the Care in the Community policy, Social Services were referring people with severe disabilities to adult education centres without prior consultation. In another LEA, basic education tutors found they were being used by Social Services as a "last resort" for the mentally handicapped, although they had no training and expertise to deal with such people.

Relations with elected members. Staff in several of the LEAs contacted referred to gulfs in understanding and perception between education staff and elected members. In some areas this had hindered the development of new work with disadvantaged and non-participant groups. An outreach worker who had been trying to set up new learning programmes in the community discovered that even the Director of Education had "little hope of effecting meaningful change because of the archaic and stubborn decision-making that goes on with elected members". This led him to conclude that even if efforts to bring in and keep new adult learners were replicable, it might be virtually impossible to accomplish such change.

Reorganisation. In some areas, adult education services have been allocated to other local government departments such as Leisure services or Recreation. In one such case, education staff reported that people in the umbrella department showed little understanding of adult education needs and processes: "They see us as a drain on resources and our work with the disadvantaged even more so. Access work is considered 'fringe'."

According to outreach development officers working across several LEAs, reorganisation of adult education services together with the introduction of ERA was having a disastrous effect on some innovative work: "LEAs are restructuring; heads are rolling and other people are coming in. We don't know who we're dealing with any more. A lot of the good stuff is going."

Community education restructuring. In one authority where the Education Reform Act came immediately on top of wide-scale reorganisation into a community education structure, the overall effect was described by an LEA officer as "total chaos. Ironically, it's come along just when there's been development towards integrated community education schemes. Now virement between schools and FE budgets is no longer possible."

In two such reorganised authorities, staff were concerned that the changes had happened too quickly and quality provision and experienced staff had been sacrificed in the process. In both cases LEA officers believed that the consequences were not fully appreciated by decision-makers:

> *Our independent centres are struggling. All income goes into a pool and they can't keep any of the funds they've raised. The problem is they [elected members] see adult education as middle class. They don't listen when we tell them that the centres serve the whole community or that a third of the people taking exam classes last year were in concessionary fee categories. [Adult education adviser]*

> *I'm concerned for the future of mainstream here. We're trying to clothe adult education in a more politically acceptable garb. Community education is much more acceptable to our politicians than "adult education", which means flower-arranging. [Area organiser]*

Unclear line management. Knowing who the decision-makers are makes it easier to expand pilot projects into larger ones. However, lines and levels of decision-making and accountability are complex in LEAs. Development staff in some authorities, particularly those undergoing reorganisation, complained that an unclear line management structure was making it impossible to bring about change:

> *We call REPLAN here journey into space! The closer you get to the middle the bigger the hole is. Nobody seems to be making decisions. [ESG development officer, shire county]*

> *The big failure of my project is to make an impact on the policy-makers. This is partly due to changes in personnel in LEA. It took me a long time to work out line management and what was going on. When I came there was no line management structure. [REPLAN officer, Midlands city]*

Insecurity and uncertainty. Uncertainty about the future had blocked development in some areas. Anxieties aroused by reorganisation, shrinking budgets and the Education Reform Act were much in evidence among the LEA staff interviewed. In some authorities there was low morale because of personal career stagnation while, in inner London, the planned abolition of the ILEA was affecting staff's ability to initiate and sustain services for new groups:

*We're marking time, marching backwards. We've already had to
reduce programmes. Our future's in the balance. Morale is very low.
We can't put on new things because we can't employ new tutors. [Head
of centre]*

Finance. Finance was the most problematic area where work with new
groups was concerned. Some of the LEAs visited had been rate-capped, which
had curtailed development work. Others were reducing fee remissions and
using adult education as a way of raising revenue. Although many of the
centres contacted wanted to bring in new clienteles, their freedom to do so
was constrained by the need to cover costs. As a result, publicity campaigns
to reach non-participants were sometimes muted: "There's a fear that special
provision might run away; we can't run things completely for them."

A dilemma identified at several centres was that campaigns to attract new
users sometimes stimulate a demand which cannot be met: "We've been ticked
off by the Inspectorate because our publicity was too effective. We were raising
expectations that couldn't be fulfilled." "We can't advertise too strongly for the
unemployed because we need full-fee payers."

Equally, although most authorities were offering concessionary fees to
certain categories of student, there were signs that some were discouraging
wide-scale take-up. According to a REPLAN development officer: "The county
want to discourage fee remissions, so the two thrusts – REPLAN and the
county – are working in opposition to each other."

Some centres were trying to juggle budgets in an attempt to find an
equitable balance:

*We're operating a kind of mixed economy. We increasingly put
successful courses onto a self-sustaining basis to free funds for
community education. Now that has become our policy. We try and
shift those students and courses which are not for local people out of
our LEA funding and shift that funding to work with local people.*

Problems arising from development budgets. Although the introduction
of special development budgets has succeeded in encouraging programme
development with new groups in some areas, the process has created
problems. In one LEA, the new schemes highlighted learning interests and
demands which could not be met from existing financial structures. As a
result, "mainstream" fees were increased and some part-time tutor fees
reduced. In two authorities there were anxieties about progression and
integration after development funding ended. The major problem identified
in two LEAs with development budgets was maintaining a balance between
good traditional practice and new areas of work:

*Already people are coming back saying "what do we do now that the
money has expired?" Some have applied for extensions, but the*

problem is, once they've established a project, how will it fit in and be co-ordinated with existing resources and ordinary work?

Is our priority supporting mainstream provision or going into new fields? Will we have to sacrifice something?

There are no policy guidelines for absorbing new work into mainstream, but you have to have good reasons for getting rid of other, more established things.

Under-resourcing of development work. In LEAs where development work in the community is not a major priority, it risks marginality through under-resourcing and lack of status. Tutors in a community education project attached to a large urban adult education centre were frustrated at the constraints under which their work had to operate:

We're running on temporary bits and pieces. All contracts are short-term. Our status was never really specified on paper. We're on the periphery of other people's programmes We haven't had staff or prestige to give us parity with other groups. To keep our end up is very hard.

An outreach worker pointed out that this kind of work is usually considered low priority because: "It isn't easy to quantify or describe and most people don't see it."

A striking finding of the research was how many LEA initiatives to attract non-traditional groups were dependent on the goodwill and often unpaid time of committed staff. A head of centre in a shire county reported that one new course was being taught by someone without payment, and research into demand for day-time opportunities had been conducted by a field worker paid for only a third of her time. Some outreach workers interviewed during the research were employed on a part-time basis but worked virtually full-time. This situation suggests that work with non-participant and under-represented adult groups needs to be put on a more secure footing in many local authorities.

Future possibilities for widening access in LEAs

Legislation. A number of pieces of legislation will affect the future extent and shape of local authority learning opportunities for adults, in particular the Education Reform Act and the Local Government and Housing Bill which imposes more stringent conditions on LEA support for learning in the voluntary sector.

The Education Reform Act will undoubtedly have a far-reaching effect on LEA provision for adults, as it imposes on each Local Education Authority in

England and Wales a duty "to secure adequate facilities for further education" for their area. Further and higher education as defined by the Act includes part-time and non-vocational education and the education of adults. One effect of this is to make the traditional separation between adult and further education increasingly anachronistic. However, the Act does not define what constitutes an "adequate service", a concept which has been explored in a UDACE development paper (11). This proposes that an adequate service would be neither purely demand-led nor purely supply-led, but the product of a "continuing dialogue" between providers and users, including employers and community groups. UDACE lists five major areas which should be included in statements of adequacy: consultation mechanisms (to determine needs); curricula and delivery mechanisms; access issues (timing, attendance modes, location); participation (client-groups); and support service.

At the time of the research some LEA staff saw ERA as presenting an opportunity to expand the scope and accessibility of educational opportunities for adults, although by summer 1989, few draft schemes of delegation had integrated adults into their plans for post-school education (12). Other interviewees feared that some aspects of the Act – such as the abolition of ILEA – would result in a reduction in services for adults, particularly programmes for the educationally disadvantaged. Another fear was that community education services for adults might be reduced as a result of pressures on school finances. Some LEA officers also expressed worries about the future of community education activities if schools opted out of LEA control. Some of these fears may have been allayed by new regulations subsequently issued by the DES (Circular 19/89), which among many provisions, refers to the need for LEAs in their planning to take account of the need to secure "an appropriate range of opportunities for adults who may be disadvantaged, including those with special education needs, those requiring basic skills or language support and the unemployed."

Finance. The financial costs of LEA adult provision are an important factor in the extent and take-up of opportunities for particular groups. In 1988–89, LEA fees for part-time study rose faster than inflation (13), although the majority of authorities continued to make available concessionary fees for certain categories of student. In many LEAs the trend is towards making general or non-vocational adult courses self-financing or using them to raise revenue. This could have a damaging effect on provision for some of the client-groups discussed. Women and older adults, for example, tend to engage most in general, non-certificated education. This highlights the perennial problem of distinctions between, and implicit value judgments about, the different types and forms of education engaged in by adults. Distinctions between vocational and non-vocational education, between education and training and between adult and further education are increasingly unhelpful and irrelevant. The UDACE paper points out that the term "adult education" has connotations of leisure which can lead to its marginalisation, but this is particularly inappropriate at a time when adults constitute "more than half the population of LEA further education – including 'returners', updating, retraining, basic and 'non-vocational' students among others "(14).

As this suggests, the clientele of further education has undergone considerable change.

Initiatives to Widen Access in Further Education

The traditional clients of further education have been 16–19-year-olds, and mainstream programmes have been weighted towards certificated courses to meet employers' requirements, with the emphasis on day- or block-release or full-time study for BTEC. According to several reports, the sector has not favoured non-traditional groups: the black communities, women wishing to enter traditional "male" occupations and groups with special needs (15).

However, changes are now discernible in the FE student intake: in 1988–89, 34% of students in colleges were women and 60% were over 19 (16). Since the 16–19 cohort will fall to its lowest level by 1994, it is likely that this trend will intensify. In addition, colleges have been encouraged to open their doors to groups who normally fall into non-participant categories by the WRNAFE (Work-Related Non-Advanced Further Education) planning process and the more flexible system of accreditation introduced by the National Council for Vocational Qualifications (NCVQ). One of the aims of NCVQ has been to promote access to qualifications for under-represented groups, and the criteria stress that awarding bodies should operate equal opportunities policies and ensure access for all groups:

> *It will not be sufficient to remove the barriers to access alone. Positive action is required to ensure that the appropriate facilities and opportunities for learning and assessment are available ... Awarding bodies applying for the accreditation of qualifications will be expected to make their policies on equal opportunities clear and the National Council will monitor delivery to ensure that practice conforms to policy (17).*

Significant changes will take place in further education following implementation of the Education Reform Act. These relate chiefly to finance and governing bodies. From April 1990, colleges will target provision according to LEA annual planning procedures. Resources will be allocated on the basis of a planned student intake (expressed as weighted full-time equivalent (FTE) student numbers). In institutions with more than 200 full-time equivalents, the management of the allocated budget will be delegated to a newly-constituted governing body, at least half of whose members are to be from the employment sector. Local management planning, like that for WRNAFE, is expected to be at two stages: for the following year and for a three-year period.

A financial change which is already starting to take effect is the reduction, by the Training Agency, in college WRNAFE funding – by 4.5% in 1989 and 10% in 1990. This is expected to have an adverse effect on work with new groups and there have been predictions that some LEAs will cut their new provision, such as Access courses. At the time the research was conducted, however, there was evidence that many colleges were making efforts to attract new groups of adult learners.

Individual college initiatives

In several colleges contacted during the project, community liaison officers had been appointed and new outreach initiatives launched in response to a number of pressures: reorganisation; new management; the need to fill course places; and requests from outside statutory and voluntary agencies. In other colleges, initiatives supported by pump-priming funding had led in a number of cases to programme development and infill to mainstream courses. Recruitment of new groups to colleges had been achieved via four different approaches:

1. Mobile units. A (REPLAN-supported) caravan taking publicity, educational information and guidance from Peterlee College to outlying council estates and pit villages succeeded, after only a few weeks, in increasing unemployed adult students by more than 25% (18) .

2. Opening up institutions to community groups. In another REPLAN-supported project, a group of single parents and their children were invited to Longlands College, Middlesborough, one afternoon a week, to meet staff and students. According to a college staff member, the sight of other adults learning in the college stimulated a desire to learn in people who would never hitherto have considered education:

> *They were surprised ... they could see people similar to themselves working in informal ways in informal settings. They were able to identify with them and though, before, they wouldn't have thought education was for them, they started to explore possibilities for themselves.*

3. The appointment of outreach staff. In 1987, a community outreach post was created in Rother Valley College. The initiative was the result of growing awareness of community needs, the college's involvement in developing an LEA adult education strategy, and a fall in the number of traditional students. The outreach worker's role was to establish contact with groups who did not use the college or its outlying centres; to discuss and evaluate their requirements and see whether these could be met by the college, and to encourage people (particularly educationally disadvantaged groups) to use existing provision.

Her initial contacts with a variety of local organisations revealed a high level of public ignorance about the college and she found it required considerable time to reach non-participants, explain the work of the college and talk through their anxieties regarding levels of courses, previous experience, appropriateness of timing and venues, before any commitments were made. Nevertheless, in the first year of the outreach worker's appointment, 172 people, most without post-school education experience, enrolled in college mainstream courses and in a wide range of newly-developed programmes – basic education, pre-vocational, creative arts and taster courses – provided free of charge to people on state benefits. Target groups included women, the mentally handicapped, people who had experienced mental illness, the elderly, the unemployed, redundant miners, parent groups and ex-offenders. All newly-developed courses were evaluated by the outreach worker, who fed back information on the progress of new groups.

According to the outreach worker, the introduction of new adult learners has brought about fundamental changes in staff attitudes and college policy. "People are now thinking more about who the college is for. Now the institution is trying to respond to expressed interests and needs rather than providing courses it thinks are a good idea" (19).

4. A "whole college" approach to access. Newham Community College, visited during the project, is in an area of multiple deprivation. Thirty per cent of residents belong to ethnic minority groups, of mainly Asian origin. There are a large number of single families in the area and problems of widespread truancy. Compared with the rest of the country, a very low proportion of children go on to post-16 education.

The college was formed in 1986 and involved the amalgamation of two further education institutions. The new Principal was faced with the task of welding discrete, traditional further and adult education departments into a unified community education system without undermining the traditional vocational work:

> The first thing we had to get across to vested interests – heads of department – was that things had to change, but we weren't going to throw the baby out. Community education was not intended to devalue vocational education. Employment is the engine of the community and a good community college also has to be a good technical college.

The process involved a corporate management and planning approach and a move towards greater cross-departmental co-operation. A Vice-Principal with adult education and community development as a special remit was appointed, and a Research, Marketing and Student Services Unit was established, with a college-wide brief to meet community, including employers', education and training needs. The Unit was described by a member of staff as "a channel through which outreach programmes can be translated into action." It identifies staff development and support needs, provides advice and guidance to enrolled students and conducts research into various aspects of the college's work.

Measures to attract new groups. As part of the new marketing approach, the college brochure has been redesigned to target three client-groups: traditional students (16–19-year-olds); adult returners and "non-participants"; and clients wishing to enrol on mainstream vocational and leisure programmes.Outside the college, outreach courses have been developed in areas where none existed before. Internally, a series of measures have been taken to assist mature student access, especially for people from the local community: departments can exercise positive discrimination in favour of Borough residents; and there is stress on assessment of prior learning, independent learning and student-negotiated aims, methods and programmes. In some departments attempts have been made to introduce greater flexibility in timing and delivery of programmes to suit adults.

The college has made a concerted attempt to provide for groups such as women and ethnic minorities, and is currently improving access for students with special needs. In 1988, provision specifically designed for mature learners included modular and open access return-to-learn courses; return to science courses; drop-in computer literacy; computer workshops; basic numeracy and return to maths open workshops. The college was also providing a range of linked skills courses: ESOL with basic education, business education, electronics, information technology and job search. In addition, a technical updating scheme for industrial workers was being set up in collaboration with a large union, the involvement of which was regarded as a key innovation and crucial in reaching working men. For students wishing to move to more advanced learning, the college was providing full-time Access courses (part of the North East London Access programme). Access students could participate in a short "Recognition Programme" (goal formation, assessment of prior learning), followed by a one-year individually negotiated programme in which "the accent is on the process of learning rather than content."

Some departmental initiatives. In the Art and Design Department, a part-time foundation course had been designed specifically for adults, and staff were addressing questions to do with outreach methods, progression routes and programmes based on the art of different ethnic groups. The Mathematics and Science Department was offering a flexible Higher National Diploma course in computing for parents, with flexible timing and creche support: "Our view is that these adults shouldn't start at the beginning again." The programme included a short induction, assessment of prior learning and three-year part-time study. In the Fashion and Hairdressing Department, accredited courses in Afro-Caribbean hairdressing had been developed in response to demand; and, to increase the pool of Asian teachers, a teacher-training course in Asian dressmaking had been introduced, with childcare, language support and bilingual staff.

Greater collaboration. The college was making efforts to liaise and collaborate with community organisations and to market programmes more effectively with employers, local schools and other agencies. One department – Engineering – had negotiated a range of courses with local employers, established a team of school visitors, initiated Open Days for sixth formers and run "very successful" taster courses for sixth form girls. Internally there was cross-departmental co-operation in providing access to learning, brush-up skills and drop-in facilities.

These new measures had been strongly supported by college management, which, in the estimation of many members of staff, had been the key factor in the institution's growing success in attracting groups of non-traditional mature learners. Problems such as rate-capping and a NATFHE strike had delayed some planned initiatives, and, in early 1988, there were some areas perceived to need development: staff training, and provision of guidance and a baseroom for mature learners. Nonetheless, the college had clearly taken important steps towards becoming a service for the whole community. In 1987 there had been 23,000 enrolments, 70–75% of which were by people belonging to groups usually under-represented in organised learning.

A college evolving towards wider access

Another urban college visited in 1988 was in the early stages of reorganisation from a departmental into a faculty system. This process was expected to bring about greater collaboration across subjects and more responsiveness to groups in the local community. According to a senior member of staff, positive changes had already been achieved, albeit with "a lot of pain and strain":

> *We ARE inflexible but things are changing and we are aware of the need to change. Two to three years ago there wasn't any real contact between departments here. We were all watertight. Now this is breaking down. We tend to discuss common problems rather than HIS problem. Internal departmental wrangling is disappearing due to the new management. We also need to counteract the fortress mentality we've developed.*

New initiatives. As part of the college action plan, a number of initiatives had already been taken to increase access for mature students. A marketing unit had been established to research needs and provide pilot courses, off-site provision, and more flexible enrolment procedures. A student services unit was planned and a working party had been convened to examine enrolment and assessment procedures and consider ways of making the college more accessible and welcoming. Among other measures to improve mature student access, the college had initiated special courses "to get adults over the threshold"; free infill for the unemployed; a staff development programme; collaborative outreach activities, and the appointment of community liaison officers.

Students. Several staff referred to changes taking place in the composition of the student body. More low-level vocational courses were being offered at the college:

> *Partly because industry is diminishing, but also because we're getting a different clientele – less academic, less vocationally-oriented people, with less certainty about what they want to do.*

One of the biggest differences identified was the increasing number of women students, a group which "had made its presence felt and was making new demands." Special attempts had been made to encourage women into male-dominated areas such as computers, engineering, technology, painting and decorating. A daytime women's course in painting and decorating leading to entry to City and Guilds was in its third year and was attracting women of all ages and ethnic backgrounds, as well as single parents. College departments were being urged to restructure timing to suit women and provide courses on a modular basis. Only one course – Women in Technology – had a creche attached (an innovation which had initially been strongly resisted by staff), and lack of childcare facilities was identified as the greatest problem associated with women's access to other provision. During the researcher's visit, a series of telephone enquiries to the Head of the Liberal Arts Department were all related to this problem.

Staff. Throughout the college there were signs that recruitment and retention of adult students was very much on the agenda. At a staff meeting attended by the researcher, eight members of staff (all white males in senior positions) discussed the areas they felt needed particular attention to assist mature student access. One problem they identified was adult drop-out from mainstream courses. This was attributed to students' uncertainty about directions and unreal expectations about what can be achieved in a short period of study. The consensus among staff was that mature students need more preparation and induction, and that taster schemes and modular programmes should be developed. The members of staff listed, in order of priority, the measures they felt would most assist mature student access:

1. Marketing policies and strategies targeted at adults, especially men.

2. Programme development designed especially for adult students.
3. More flexible timetabling arrangements.
4. Specific induction procedures.
5. Better interview and assessment procedures at enrolment.
6. Provision of counselling and guidance.
7. Language and literacy support.
8. More off-site access provision.
9. Clear and identifiable progression routes.
10. Collaboration with other providers.
11. A more welcoming atmosphere for adults.
12. Information about skills shortages and employment prospects.
13. Staff development programmes.
14. Childcare.

Perceptions of change. According to one head of department, there had been a significant change in staff attitudes to adult students:

> *They recognise now that people other than traditional groups exist and can succeed. The whole focus has changed. We're more aware now of the needs of the total person.*

This perception was not shared by the community outreach officer, who was finding institution-based staff extremely resistant to expressed community demands. She referred to the college as a "bastion of white male domination" in which even the most well-meaning staff had "absolutely no idea of how to respond to community need". Her view was that the college still had a very long way to go in order to become really accessible to different groups in the community.

The overall impression gained during the visit was that most staff at the college had a clear and sincere commitment to increasing access for mature learners, and a considerable amount had already been achieved. However, there were some contradictions. The main building was surrounded by a high wall topped with barbed wire and the only entrance was manned by a uniformed security guard. This made the college appear physically unwelcoming and intimidating. Secondly, although the college is located in an area with a large ethnic minority population, there were relatively few black faces in evidence in the institution and none among the staff. Moreover, in spite of the increasing numbers of women students there appeared to be few female staff and none in senior positions. Thus, despite the new impetus to attract mature students, the college still projected a very traditional image.

Initiatives to Widen Access in Higher Education

Between 1979 and 1986 the number of first year mature students in higher education increased by 42%: 83% of them, however, were in polytechnics and colleges, mostly engaged in part-time courses below degree level (20). As this suggests, public sector higher education has done more than universities to attract mature entrants, although some believe that because of the principle of comparability with university degrees, it has failed to become more than a "less privileged variant of the middle-class university" (21).

It has often been observed that the proportion of students from working-class or ethnic minority backgrounds has not significantly increased in higher education, in spite of the introduction of the public sector system, the Open University and more flexible entry policies promoted by the Council for National Academic Awards (CNAA). Mature students taking degree courses tend to be from middle-class backgrounds who missed out the first time round or who wish to acquire more qualifications. A review of students on CNAA part-time first degree courses showed that two-thirds were male, with an average age of 30 and most were in employment (22).

There has been, however, a gradual move towards facilitating entry for non-traditional student groups. In 1984 the two higher education funding bodies jointly accepted the principle that people without formal qualifications "may demonstrate ... considerable ability to benefit from higher education." In 1985, the CNAA introduced the Credit Accumulation and Transfer Scheme (CATS) promoting exemption from qualifications and credit for prior and experiential learning. Two years later, the same body revised regulations to admit unqualified students and ended the distinction between "standard" and "non-standard" students. In 1987 and 1988 a series of documents were published advocating a range of measures to facilitate entry for students without A-levels: the White Paper *Meeting the Challenge* and publications from the Further Education Unit and the National Advisory Body (23) all urged increased development of modular courses, flexible and distance learning, credit transfer and accreditation of prior experiential learning schemes, equal opportunities policies and a range of student support mechanisms. In 1989, a new national framework for Access courses was announced and the Scottish Wider Access Programme launched. An additional push for change has been the fact that other parts of the education system have become more flexible and accessible as a result of initiatives such as TVEI, GCSE and NCVQ.

During 1988 and 1989, pressure on higher education to increase and diversify its student intake mounted (24) and culminated in the announcement of a shift from public funding to funding by fees: a strategy designed to persuade institutions to increase numbers and become more "market-led". Whether higher education institutions will respond to this change by seeking more mature students and under-represented groups has yet to be seen. Research conducted in 1988 found institutions and individual departments generally unwilling to develop strategies to prepare for the 1990s, with universities still reporting a rising demand from their traditional pool of school-leavers. Within the sector as a whole:

> *The commonest response even among those facing serious recruitment difficulties has been to try and increase the "market share" from a fixed and diminishing pool of "good" A-level candidates (25).*

The same research found a "vague desire" among higher education admissions officers to increase the number of students from disadvantaged and under-represented categories, although action to achieve this aim had been somewhat token. In the universities, the reasons generally given for lack of action was the fixed quota of places set, until recently, by the funding council, and the use of admission statistics for resource allocation:

> *Most university managers were convinced that standard offers and average A-level point scores were still seen as a key indicator of departmental and indeed institutional policy (26).*

This situation could change if the new funding arrangements persuade institutions to recruit more non-traditional students.

Non-traditional access routes

There are various ways in which students without A-levels can currently gain access to advanced higher education courses: by direct entry; participation in shorter courses such as DipHE or HND; through collaborative "franchising" arrangements between further and higher education establishments; or, most frequently, via Access courses.

Access courses

Access courses are designed specifically to facilitate entry to higher education for people without formal qualifications and groups who face particular barriers to entry. The majority of courses are in colleges of further education and are validated by higher education institutions. It is estimated that there are over 400 Access courses in England and Wales. Courses can be full-time or part-time and most guarantee progression to specified courses at particular institutions, although some more recently developed courses have a variety of exit routes. Some of the newer Access developments have come about as a result of the increasing collaboration between the open college networks burgeoning around the country.

Targeted access

Reports have indicated that Access courses are particularly effective in recruiting students from Afro-Caribbean backgrounds (27). Some courses have been specifically designed to encourage ethnic minority individuals into occupational areas where they are under-represented: the caring professions (Matlock College); teaching; (Sheffield Polytechnic; Bradford and Ilkley Community College); public sector agencies: (Bradford and Ilkley Community College); management and supervisory occupations (Liverpool University); business (Sandown College); childcare, catering (South Fields College).

Although such targeted opportunities have been generally welcomed, some black groups view them with suspicion, fearing that they will become ghetto areas or soft options. The opposite, however, can be the case. According to one lecturer, a black Access course in a Midlands college "attracted the middle classes in droves" once it had been accepted for JMB accreditation. A lecturer in another institution also claimed that black Access courses had been "highjacked by the middle classes."

Some of the reservations about Access courses expressed by staff interviewed during the project prompted the following questions:

Motives for development. Is an Access course viewed as a convenient way to fill empty places or as a genuine service to the community? If the former, courses may be developed more to suit the institutions involved than potential students, and conditions for entry may deter all but the most highly motivated. A research report (28) on the experiences of Access candidates at two London institutions catalogues a series of off-putting factors: inadequate information; lengthy queues at open evenings; formal interviews followed by brusque, unhelpful letters of rejection. Some courses are preceded by lengthy diagnostic tests which, in the view of a polytechnic lecturer, intimidate all but the most confident of applicants: "I find it bizarre that an Access course should set up hurdles to access at the outset."

Recruitment of educationally disadvantaged groups. How effective are Access courses in reaching people in educationally disadvantaged categories? The paucity of places on some courses raises questions about the selection process. In 1988 a college in Derbyshire had nearly 100 applicants for 12 places on a black Access course. Given such competition, the chances are that the process of "Second Creaming" referred to on page 19 will be repeated, with those people in better material circumstances, with more confidence and a higher level of initial schooling benefitting most from the opportunities offered. It has been claimed that Access courses attract self-selecting and highly-motivated individuals (29) and the timing of the higher education application process – usually one year in advance – may reinforce this tendency. Many people returning to education (especially those in educationally disadvantaged categories) do not have an adequate idea of what they want to do at that stage and may prefer broader-based courses with multi-exits to specialised ones (the majority) leading to specific advanced courses. A consortium of higher and further education institutions in Essex has devised a scheme to provide open access to all mature students, leading to a diversity of exit routes. All candidates are accepted for the course, which involves a preparation stage and an individually constructed full or part-time programme of core studies and subject options, negotiated with the participating institutions. On successful completion of the programme, students receive an Essex Access certificate with details of what they have covered and achieved (30).

Some reports imply that there can be covert discrimination in Access recruitment methods. A survey (31) found that an Access to law course was publicised in such a restricted way that it ensured a very narrow candidature – a strategy that contradicts the whole concept of an Access course. A black lecturer at a Midlands college claimed that selection interviews effectively discriminate against black applicants:

> Our students don't have the same confidence and ability to communicate. They're used to being reticent and not putting themselves forward, so can fail interviews. Our biggest difficulty is with the Admissions Tutor who has no conception of what "access" is about.

Lack of support structures. Many groups – unwaged women, the unemployed, people on state benefits or low incomes – cannot take advantage of Access courses for purely financial reasons. There are a small number of targeted courses which are free or qualify for mandatory awards, but since Access courses are defined as "non-advanced" most attract only discretionary grants, although not in all LEAs. In the ILEA there have been discretionary grants for Access courses with a set of criteria administered by County Hall – a situation that many people believe will not outlive the ILEA – while for part-time courses, financial support has been up to individual institutions. Elsewhere, the evidence suggests that opportunities for discretionary grants are dwindling and the future prospects concerning financial support for Access students are not considered bright.

Access courses also generally lack support structures such as childcare and bilingual support. A polytechnic staff member reported that the black communities in particular feel that there is inadequate help with language:

> Locally there's a bit of a backlash against Access courses because people feel they're not serving the black communities and bilingual students. The issue of support for bilingual students is being side-stepped.

The future of Access courses. Ostensibly, the principle of mass higher education implied by new funding arrangements secures the role of Access courses as a means of assisting non-standard entrants. The new national framework for the recognition of Access courses has several aims: to enable courses to achieve a "wider acceptability and currency" across the higher education system; to act as a safeguard against any erosion of standards; to provide a more coherent and uniform framework; and to act as a catalyst for innovation.

In spite of this initiative, there are fears that the number of Access courses will diminish, since components such as guidance and small group work make them more expensive to run than standard courses. One polytechnic staff member in London had already discerned a "downward curve" in Access course development and a definite reduction in the number of part-time courses which particularly attract groups such as women.

Co-operation with other institutions: open college networks and credit transfer

Access courses require collaboration between institutions – a process which has been increasing in recent years partly as the result of open college networks. Open college networks or federations have been established in a number of areas – north-west England, west and south Yorkshire, the west Midlands and London – and others are in various stages of development. The federations aim to make education and training more accessible by developing collaborative links between institutions and individual courses. They accredit learning opportunities across a range of providers and allow credits to be transferred between different sectors (including, in some areas, the voluntary sector, which assists non-traditional learners to gain access to qualifications). Many of the federations belong to a national open college network, which allows credits earned in one area to be accredited in another. Credits can be used as a personal record, as a basis for further study or to support job applications. In many cases they have reputedly raised the confidence and self-esteem of people without formal educational qualifications.

Residential college courses

Residential colleges have traditionally targeted people from working-class backgrounds. Their aim has been to offer a radical alternative to people failed by the education system. The long courses provided at the colleges are now generally accepted as an alternative entry route to higher education.

At Fircroft College in Birmingham there is a one-year full-time (two-year part-time) residential course with bursaries for full-time students. Students choose three major discipline areas and there is no final assessment. On completion of the course they receive a transcript – a factual record of their work – which is accepted by JMB as exempting them from A-level entry requirements for university degree courses.

Students are selected on the basis of an interview and a short essay, with the college tending to accept those who give some evidence of motivation and commitment to study. Typical applicants are unemployed, unqualified men in their twenties from socio-economic groups D/E who left school at between the ages of 15 and 16. Many have been involved in the Trades Union movement. In 1988 about 25% were from ethnic minority groups. The part-time course attracts mainly unwaged women from socio-economic group C, many of them single parents (although the college has no childcare facilities). According to staff, it has proved difficult to recruit working-class women because of cultural barriers and male hostility to their involvement.

Most applicants come with the intention to progress to higher education and in this respect the college enjoys a "spectacular success rate: 75% come with the desire to go to higher education and about 95% actually go." However, the use of the college predominantly as a route into higher education was worrying some members of staff. Some felt that the original purposes of the college were becoming increasingly peripheral to individual aspirations. One lecturer referred to growing "higher education paranoia" at the college: a feeling among students that if they do not start to make applications they will "miss out". A problem he identified was that full-time students have to start applying to higher education institutions virtually at the time they enter college, although at that stage few have a realistic view of the available options. He also referred to the conflict experienced by staff who are expected to support students' applications to universities and other institutions, even though they may feel that some students are unprepared for advanced courses.

A fear expressed by staff in two of the colleges was that the residential route into higher education may come to be viewed as uneconomic as the number of Access courses increases. Thus some staff members argued for a change in role and a shift in emphasis towards short residential courses for the local community.

Assessment of prior experiential learning (APEL)

Assessment of prior experiential learning schemes provide another means of assisting people without formal education qualifications to gain entry to formal courses. A number of institutions now incorporate APEL into Access, foundation or induction courses sometimes under other names such as Portfolio Preparation (North London College, South Bristol College), or Making Experience Count (Thames Polytechnic). A CNAA investigation of 12 schemes showed that APEL schemes can result in a number of positive outcomes for non-traditional students: increased confidence and self-esteem; admission to advanced courses; employment or promotion; general career and direction change (32).

There are, therefore, a number of alternative routes into higher education for non-traditional students. However, measures to widen access have not been universally welcomed. Changes in entry criteria have prompted concern about quality, entrance standards, completion rates and performance indicators. Moreover, suspicion has been voiced about the motives underlying the impetus to increase the numbers of mature students. One suggestion is that innovations such as part-time study, modularisation and credit accumulation "masquerading in the sheep's clothing of affirmative action" may turn out to be a "second-rate education on the cheap", camouflaging reductions in opportunities for school-leavers and intensifying the gap between universities, which take few adult students, and public sector higher education, which takes the most (33). Relaxed entry requirements have been described in another quarter as: "Further assaults on university standards ... soft options being prepared for young people from the ethnic minorities and the working class" (34). This view is contradicted by the evidence: research has consistently demonstrated that students without standard A-level qualifications achieve better degrees than many other groups in public sector higher education (35), and it has been accepted by Government that "achieving a more open system is wholly compatible with maintaining high standards" (36).

Institutional Support for Non-Traditional Students

> *How people get to the starting gate can't be an end in itself. It's not enough to admit people. We have to ensure that they can fully participate and benefit. [Deputy Director of a polytechnic]*

As support issues are substantially the same for students in further and higher education, both sectors are covered in this section.

The evidence from practitioners and surveys suggests that a high proportion of non-traditional students drop out of further and higher education through lack of support. In the US, attention has been drawn to the *laissez-faire* approach in education institutions which react to "the new majority" (mature students) simply by removing barriers in admissions and eligibility procedures. Adults are then left to cope within the system without support (37). All the evidence suggests that a comparable situation obtains in this country. According to a mature student co-ordinator in a London polytechnic, there has been a move to open up higher education but a failure to recognise that people are not ready for it. "The real principles of equal opportunities are: 1. to go out and get people in, and 2. support them!"

Support stage 1: Publicity

Non-traditional student groups require support at all stages of their involvement with education institutions, even before they actually step inside them. For those institutions without outreach activities, the only way of reaching non-users is through marketing and publicity. Traditionally, further and higher education publicity has assumed a single market and focused on traditional younger learners. Now, institutions are making efforts to target mature students. Examples are Manchester Polytechnic and the Polytechnic of North London, both of which have mature student guides dealing fully, in an informal and readable style, with the questions and worries new students are likely to have. However, some institutional attempts to attract mature students have been unfortunate. A totally inappropriate approach was employed by one FE college, which, in an information hand-out advertising a course for unwaged women, referred to: "Methods of study with elements of both formal information input and interactive student learning ... through research and seminar to role play and simulation using CCTV" (38). Other institutions have gone too far in the opposite direction. A research report (39) complains of the coy or patronising nature of some publicity for women: "For the fair sex", "This means you too, ladies!". Similar complaints have been made about publicity directed at older people.

Support stage 2: First contacts with institutions

Several research reports suggest that scant attention is given by institutions to assisting individuals in their first contacts with them. In many cases this contradicts and undermines a genuine wish to bring in new students. Visits, telephone calls and correspondence involve expenditure of time, money and effort by the individuals who respond to publicity: if new hurdles are then put in their way, many potential clients will fall by the wayside. Several studies have detailed the immense difficulties faced by people who have tried to obtain information on available educational opportunities and entry criteria. A REPLAN investigation (40) of contacts between unemployed adults and a range of adult, further and higher education establishments found that responses to telephone enquiries were "almost always unproductive", and often "abrupt and dismissive", with callers either being given no information or being referred to other agencies. Another study (41) describes how adults' first contacts with colleges can be marred by inadequate reception facilities and poor signposting. The first people encountered by visitors or callers are switchboard operators, receptionists, secretarial staff and security guards, few of whom are experienced or trained in giving information. Similar problems are outlined in an investigation (42) of the experiences of Access course applicants at two London colleges. This report describes a range of offputting factors such as:

☐ preliminary advice evenings held for all prospective college students, leading to long queues
☐ inadequate telephone systems
☐ inappropriate conditions at open evenings: badly-lit, unmarked approaches to colleges; inadequate internal signposting and directions
☐ insufficient information on the nature and purpose of assessment
☐ referrals to Return to Study courses that were not connected or integrated with the content of Access courses
☐ failure to pick up at an early stage that some people were not ready for Access courses
☐ formal and unfriendly interviews at which inappropriate questions were asked
☐ brief letters of rejection that were not clear about reasons for failure.

These findings are generally consistent with what was learned from informants during the research, in particular the almost universal inadequacies of telephone contacts. Many of the institutions visited during the research had very few outside lines. One very large college had only eight, leading an outreach worker to complain: "It's almost impossible to get a line out. How do they expect the community to get one in?"

The evidence cumulatively suggests the following priorities for assisting adults in their first contacts with institutions:

☐ more outreach work by institutions
☐ specific publicity for mature and part-time students
☐ application forms tailored to non-traditional students
☐ publicity which states the hours when course tutors are available
☐ more telephone lines or answering machines
☐ college-based advice and counselling services
☐ preliminary screening and constructive referral so that unready candidates are identified before interview stage
☐ front-line staff with access to information containing names and availability of staff
☐ in-service training for office and reception staff
☐ separate open days or evenings and enrolment times for mature students at which clear information on courses and all aspects of institutional life is provided
☐ interviews which encourage people to demonstrate their potential rather than inadequacies
☐ "positive" letters of rejection, giving candidates an idea of their strengths as well as weaknesses, and information about other opportunities and details of advice and guidance services (43).

Support stage 3: The institutional environment

The nature of new students' first impressions and experiences in an institution can be crucial to their continuation on a course of study. On the whole, however, institutions have been slow in their response to an increased intake of mature students. An HMI survey of thirty-five further and higher education colleges criticised them for "dreary, poorly lit and sometimes dirty classrooms" and for their "lack of expertise in adapting teaching strategies to meet the needs of adult learners" (44).

Mature students often feel conspicuous in institutions geared to a younger clientele, especially if their educational, economic and social background, not to mention age, colour or gender, differ from those of the majority. They also experience discomfort and alienation if there is too great a mismatch between their experience and life-style and an institution's ambience and environment. A REPLAN worker in the north-west described how a well-meaning initiative to attract unemployed manual workers to a college totally misfired on their first visit: "They were taken into an oak-panelled room and given coffee in really tiny cups. They felt totally out of place and there's still a hard core that won't have anything to do with the college because of that one experience."

Many institutions have no separate rooms or facilities for adult students, despite the clear need for them. There were some exceptions: Longlands College has a "cushion room" where adult learners can meet informally. Some institutions have separate entry points for adult students – often entitled Adult or Access Units – which ease transition for new groups. An example is the Access Unit at Bradford and Ilkley Community College, established to improve community access to the college and "provide a human face to a large and complex organisation". Childcare facilities or assistance with childcare arrangements is an essential support measure for women students, but few institutions have adequate facilities.

Support stage 4: Guidance and induction

The importance of initial and continuing guidance was constantly stressed by staff working with non-traditional mature students. Adults entering institutions after a long interval are vulnerable to early drop-out, often because they have joined the wrong course at the wrong level. It has been suggested (45) that guidance is required at five stages of access: "recruitment, induction, experience (developing through course), transition (to next step) and post-course (coping with the next step)". A crucial stage in this process is on entry when it is essential to assess prior learning; to discover which courses and learning levels are appropriate and to refer individuals accordingly. A number of institutions now provide some form of guidance, either as a separate service or as part of induction or taster programmes.

An FEU document (46) promotes the concept of "sheltered entry" and a "base course" open to entrants all year round, enabling them to discover what colleges have to offer, to sample courses, meet staff, and obtain guidance before commitment to programmes of study. The wisdom of this has been confirmed at several colleges where it has been found that induction and taster programmes increase mature student enrolments and reduce drop-out. At Stockton Billington Technical College, a range of short access courses co-ordinated between departments and preceded by counselling significantly increased enrolments of the unemployed. At Bilston Community College, new students can select from a "honeycomb" of modules. This allows people to try a variety of educational activities before they make a definite decision on the course of study they wish to pursue. Entry into the honeycomb can be made every five weeks and there is continuous advice and guidance through a personal tutorial system. Some higher education institutions have developed special foundation courses to assist mature students on entry (for example Newcastle-upon-Tyne Polytechnic). In Birmingham, colleges have an induction fortnight with guidance and assessment for pre-Access students.

Associate Student schemes fulfil basically the same function as sample or taster courses. A number of polytechnics operate such schemes (for example Hatfield, Newcastle-upon-Tyne, Leeds) which allow people to try different courses without committing themselves to a whole programme (although assignments can be accredited). In one Associate Student scheme, at Newcastle Polytechnic, people over 21 can "pick and mix" units of courses, join any programme without having to enrol for the whole course, and put together a personal programme for as long or as short a time as they can manage.

Support stage 5: The curriculum

The further and higher education system has been described as "an academic conveyor belt in which subject and method are rigidly predetermined, and rarely developed with the needs of working-class or black people in mind" (47). Some colleges have tried to recruit mature students not out of concern to widen access to the community but to compensate for a shortfall in traditional student numbers. In such cases the tendency has been to fit adults into existing programmes, which according to an FEU survey "severely limits the number who can benefit" (48). Other institutions provide short initial programmes as a carrot to attract specific groups of adults who are then steered into mainstream courses: "Our approach is to provide programmes in those areas they find non-threatening, then encourage them into other areas" (staff member in a college in the north-east).

By providing pump-priming funding, several national programmes have enabled institutions to develop a curriculum for under-represented groups. With REPLAN support, Sandown and Weston-Super-Mare Colleges were able to offer a range of flexible courses for older adults and the unemployed.

Pump-priming funding from UDACE contributed to the organisation of taster courses for the black community at Luton College of Higher Education.

Some institutions with a commitment to encouraging mature students, have developed certificated programmes specifically for adult learners. Bradford and Ilkley Community College, for example, offers part-time certificated courses for mature students. One, in the Department of General and Basic Education, prepares students for entry to advanced study; the other, in the Department of Business Studies, prepares them for entry to HND or HNC in Business Education or other higher level courses.

In some institutions, existing curricula have been modified to take account of mature learners, for example by modularisation. Modularisation, which permits sampling and varied and flexible modes of attendance, has most often been introduced in Humanities and Social Science departments, although the practice is slowly spreading to other disciplines.

Support stage 6: Learning support

The value of induction programmes or sampling is that individual learning levels and support needs can be picked up at an early stage. Many adults enter advanced learning programmes without real awareness of what they entail. They may need preparation in study skills, English as a Second Language, or support courses in basic mathematics and English. A number of institutions have established support programmes in these areas. At South Bristol Technical college, a wide-ranging Foundation Service has been operating on mainstream budget since 1987. This provides:

☐ individual guidance and tutorials
☐ study skills (rolling programmes with initial interviews and assessment)
☐ weekly guidance drop-in workshop (with careers advice and portfolio preparation)
☐ preparation for mathematics.

The service was initiated by a staff member who was concerned about mature student drop-out:

I've seen so many people give up through not having this kind of support. The drop-out rate, particularly in maths, is phenomenal. A lot of the problems arose from lack of counselling. Adults join classes without knowing what's expected of them.

During the spring and summer terms the accent is on preparation for study and, during the autumn term, on support for study. The guidance workshop assists people with career advice and financial questions such as eligibility for grants. The service therefore provides progressive stages of guidance. This requires team work and inter-departmental cross-referrals, with the guidance worker as the first point of contact:

> *I discover needs, offer information and identify the next step. Once the person is in a group, the tutor will identify the next need and suggest ways of meeting it. Hence there is a great deal of cross-referral as the student becomes ready for the next step. If I gave all the information in one go it would be too much: the person would be overwhelmed and back off, so I have to rely on the referral structure.*

The support offered by the Foundation Service has been an effective means of reducing drop-out. The Service also provides considerable personal support for individuals.

Support stage 7: Personal support: financial and pastoral

Concessionary fee policies and discretionary grant arrangements vary greatly between local authorities and institutions. A common personal problem experienced by mature students is lack of finance. Apart from those on special schemes or people with basic education needs, the majority of part-time adult students receive no financial support. Several institutions try and assist students with financial problems. The Access Unit at Bradford and Ilkley College, for example, helps to seek funding for those students in financial difficulty and handles fees and funding for unemployed students. Other colleges allow low-paid workers and unwaged people who have difficulty paying for mainstream courses to pay by monthly instalments. Richmond College has introduced a successful voucher system allowing unemployed people and people on state benefits to enrol for a number of courses for only a small amount per term.

Adult students come into institutions from a range of complex work and family situations and many need more than just practical support. A number of reports have described the problems experienced by non-traditional mature students moving across class and cultural boundaries into educational environments that have traditionally been the preserve of a small, elite section of society. Black students moving from a "sheltered" feeder course to a large college in Bristol were described by an outreach worker as "dropping out like flies" through lack of support:

> *The common theme is alienation. Even those who are very keen, after a couple of weeks, they get some nervous disorder. That college is a lumbering dinosaur; a middle-class, hostile environment. You have to understand the experience of people who've never been employed, come from a different route and background, and perceive themselves as failures, but they're expected to perform at the same rate as other*

people. There's nothing to buttress them; there's no black staff, no support system, no one to turn to.

This example underlines the need for pastoral support services. Non-traditional students require access to empathetic individuals (counsellors or personal tutors) who can understand their experience and problems. An outreach worker in Bristol felt that recruitment and retention of non-participant groups depended on a "push factor" – individuals or agencies outside institutions encouraging and referring people – and a "pull factor" – people inside institutions encouraging and supporting them. Ideally these should be pastoral staff of the same sex or ethnic background who can empathise with students and mediate on their behalf within the system.

Support stage 8: Staff attitudes and practice

The flexible, supportive approach used in work with adults in the community can contrast sharply with institutional practice and teaching methods. In some institutions, mature students have experienced problems with staff attitudes and teaching styles. Tutors who work with adults at the point of entry are usually aware of their needs and problems, but as students progress into mainstream they often do not encounter the same understanding. A formal lecturing style does not suit all adults. Many prefer a more participative, open-ended discussion approach which draws on their maturity and experience. Some staff find this threatening and those accustomed only to traditional younger students sometimes have difficulty adapting their long-established teaching practices to the requirements of mature students or specific groups. Several tutors interviewed during the project commented on colleagues' insensitive reactions to ethnic minority students: they referred to lecturers who made no attempt to modify their accents or terminology for immigrant groups, produced jargon-filled handouts, and often expected people with limited English to follow vocational courses at the same pace as other students. Access Liaison Officers and outreach staff complained that some colleagues regarded adults as "inappropriate" students and generally ascribed any drop-out to lack of commitment rather than any lack of institutional support. Research evidence suggests that this situation is not uncommon. One report on the experience of women moving into education institutions referred to "aggressive" selection interviews and staff who seemed to regard them as potential nuisances (49). In many institutions, resistance towards non-traditional student groups – women, black people and adults generally – appeared particularly prevalent in the traditional vocational departments.

Staff development. To reduce these problems, attempts have been made in some institutions to involve as many staff as possible in the induction process and subsequent work with mature students. The involvement of staff in curriculum development and introductory work with mature students has turned out to be a valuable staff development exercise in some establishments. According to a tutor, actual contact with new learner groups "can achieve more in terms of attitude change and awareness in a few weeks than all the textbooks in a year."

However, the research suggested that there is generally a wide gulf in understanding between full-time staff teaching traditional student groups and those working with mature students in outreach and institutional settings. Some outreach staff reported that institution-based colleagues tended to dismiss their work as unprofessional and trivial. In one college, outreach workers were perceived to be doing little other than wandering about having "chats" on college expenses.

At a time when adult students are entering further and higher education in greater numbers than ever before, staff development is urgently needed to bridge this gap in understanding, and to sensitise institution-based staff whose experience has been restricted to conventional students to the very different circumstances and requirements of mature learners. These were the aims of staff training sessions conducted at colleges in the north-west with GRIST funding. According the organiser, the sessions were designed for all levels of staff:

> *I think staff development is crucial only if it affects the whole system. I won't just work with people who are outreach workers. There's no point unless we get mixed groups of full- and part-time staff, senior management and organisers. There's a particular need to feed in outreach experience otherwise mainstream just won't change. I feel that all full-time workers should do some outreach sessions to see why people have certain needs. Outreach workers need two-way channels and in my sessions I look at these.*

In this instance, the organiser found that the staff most resistant to change were senior management: "It's not easy but it's a good exercise for them to listen rather than talk. They have to be told to shut up and can get very upset. But I can say things because I'm from outside!"

Support stage 9: Accreditation

Mature students require tangible benefits for time put in: "value-added" incentives such as credits or qualifications which give status and legitimacy to learning. The more flexible systems of accreditation encouraged by Access courses, open college networks and NCVQ, and the widening of the curriculum to embrace a range of community activities and skills (as in RSA-accredited courses) have opened up access to qualifications for a much wider group of adult learners.

With short courses which do not lead to qualifications, it has been found that a certificate of completion is greatly appreciated by students. A guidance worker in Yorkshire stressed that adults generally want their participation recorded and recognised: "This was perceived as having an important market value as well as marking a passage through the educational system " (50).

Support stage 10: Progression to different levels of learning

One argument for having introductory programmes located inside rather than outside education institutions is that people get to know the college environment, making the transition between study modes and different types and levels of education easier. In some institutions it has been found that provision of part-time courses promotes enrolments in more advanced full-time courses.

A common observation, however, is that the gap between introductory and mainstream programmes is too wide for many students. The aim of an ALBSU special development project in Richmond Community College was to explore ways of easing transition for post-basic education students. The project worker found that the starting level of mainstream courses was too high, and the pace of learning too fast, for this group. To assist their progress to more advanced programmes, a series of intermediate courses and taster sessions was developed, linked to the full range of work in the college. Students had access to guidance and counselling at all stages and this was considered a crucial element in the success of the scheme: 74 students subsequently joined 159 mainstream courses and the drop-out level was very low (51).

Equal Opportunities Policies

To ensure genuine access to all stages of further and higher education, student support structures need to be underpinned by strong equal opportunities policies. However, the majority of institutions do not have well developed policies and surveys suggest that those that exist frequently do not go beyond a general statement of intent or code of conduct (52). As one research report has pointed out: "It is clearly not enough simply to proclaim a commitment to equal opportunities without confronting the question of sexist attitudes or practical difficulties such as childcare" (53).

Different student groups

Institutional policies vary enormously in the emphasis they give to different groups. An unpublished survey (54) found special needs to be the most highly developed dimension of equal opportunities. Twelve out of 30 further and higher education institutions surveyed provided special facilities, courses and support for students with special educational needs, 10 had special access measures, courses and support mechanisms for women, but only five had adopted special measures and developed courses to encourage the participation of ethnic minority groups. This trend was confirmed in another survey, published in 1989, which found that the majority of universities and 14 out of 26 polytechnics had "barely begun to think about" the issue of ethnic minority participation (55). More has been achieved in the further education sector, but there is no cause for complacency. An examination of NAFE plans in 1987 found LEA rhetoric on equal opportunities for ethnic minorities falling into several categories:

☐ stated intentions without strategies for implementation
☐ "catch-all" references (general policies but no targeted measures)
☐ collections of statistics on ethnic minorities without saying how these were to be used
☐ limited references to ethnic minorities in some parts of plans but no coherent overall approach to equal opportunities
☐ concentration on specific ESL and Access courses or courses for low achievers (56).

Unwaged or unemployed people are not often specified in equal opportunities policies. A survey of colleges in a Midlands county found only one with a clear policy on helping to facilitate access for unemployed people (57). Even fewer institutions, it seems, have a policy which embraces older learners.

It has been found that separate policies for different groups often lead to a fragmented approach to equal opportunities. The case for an integrated approach which "articulates age with gender, race and disability" has been persuasively argued by Cooper and Bornat (58). They complain that references to older adults are usually only made in policies for people with special needs – a medical model which "stresses physical and mental changes and does not give prominence to learning potential and educational development."

Staff responsibility for equal opportunities

A report on Access and equal opportunities (59) observes that the shortfall in provision of resources for staff has had a "strong impact" on the development of equal opportunities in institutions. Few further and higher education establishments have a full-time member of staff to co-ordinate equal opportunities throughout the institution. Responsibility is often given, on a part-time basis, to an existing staff member. This results in the whole issue of equal opportunities remaining marginal and associated only with a specific department or teaching area.

In some institutions, however, outside funding has enabled the creation of special posts to facilitate access for particular categories of students. In one college of higher education, a full-time multi-ethnic co-ordinator has been appointed, using Section XI funding, with a brief to work across the whole institution.

Staff attitudes

The introduction of equal opportunities policies is not always welcomed by staff. Interviews conducted at several institutions revealed attitudes of hostility and defensiveness:

> *People here are affronted at the idea that they might be racist. There's no awareness that their assumptions bear no relation to black people's experience. [FE lecturer, West country]*

A lecturer at a higher education college reported that colleagues were unwilling to participate in staff development on equal opportunities because they felt that it was an additional pressure and it implied that they were not aware of race and gender issues. Some were sceptical of the motives behind the initiative, suspecting that the principal aim was to give the college a "progressive image". The tendency among many teaching staff is to consider that simply having a policy is enough.

> *Lots of people didn't think we needed a policy. There was some bad feeling. Some thought it was unnecessary and already part of the rules. As usual people thought that the work was finished after the policy was produced. [Equal Opportunities co-ordinator, HE college, Midlands]*

The drafting of an equal opportunities policy can in itself be an effective staff training exercise. One college staff member found that involving colleagues in discussing and drafting a policy resulted in commitment to its implementation and focused attention on shortcomings in their respective teaching areas. Equal opportunities committees with a whole institution remit have also been effective in raising staff awareness. One established in a college of higher education was reported to have "massively raised the profile of equal opportunities."

Implementing policies

A handbook on NAFE planning in relation to the ethnic minority communities pinpoints the following 12 areas where action on equal opportunities is required: policy; priorities and resourcing; monitoring; consultation and needs analysis; marketing; access and recruitment; course programming; delivery mechanisms; progression; student support; evaluation and review; staffing and staff development (60).

As this suggests, equal opportunities is a concept that impinges on all aspects of an institution's work. An FEU report, *FE in Black and White* (1987), argues that only a whole college approach to equal opportunities, involving all staff, and given high enough priority in terms of time and resources, will achieve positive change. The NAB report *Action for Access* (1988) agrees with this view, arguing that equal opportunities policies should be integrated in corporate plans, agreed by governing bodies, and should underpin all areas of practice. The report maintains that if there is no real commitment to equal opportunities at senior levels, no real change can be achieved in institutions.

The research highlighted another reason for lack of progress: few institutions appear to have any mechanisms for monitoring the implementation of equal opportunities policies.

Monitoring

It is now widely recommended that education institutions monitor and analyse their student and staff composition annually in terms of gender, ethnic origin, disability and current or previous occupation. The Principal of Newham College has maintained that such an audit should be carried out in the interests of equity, which he proposed as a third performance indicator to be added to the criteria of effectiveness and efficiency identified in the Responsive College Project. To meet the new criterion, the college was proposing to collect data on the age, ethnic origin, gender, geographical location, disability, employment status and social class of its primary clients. The audit was to be made at three stages:

☐ Access (publicity, recruitment, enrolment)
☐ Process (course induction, content delivery, assessment, support services, progression arrangements)
☐ Success (placements in further and higher education, employment, usefulness of education) (61).

Few institutions currently record such comprehensive details, although many now monitor for ethnicity, and the DES has added this dimension to the Further Education Statistical Record. Nonetheless, this kind of monitoring can be problematic. A researcher in higher education referred to the problem of identifying accurate and reliable statistical data concerning the ethnic origins of students and staff:

The college has tried to implement an ethnic monitoring form when students register, but it is frequently not filled in or filled in incorrectly, so the figures produced may not be reliable.

Some groups may detect sinister motives behind questions about race, previous occupation and social class. Only when an institution has proved itself to be accessible to all groups, with a genuine commitment to equal opportunities, will such suspicions be allayed.

Factors Which Have Favoured Access for Non-Traditional Students in Further and Higher Education

The research took place at a time when a variety of social, demographic and political pressures were encouraging further and higher education institutions to seek ways of attracting a greater number of non-traditional students. Certain factors, however, appeared to have particularly favoured innovation.

Financial resources for innovation

In most institutions contacted during the project, improved access had depended on securing the necessary resources to finance outreach activities, new posts, new programmes, support services and other equal opportunities measures. A principal attributed his college's success in attracting groups of mature students to diversity or plurality of funding: "We're not just in hock to the Borough and aren't as hamstrung as other places in what we can do." In other institutions, staff had been able to use base funding "creatively" to initiate new programmes and student support services.

In a majority of institutions contacted, initiatives for new learners had been developed with pump-priming finance from ESG, MSC/Training Agency, Urban Programme, ALBSU, and the REPLAN programme. Where external funding had financed staff time for access initiatives, this had sometimes created an atmosphere conducive to change in an institution.

Management support

In a number of institutions, the commitment of senior management was considered to have been a key factor in widening access.

Efforts and commitment of individuals

In many institutions, initiatives to assist access for new student groups had come about as a result of the efforts of dedicated individuals. These were not necessarily in managerial positions, and most claimed to have achieved things through persistence, persuasion of others and a refusal to be "fobbed off". According to one report, it is necessary for change agents in institutions to have: "A level of stubbornness and sometimes lack of regard for a system which left to itself would always be reluctant to change" (62).

Several people reported that simply getting things started was the only way to achieve innovation: "Getting things known at the planning stage sometimes stimulates resources for them" (open college network co-ordinator).

Staff involvement in innovation

Individuals working with mature student groups have achieved most success when they have secured wider staff co-operation and involvement across departmental boundaries. This has often happened when colleagues have been brought in at a planning stage:

> Who owns things and ideas matters because then things tend to work and there's a commitment. We had some staff development for staff unused to dealing with non-traditional students. Because it was THEIR idea, it worked well. [Polytechnic staff member]

Colleges with a staff matrix structure have been able to break away from hierarchical departmental structures and form course teams. In some cases, the establishment of cross-institution working parties in areas such as curriculum development has resulted in changes affecting whole institutions.

The influence of outside agencies

Changes in institutional practice have frequently occurred in response to requests, recommendations or pressures from outside agencies.

LEAs. Institutions in local authorities with a strong commitment to equal opportunities have sometimes been drawn along in that direction:

> We were lighting matches in the dark for a long time and suddenly they caught light. The poly decided, comparatively recently, that they had a community role. ILEA was the catalyst. [Mature student co-ordinator]

Guidance services. By feeding back community interests and demands, guidance agencies have contributed substantially to the development of new programmes in some institutions.

Local and open college networks. In some areas local networks have succeeded in raising provider awareness and changing the climate for mature learners in institutions. A further education college staff member in London referred to the influence of Brent Information and Learning Links for Adults (BRILL) as:

> *An incredible catalyst: in 18 months they have brought people together, making us know who all the other agencies are and how bad we've been at making efforts to find out what our community wants and how to go about it.*

Other educational institutions. Successful innovations in some institutions have provided models for others. A London polytechnic lecturer maintained that the introduction of a mature student enquiry office with its own telephone line had inspired widespread imitation: "Now everybody's doing it."

Trickle-down effects of new measures in institutions

Introduction of new procedures such as Assessment of Prior Experiential Learning schemes has stimulated some institutions to re-examine their recruitment policies, admission systems and curriculum content. In some cases, the development of new curricula and support services for mature learners has had an impact on the whole institution. At Hinckley College, an innovative programme for unemployed adults became "proactive and an organic growth which changed the nature of college provision for other learners."

The influence of new groups

New student groups have frequently been potent catalysts for change. A college staff member referred to the "dynamic" impact of non-traditional students on teaching and learning styles: "Group entry of women students really brings about changes in areas such as timetabling and staff development."

An influx of black students on Access courses in another college was reported to have had a significant impact on the assumptions and attitudes of teaching staff and on the language used in teaching and materials:

> *Having ten black students in a class makes a great difference. It really challenges practice. There was a certain degree of discomfort among staff at first. We'd had a number of staff development days to talk about the importance of recruiting black students but if you have live*

representatives of another culture in your class it's better than the theory. You have to harness new ideas. [College lecturer]

Sustaining change

Staff who had succeeded in introducing measures to widen access claimed that the best way of making short-term initiatives permanent was by ensuring that they spread into the system:

I knew there was a crying need for this [student learning support] so I flooded the system. There was so much demand that when funding ran out, they couldn't just cut the service off as by then it was too embedded in the system. They had to fund it from the mainstream budget. [Adult student organiser in an FE college]

However, it was clear during the research that, to become embedded, innovations need to be perceived as being in the best interests of the institution and those working in it. In one polytechnic, Access staff had adopted two strategies for change: persuading senior management and "a pincer movement on the ground trying to take the institution with us". New measures were promoted by appealing to the institution's self-interest.

The programmes and initiatives which contribute to institutional goals are the most likely to survive and be nurtured. This implies some measure of compatibility with, or adaptation to, the established norms and values of an institution.

Factors Which Have Impeded Wider Access for Non-Traditional Adult Groups in Further and Higher Education

Traditional structures and practices

I asked the [FE College] Principal how they monitored community demand. His face was a picture. He didn't know what I was talking about. [ESG Development Officer, shire LEA]

In further and higher education, entry and recruitment policies are still largely oriented towards young people with A-levels. A polytechnic staff member referred to resistance to change from "a hostile mainstream seeking to protect its own powers and resources". He argued that when institutions start to recognise that the "problem" of access lies not within community groups but within their own structures and procedures, there is an implied challenge to power structures and existing resource allocation which may be fiercely resisted.

Traditional departmental structures constitute a particularly strong barrier to innovation because of the vested interests involved:

> In most places institutional policy is still in an important sense the sum of the policies of separate departments ... Success in implementing institutional policy usually depended on how successfully it could be reconciled with departments' current policies or practice" (63).

The greatest resistance to change in institutions appears to be within traditional technical departments. Most of the outreach and Access workers attached to further and higher education establishments referred to this, as did development and guidance workers working in the community:

> We've had no success in the traditional technology areas. A lot of the problem is to do with ingrained attitudes, prejudice, resistance to change. We've sometimes been used by people inside institutions to put on pressure from outside to achieve change because their internal channels were blocked! [Guidance worker, West Yorkshire]

In further education, subject departments have been oriented towards employer rather than community needs. Posts and salary structures are related to levels of work, with higher level work attracting greater resource allocation and offering better promotion prospects than programmes for the unskilled. This situation largely explains the reluctance of staff, particularly those in vocational and technical departments, to support measures to improve access for non-traditional students, such as the unemployed, black people or women.

No perception of need

Institutions attracting sufficient numbers of their traditional student clienteles have no incentive to pay attention to other groups' needs, especially if this means extra work:

> Staff dislike assessing the experience of mature students for entry purposes: their attitude is: "why should we spend time doing that when we've got A-level students?" [Access course tutor, London]

In some institutions contacted during the research, staff did not anticipate any large-scale changes in student intake. In one technical college visited, recruitment was directed at traditional and foreign students and the director had no plans to target under-represented groups in the community:

Our policy is not to turn anyone away, they can come if they can pay, but we don't target specifically.

Changes and reorganisation

At the time the research took place, attention to access issues was taking second place to preoccupations with the forthcoming changes resulting from the Education Reform Act: "The Directorate has been much too involved in preparing for corporate status to look at mature student entry" [polytechnic staff member].

Staff attitudes

Negative attitudes to mature students among institutional staff also constitute a formidable obstacle to change. In some institutions it was reported that certain teaching staff automatically considered groups such as black students and older adults as low level learners. Individual interviewees were resistant to mature students *per se*. The head of a college construction department contended that mature students were only appropriate for evening provision; another head of department (mechanical engineering) insisted that since all his students (16–19 white, male) were adults, questions about access for mature learners were irrelevant.

Staff composition

Staff resistance to mature learners appears to derive partly from a view of adults as "inappropriate" learners, partly from anxieties about changing established practices. However, it could also be related to the fact that the majority of teaching staff in many education institutions belong to a relatively homogeneous group: white, middle-class males. This, it may be inferred, constitutes a substantial obstacle to change. Very few ethnic minority teachers had been recruited in any of the institutions contacted and few women were in senior teaching or administrative positions.

Lack of staff involvement in planning

In colleges and polytechnics where there had been whole institution shifts towards greater responsiveness to the community, staff had generally been involved in planning for anticipated changes in student intake. In many institutions, however, there appears to be little overall staff involvement in planning. Two reports (64) have highlighted staff ignorance of and confusion about decision-making structures in further education.

Lack of funding

Lack of resources was cited by many staff as the greatest impediment to progress in widening access:

> *It's our biggest problem. It's impossible to put on new programmes. We get no financial support for that from the LEA; it's up to us but we have no money to do anything. [Principal of FE college]*

In a county with a large ethnic minority population, a college lecturer had experienced immense difficulty in obtaining resources for work with this section of the community: "You get bugger all unless you raise it yourself. We've had to go outside the county to find finance."

External funding problems

A large proportion of initiatives for mature students in further and higher education have been financed from external sources. In some cases, however, short-term funding has created more problems than it has solved. There can be wide differences between the aims, regulations and criteria of external funding agencies and those of the host institution. As a result, some short-term innovations had been fraught with administrative and organisational problems. External funding requires renegotiation and resubmissions, but staff complained that criteria and regulations were constantly being changed. Another problem mentioned was the time-lag between applications for external finance and actual receipt of funds. In some cases this had resulted in loss of momentum and the abandonment of planned initiatives.

Some respondents feared that special funding had come to be perceived as the only way to finance work with non-traditional groups. One lecturer referred to Section XI funding as "financial apartheid". Although pump-priming finance has led to new programmes becoming "base budget" in some institutions, in others where it has been taken up purely for expediency, it has had little general impact: "Specialist initiatives were 'add-on' provision with no guarantee of continuation, consequently seen as marginal" (65).

Short-term funding has resulted in a tendency for innovative measures for non-traditional students to be clustered around the edges of institutions and staffed by people on a part-time or short-term basis. The overall result is that the whole area of wider access can be inherently marginal:

> *If you're in innovation, access, black students etc., there's always a*

danger of being marginalised; of not having a high enough profile in an institution. [Mature student co-ordinator, London polytechnic]

Lack of monitoring mechanisms

In some institutions with a policy commitment to wider access, there can be a wide discrepancy between stated intentions and practice: no childcare; few black or female teaching staff; no guidance or learning support services. Some colleges had appointed community outreach officers but were not responding to the learning demands they identified:

Who can I report to? Who can implement the courses I suggest? People say to me: "who's going to do it? where's the money coming from?" There are more barriers here than out there! [College outreach worker]

Equal opportunities policies without detailed plans for their implementation and monitoring mechanisms do not have any real impact on an institution.

Contradictions in policy

The research revealed some tension between the promotion of "equity" in access and the imperative to market courses and raise revenue. A mature student co-ordinator in a London polytechnic referred to the inherent contradiction between her role and the institution's marketing policy: two thrusts which appeared to be working against each other. Raising finance was taking precedence over access initiatives in several institutions contacted during the research, and the growing tendency was to seek foreign students.

The impact of outside agencies

In some instances, the actions of external agencies had slowed the pace of innovation. Union disputes and rate-capping had delayed action in some institutions, while lack of Local Authority understanding and support had impeded development in others:

We have to convince a hostile county that the work we do with ethnic minorities is valid and will bear fruit. We get a lot of flak and obstruction from them. [Multicultural co-ordinator, HE college]

We wanted to start some work with black groups. I asked the county

what they knew about Section XI funding and they said "what's that"?
[FE college outreach worker]

Staff working with some groups of mature students have experienced problems with the bureaucratic procedures employed by official bodies. Difficulties were reported with the DSS, the former MSC and various local government departments in connection with the position of unemployed and other students in receipt of state benefits, eligibility for grants and definitions of part-time study. In some cases this had led to proposed courses being abandoned. A tutor in a London college cited instances of unemployed students being "harassed" by the DSS on account of their participation in a Second Chance to Learn course.

Difficulties in liaison and collaboration

Collaboration with other agencies in the development of new courses and access measures is not always a smooth process, and in some cases conflict has delayed innovation. A polytechnic and the Commission for Racial Equality were locked in dispute over arrangements for Section XI-funded posts, and as a result no ethnic minority staff had been appointed. In some cases tension had arisen between higher and further education institutions over Access course arrangements.

Staff have found some accreditation and assessment bodies "reactionary" in their attitudes to more flexible arrangements for mature students. A college head of department who wanted to set up a computing course for parents reported that it took three-and-a-half years to negotiate a more flexible formula with BTEC. Other staff had found negotiating with external funders extremely difficult: "MSC asked for our suggestions. We want to introduce modular packages and we keep suggesting this to them but they never respond."

Some institutions were being hampered by the very groups they wished to help. In one college, an attempt to involve local ethnic minority groups in initiating creative arts programmes derived from their own culture had generated "a fierce separatist debate. They said this white college shouldn't be doing it. But if we don't, who will?"

Loss of momentum

Some innovations had become the victim of their own success. When new measures become embedded in institutional practice they can become subject to what a mature student co-ordinator described as "institutional drift" – bureaucracy takes over, measures lose momentum, get watered down, and sometimes lose their original intention. Examples reported included a women-only science course which became open to all students; access units being taken over and given unfamiliar and intimidating academic names; adult services becoming open to the whole student body thereby losing their sheltered and supportive ambience. An interviewee in a polytechnic observed that once a change becomes institutionalised, the student-centred approach rapidly reverts to an institution-centred one and "it becomes difficult to keep student needs paramount."

Views on Non-Participant Access

Although many education institutions have introduced measures to widen access, efforts have generally been fragmented and piecemeal. Few appear to have approached the issue of mature student access in a broad, whole-institution way, with attention to all aspects of practice that affect adult learners. This failure may be partly attributable to doubts about the feasibility of attracting more non-traditional students into advanced education without substantial additional funding. Some administrators and teaching staff expressed suspicion of the motives behind current moves to increase student numbers in higher education, one view being that coherence and quality might be destroyed in piecemeal attempts, "masquerading as social justice" to provide a cheaper service for more people (66). However, other staff argued that further and advanced education could be opened up to working-class and other mature student groups relatively easily, simply by diverting existing resources:

> To reach non-participants we don't have to go very far. We have our own administrative, secretarial, clerical and manual workers. If we are really serious about access we need to clean up our own backyard. [Deputy director, polytechnic]

The same respondent maintained that higher education has the resources but not the will to widen access to non-participant groups. The research as a whole suggests that institutions should have a clear policy towards mature learners, underpinned by a genuine commitment to equal opportunities and coherent strategies for planning, implementing and monitoring such a policy.

References

1. McIlroy, J. & Spencer, B. *op. cit.,* pp85, 100.
2. Department of Education and Science, Statistical Bulletin. DES, 1988.
3. Bird, M. & Varlaam, A. *Changing Course: Community education in Inner London.* Report PS 7114, ILEA, 1987.
4. Higgins, A. LEA provision. Paper delivered at a conference in Gwent, 1988.

5. Annual surveys of the levels of fees for part-time adult classes charged by LEAs are produced by NIACE, Leicester.

6. McPherson, J. *op. cit.*

7. Bateson, G. *op. cit.*

8. *The Challenge of Change.* UDACE, 1986, p95.

9. *Developing Educational Provision for Unemployed Adults.* NIACE/REPLAN, 1988, p11.

10. *Ibid.*, p12.

11. *Securing Adequate Facilities: Planning for the education of adults. A development paper.* UDACE, 1988.

12. Monitoring of draft schemes of delegation prepared by over 60 LEAs indicated that few LEAs were planning for when there were fewer school leavers by integrating adults into a comprehensive plan for post school education. Reported in *Education,* 173,22, p515, 2 June 1989.

13. Charnley, A.H. *Fees Charged to Part-time Students in LEAs 1988–89.* NIACE, 1989.

14. UDACE *op. cit.*, 1988, p3.

15. *Access to Further Education and Higher Education: A discussion document.* FEU, 1987; and *Students with Special Needs in FE. Education Observed, 9.* HMI, 1989.

16. Maloney, K. Priming the system. *REPLAN Review,* 4, 1989.

17. Information leaflet 3, NCVQ, p4.

18. *Partnerships in Action: Report of REPLAN activities in the North East.* NIACE/REPLAN, 1989, p14.

19. Information supplied for the project by Jan Eldred.

20. Department of Education and Science. Mature students in higher education 1975 to 1986. Statistical Bulletin 11/88. DES, 1988.

21. Rustin, M. The idea of the popular university. *In* Finch, J. & Rustin, M. (eds) *A Degree of Choice? Higher education and the right to learn.* Penguin Books, 1986, p44.

22. Bourner, T. *et al. Students on CNAA's Part-time First Degree Courses.* CNAA Development Services Publication 16. CNAA, 1988.

23. FEU *op. cit.*, 1987, para 31; and NAB *Action for Access.* NAB, 1988.

24. *See,* for example, Training Agency *Admissions to Higher Education: Policy and practice.* Training Agency, 1989; and Industry Matters *Raising the Standard: Wider access to higher education. Report of a national one-day consultation.* Industry Matters, 1988.

25. Fulton, O. & Ellwood, S. *Admissions to Higher Education: Policy and practice.* Training Agency, 1989, p12.

26. *Ibid.*

27. *see* Millins, P.K. *Report on Access Courses.* DES, 1984; and Woodrow, M. Access courses: some questions and answers. *Journal of Access Studies,* 1,1, p72, 1986.

28. Payne, R. *The Access Enquirers Project: From enquiry to interview.* ILEA/ALFA, 1988.

29. Pelissiet, C. & Smith, R. Student-centred continuing education: a county strategy for access. *Journal of Further and Higher Education,* 12, pp 64–71, Summer 1988.
30. *Ibid.*
31. Payne, R. *op. cit.*
32. Evans, N. *The Assessment of Prior Experiental Learning.* CNAA Development Services Publication 17. CNAA, 1988, p2.
33. Duke, F. Degrees of experience: are the needs and expectations of mature adults and school-leavers compatible? *Journal of Access Studies,* 1,1, pp54–63, Spring 1987.
34. Sherman, A. Relevant steps in a wrong direction. *The Guardian,* 20 September 1988.
35. Bourner, T. & Hamed, M. *Non-standard Entry Students: Entry qualifications and degree performance.* CNAA Development Services Publication 10. CNAA, 1987.
36. Jackson, R. Under Secretary of State for Education, at Royal Society Conference, 1988.
37. Holtzclaw, L.R. Flexible admission practices for adult learners. *Lifelong Learning,* April 1988.
38. Quoted in Morton, S. An Exploration of the Educational Circumstances and Needs of Mature Unwaged Women who are Non-participants in Continuing Education. Unpublished MEd dissertation, University of Sheffield, 1985.
39. Bridger, S. *op. cit.*
40. Blamire, J. & Nielsen, F. *Don't Call Us.* REPLAN, 1987.
41. Lowen, D. *Barriers to Educational Opportunities for Adults. A report on the institutional barriers to educational opportunities for adults.* Central and West London Open College, 1986.
42. Payne, R. *op. cit.*
43. *Ibid.*
44. HMI *Contribution of Further and Higher Education to Professional, Industrial and Commercial Updating.* HMSO, 1988.
45. FEU *Preparing Adults: An appraisal of MSC-sponsored adult preparation courses.* FEU, 1987.
46. *Ibid.,* p116.
47. Bridger, S. *op. cit.,* p125.
48. *Anxious to Work.* FEU/REPLAN, 1987.
49. Bridger, S. *op. cit.*
50. *EASA: survey of use: 1986–87.* Bradford EASA, 1987.
51. *Report of the Special Development Project at Richmond Community College 1984–1986.* ALBSU, 1987.
52. National Advisory Body *Action for Access.* NAB, 1988.
53. Bridger, S. *op. cit.,* p119.
54. Crossland, G. Equal Opportunities Policies in Further and Higher

Education Colleges in England and Wales. Unpublished, Wolverhampton Polytechnic, Equal Opportunities Unit, 1988.

55. Williams, J., Davis, L. & Cocking, J. *Equal Opportunities and Racial Equality in Higher Education.* CRE, 1989.

56. *Equal Opportunities for Ethnic Minority Groups in NAFE.* FEU Project Bulletin. CRE/FEU, 1987.

57. FEU/REPLAN 1987 *op. cit.,* p10.

58. Cooper, M. & Bornat, J. *op. cit.*

59. National Advisory Body *op. cit.,* 1987.

60. Borthwick, A. *et al. Planning NAFE Equal Opportunities for Ethnic Minorities.* FEU, 1988.

61. Baillie, J. *Reponsive College Proposal.* Newham Community College, 1987.

62. *Charting the Change.* NIACE/REPLAN, 1987, p15.

63. Fulton, O. & Ellwood, S. *op. cit.*

64. FEU *Black to White.* FEU, 1987, para 33; and Smith, V. Decision-making in FE. *NATFHE Journal,* March/April 1983.

65. FEU *op. cit.,* 1987, para 145.

66. Duke, F. *op. cit.,* p60.

Section 5

Concluding Observations

General Findings

Non-participation is an indictment not of public apathy but of an education system which still projects a narrow and elitist image.

The public as a whole has little knowledge of the nature and extent of educational opportunities for adults. Post-compulsory education is complex, fragmented and diverse. Professionals working in one part of the system often have little knowledge or understanding of the others. It is unrealistic to expect the public to understand the system if educationists themselves have little sense of the whole.

People in non-participant categories have a widespread tendency to equate all forms of learning with formal school education. Most perceive education as the preserve of younger people belonging to an exclusive, affluent and intellectual circle. The surveys conducted during the project revealed considerable anger and hostility towards a system which was widely seen as trying to impose and uphold the values of a particular social class and culture. Thus, the major barriers to participation are attitudes, perceptions and expectations, although life situations and material circumstances also play a crucial part. Attitudes related to social class and gender roles are particularly resilient and difficult to change.

For their part, people working in education tend to regard non-participants as the "problem", rather than exploring how the system itself has failed to be relevant and attractive to a large proportion of the adult population. Traditionally, adult learning opportunities have been determined by education providers for a self-selecting client group. A service that operates from an assumption that all adults are self-directed and in circumstances that favour participation makes unequal access inevitable. The research provided little evidence of any general thrust for change:

> What people really want is access, access, access at different points in their lives, but the political will to help people without clout or a large profile – pensioners, for example – isn't there. [Adult education worker in London]

> There's been a lot of questions, a lot of research, a lot of reports but not a lot of action. [Member of ethnic minority group]

> I know lots of genuine, sincere people but nothing ever happens. The

> *traditional system is so firmly entrenched. I've had Prince Charles sitting where you are, and Kenneth Clarke; both very interested. They said how good it was, but nothing's changed. [Outreach worker with the black communities]*

Short of a major evolution in societal structures, mores and attitudes, to get people to the point where voluntary participation in education is part of normal behaviour requires significant intervention by education providers. This would involve major shifts in priorities and resource allocation and a greater readiness to reach out to the community.

Current Provision

The research revealed a system in a state of considerable flux, with enormous variations in provision and practice between locations and institutions.

There have been a variety of educational initiatives for non-participant groups in different parts of the country, but learning facilities and opportunities for different groups are not available in all localities and are not always provided by the local education authorities. Some councils look on adult education as a middle-class leisure pursuit and do not see the need for a publicly-funded service. Others have made laudable efforts to redistribute resources in favour of disadvantaged adults, but this has sometimes been at the expense of education provision that was already attracting significant numbers of people in non-participant categories. Thus the argument for widening access should not be polarised into *either* traditional adult provision *or* work with new groups, but should make the case for a more flexible, multi-targeted service, operating from the recognition that the community is composed of different groups with equally valid learning interests and requirements. The fact that some groups are more vocal in their demands than others does not mean that opportunities should be targeted exclusively at them.

Entitlement to financial support also varies widely according to a person's place of residence, the type and level of course taken, and mode of attendance. LEAs differ enormously in their treatment of adult learners and there is little coherence in concessionary fee structures for part-time students or recoupment arrangements. Variations in fee levels and complicated arrangements for different categories of student lead to confusion and resentment and may deter potential students.

Creating Conditions for Wider Access

For adult learning opportunities to be genuinely accessible to all sections of the community, there need to be:

☐ Clear policies for adult learners.

☐ Co-ordinated links between different parts of the post-school system.

☐ Links between education and other services, agencies and areas of expertise.

☐ Programmes and delivery mechanisms based on recognition of adults' employment and family responsibilities.

☐ A curriculum that acknowledges and uses adults' experience.

☐ Greater institutional flexibility.

The research indicates that two stages of access are particularly vital in work with under-represented adult groups:

1. The introductory stage: getting people to the point where they will voluntarily engage in learning opportunities.

2. The transition stage: helping people to progress from informal first stage learning to other forms and levels of education.

Currently, neither of these stages appears to be receiving sufficient attention and resourcing.

The First Stages of Access

The major emphasis in official measures to widen access has been on facilitating access to higher education. However, most people in non-participant categories perceive higher education as completely beyond their reach. Getting people to the point where they will cross the threshold from non-participation to participation requires attention to the first stages of access: reaching people and mounting informal learning activities in the community.

Peer and reference group influence is very powerful within the groups with the most negative attitudes to education. Individuals in such groups do not readily depart from accepted norms and behaviour patterns. Outreach approaches, group targeting and using key individuals as change agents have been found the most effective strategies for recruiting people for whom participation in education is not a normal activity. The initial support offered need not always take the form of classes with paid tutors. People have been attracted back to learning through information and advice on local learning opportunities, access to premises and use of facilities for meetings and self-generated activities.

Consultation and negotiation with non-participants on learning needs, curricula, methods of delivery, modes of attendance and styles of learning emerged as key processes in work with new groups. A participatory approach characterises informal outreach work in the community, but it is less in evidence higher up the system, and the research found few cases of negotiated programmes in education institutions where every level of interest was involved – student, tutor, providing institution and funding agency.

Collaboration

Outreach work requires collaboration with other agencies, a process frequently hampered by the fact that in some areas the education service operates in isolation from other local authority services. Moreover, the departments and agencies in contact with socially and educationally disadvantaged groups frequently have no structural mechanisms for communication or collaboration.

Costs

Financial constraints largely explain why some providers have been reluctant to initiate work which is expensive and labour-intensive and can be slow to build up. It takes time for educators to win the trust of people in non-participant categories and there is often a slow initial response to recruitment measures. This means that a "viable" class may not be achieved in the early stages, creating difficulties for providers affected by ESH (Effective Student Hours) criteria. Some development work has succeeded only because it was allowed to run with small numbers for the first few weeks.

The practical costs of outreach are high. A community outreach worker recruiting for a Second Chance course estimated (early in 1988) that it cost approximately 3 per student contacted and 6 per student recruited. Thus, in services operating on a limited budget, group targeting and outreach approaches can only be undertaken with the support of special funding. Pump-priming funding has supported a variety of innovative work with non-participants and enabled many individuals to engage in learning for the first time as adults. However, a disadvantage of such funding is that the work undertaken is often short-term, marginal and not integrated with mainstream programming. As a result, it often has a low priority in comparison with other work in an institution. An additional problem has been identified as the tendency of funding agencies to change their regulations and criteria, as a result of which many development officers have experienced difficulties in ensuring the continuation of work they have started. Although some short-term initiatives have been continued by LEAs and education institutions, many have not outlived their initial funding and have left little trace:

> At the end of a lot of work you've often got little or nothing to show. The rules keep changing and the parameters shift. This means that

*planning is difficult and everything's so short-term. [Outreach
guidance worker]*

The research made clear the urgent need for the financial underpining of
measures to widen access, without which many may continue to be *ad hoc* and
short-term.

Development staff

Short-term development work is often undertaken by staff working on a
temporary or part-time basis in low-status positions with no career
structures. Workers at contact level are characterised by motivation,
enthusiasm and dedication and many appear to put in more hours than they
are paid to do. The research demonstrated that a variety of skills are required
in outreach work with non-participant groups:

☐ Ability to deal with people at different levels and from a variety of social
  and cultural backgrounds.
☐ Communication and listening skills.
☐ Negotiation skills.
☐ Counselling skills.
☐ Resourcefulness.
☐ Patience.
☐ Ability to handle rejection.
☐ Multi or bilingual skills.

These skills are generally unquantifiable and not always recognised and
appreciated by institution-based staff.

Outcomes

The outcomes of introductory programmes are also largely unquantifiable.
Learning activities developed for non-participants are often more to do with
developing confidence, self-sufficiency and autonomy than acquiring
qualifications. This means that new programmes can be difficult to justify to
managers and funders, who are increasingly concerned with certificated and
employment-related courses.
    A fundamental problem in working with deprived people is that education
by itself cannot solve problems arising from social and economic factors,
unemployment and racism. Adult educators recruiting new groups have to
maintain a fine balance between giving people realistic expectations of what
can be achieved through participation and not raising their hopes too high.

Access to Advanced Formal Education

The research highlighted the need for bridging and induction programmes to ease transition for mature students between very different levels and styles of learning. The development of Access courses as a major means of facilitating entry to higher education raises a number of questions, the most salient being whether such courses actually recruit the real non-participants. Other institutional access measures such as Assessment of Prior Learning schemes, new curricula and learning support programmes are expensive because they require intensive individual and small group work. Consequently, as in the first stages of access, much of the work undertaken with new groups in further and higher education has been short-term funded, with all the attendant problems.

Many initiatives for mature students in education institutions have resulted from the efforts of individual staff members rather than from an overall institutional policy. Access and equal opportunities policies and the extent to which they are implemented vary enormously between institutions. Often such policies are contradicted in practice and there can be a large gap between what an institution is doing and what staff believe it is doing. Few institutions appear to have established performance indicators and structures for monitoring and evaluating how actual practice meets aims.

The majority of support measures for new students have been reactive rather than proactive and most have been at entry point only. Mature students require a range of support mechanisms – guidance, counselling, a baseroom, childcare and learning support (study skills, language and numeracy support) – but few institutions provide all of these services.

The introduction of new groups and innovatory practices in an institution is often perceived as a threat to staff roles and established work, and in some cases this has led to tension and lack of co-operation. It is clear that there are as many misconceptions about adult learners within education systems as there are misconceptions about education outside the system. Since the numbers of mature students in higher education are expected to increase, this underlines the need for extensive staff development programmes, explicitly for teaching and non-teaching staff who come into contact with mature students.

The Effects of Policy Changes on Non-Participant Access

Equity – improving opportunities for the under-privileged – is rarely the principal goal of education-providing agencies and institutions. Subsidies to providers are usually related to the numbers of participants and courses mounted. Many organisations, to a large extent, rely on students' fees, which can skew provision towards the better off. Increasing pressure on education providers to become more market-oriented is, in some cases, impeding attempts to improve access for economically and educationally disadvantaged groups. Most local education authorities have raised their part-time fees above the level of inflation and in some areas adult education services have been "floated off" to semi-private status.

Changes in funding allocation to Responsible Bodies have led to shifts in some university extra-mural and continuing education departments in favour of professional training. Others with a fine record of providing wide-ranging, reasonably priced adult courses have, since September 1988, raised fees, shortened course length and changed to certificated and examination programmes, all of which are measures which erect barriers against the less well-off, less educated, less confident adult.

Theoretically, the Education Reform Act should improve education services for adults by making the provision of "adequate facilities for further education" for people over compulsory school age a legal obligation, and by urging LEAs to be responsive to local community needs. Subsequent DES regulations and accompanying circulars guarantee a secure statutory base for adult education within the FE sector and require planners to take account of disadvantaged categories of adults. Other results of the Act, however, may negatively affect access for disadvantaged adult students. The future of the ILEA adult service, with its unparalleled record of attracting non-traditional learners with its low fee and equal opportunities policies, is uncertain when it is dispersed to 13 boroughs. In the FE sector, the Act, according to one observer, "embodies major tensions ... between the values of equity, access and entitlement and those of differentiation and competition implicit in the market assumptions underpinning the Act" (1). The need to market courses effectively may reduce an institution's incentive and ability to cater for under-represented groups, particularly those without financial resources. According to one college Principal interviewed during the research: "The new budget procedures and targets necessitate the generation of income to maintain staffing levels and this has major implications for sections of the community which are traditionally under-represented in the sector."

Some further education staff feared that changes in college governing bodies might also have a negative effect on burgeoning work with disadvantaged sections of the community.

Thus, some developments in the further and higher education sectors appear to run counter to the general momentum towards increasing access for non-traditional students. The steady cuts in universities' finance and staffing over the last decade, together with proposed cuts in the numbers of lecturers in further education and public sector higher education, suggest a service that is shrinking at the same time that it is being required to expand.

In higher education, the shift towards funding by fees is intended to make institutions more competitive by giving them the incentive to recruit more students. Although the change has been generally welcomed, there are fears that the change will strengthen the division between universities and public sector higher education. Universities cream off the majority of highly qualified school-leavers and, as the birth rate in the middle classes has not fallen to the extent it has in other classes, this situation seems likely to continue. As a result, public sector higher education will continue to take the greater proportion of non-traditional students and this, some believe, will reinforce a basically unequal two-tier system.

The student loans proposal has raised fears that such a system will discriminate against disadvantaged sections of the community, particularly women, who traditionally earn less than men, and ethnic minorities. The signs are that women, black and older entrants – the groups least represented in higher education – are most hostile to loans and in consequence, a large question mark hangs over the composition of the future student body.

The future position of part-time students – the majority of whom are mature learners – is not clear. Part-time students have never received financial support, and a number of changes – reorganisation of social security benefits, stricter application of Availability for Work regulations, confusion about the 21-hour rule and definitions of part-time study – have made it more rather than less difficult for those in disadvantaged categories to study part-time.

Thus, alongside the laudable national aim to make post-compulsory education accessible to a wider cross-section of the community, are developments, particularly those to do with finance, which appear to be undermining moves towards wider access. It became apparent during the project that one effect of the current stress on marketing provision has been to encourage institutions to seek high-fee-paying overseas students at the expense of under-represented home students. Recent research into higher education admission policy found "more instances of quotas for overseas groups than for any other group" (2).

Stress on market forces may mean that the most popular, income-generating courses will survive, while expensive small group and minority interest courses will be dropped. For non-traditional students who need a small staff–student ratio and a period of preparation and guidance before they make educational choices, this implies a closing rather than opening of doors. Already there are signs that the curriculum in some areas is shrinking towards more instrumental, vocational and Euro-centred programming. As one outreach worker rhetorically asked: "If you let market forces reign, what happens to those who have no money and no real clout?" These, unfortunately, are the people predominantly found in non-participant groups, for whom a system financed increasingly through fees may have progressively less to offer.

References

1. Farley, M. The core mission of LEAs. *Education,* 5 August 1988.
2. Fulton, O. & Ellwood, S. *op. cit.,* p6.

Bibliography

Addams, B. (1987) *Listening To You, Listening To Us: Expanding education provision for unemployed adults in Birmingham.* FEU/REPLAN.

Adlington, E. (1988) *Educational Vouchers for Unemployed Adults.* NIACE/REPLAN.

Adult Learning Federation (1988) *Report on Activities 1 Dec 1987 to 1 July 1988.* ALFA.

Adult Literacy and Basic Skills Unit (undated) *Sheffield Outreach Project Report.* ALBSU.

Adult Literacy and Basic Skills Unit (1983) *Organising Provision: Good practice in adult literacy and basic skills provision.* ALBSU.

Adult Literacy and Basic Skills Unit (1985) *Publicising Adult Literacy and Basic Skills.* ALBSU.

Adult Literacy and Basic Skills Unit (1987) *Annual Report 1986–87.* ALBSU.

Adult Literacy and Basic Skills Unit (1987) *Report of the Special Development Project at Richmond Adult and Community College: July 1984–March 1986.* ALBSU.

Adult Literacy and Basic Skills Unit (1988) *Bedfordshire Project: Interim report.* ALBSU.

Advisory Council for Adult and Continuing Education (1979) *Towards Continuing Education: A discussion paper.* ACACE.

Advisory Council for Adult and Continuing Education (1982a) *Adults: Their educational experience and needs.* ACACE.

Advisory Council for Adult and Continuing Education (1982b) *Continuing Education: From policies to practice.* ACACE.

Akins, A. (1985) Barriers to access to learning opportunities in New Zealand. *ACE Bulletin* 15, pp25–28.

Alexander, D. & Stewart, T. (1974) An educational perspective on community education in Scotland. *Scottish Journal of Adult Education,* 5,3.

ALFA (1987) *Annual Report 1986–87.* ALFA: Access to Learning for Adults. The North London Open College Network.

Allen, G. (1988) *Community Education: An agenda for educational reform.* Open University Press.

Alloway, J. & Nelson, P. (1987) *Advice and Guidance to Individuals.* SIACE/UDACE.

Ames, J. (1986) *Financial Barriers to Access.* UDACE.

Anderson, R. & Darkenwald, G. (1979) *Participation and Persistence in American Adult Education.* Papers in Lifelong Learning, College Entrance Examination Board.

Anderson, D. & Niemi, J.A. (1969) *Adult Education and the Disadvantaged Adult.* ERIC Clearing House on Adult Education.

Aslanian, C. & Bricknell, H. (1980) *Americans in Transition: Life changes as reasons for adult learning.* New York College Entrance Examination Board.

Barr, J. (1987) Keeping a low profile: adult education in Scotland. *Adult Education, 59,4.*

Bateson, G. (1988) Radical community education in local authority settings – a contradiction in terms? *Journal of Community Education, 6,4, pp21–23.*

Beder, H. (1980) Reaching the hard-to reach adult through effective marketing. *New Directions for Continuing Education, 8.*

Beder, H. & Valentine, T. (1987) *Iowa's Basic Education Students: Descriptive profiles based on motivation, cognitive ability and socio-demographic variables.* Department of Education, Iowa.

Benseman, J. (1979) Continuing education clientele: present realities and future possibilities. *Continuing Education in New Zealand, 11,1.*

Bird, M. & Varlaam, A. (1987) *Changing Course: Community education in Inner London.* Report PS 7114, ILEA.

Blamire, J. & Nielsen, F. (1987) *Don't Call Us.* REPLAN.

Boshier, R. (1971) Motivational orientations of adult education participants: a factor analytic exploration of Houle's typology. *Adult Education* (US), 21,2, pp3–26.

Boshier, R. (1976) Factor analysts: a critical review of the motivational orientation literature. *Adult Education* (US), 27,1, pp24–42.

Bourner, T. *et al.* (1988) *Students on CNAA's Part-time First Degree Courses.* CNAA Development Service Publication 16. CNAA.

Bourner, T. & Hamed, M. (1987) *Non-standard Entry Students: Entry qualifications and degree performance.* CNAA Development Services Publication 10. CNAA.

Bridger, S. (1987) *Women Learning: A consumer view of access provision.* Bradford Women's Employment Group.

Brookfield, S. (1978) Learning to learn: the characteristics, motivations and destinations of adult study skills students. *Adult Education,* 50,6.

Brown, J. (1987) Some aspects of access to adult education. *Journal of Community Education,* 6,2.

Burgess, P. (1971) Reasons for adult participation in group education activities. *Adult Education* (US), 22,1, pp3–29.

Canadian Association for Adult Education and Learning (1982) *From the Adult's Point of View.* Institute Canadien d'Education des Adultes.

Cannon, P. (1988) Thoughts on adult education. *AONTAS Newsletter,* 1,9, p6.

Castle, E. & Selby, A. (1987) Then and now: a course for old people. *Adult Education,* 60,2, pp122–126.

Challis, J. (1982) *Building and Communication: Report on MSC-sponsored linked-skills project at the Lee Centre 1981–82.* The Lee Centre.

Charnley, A.H. (1989) *Fees Charged to Part-time Students in LEAs 1988–89.* NIACE.

Chatfield, M. & Mills, J. (1987) The Bridge Project: training for women in Washington. *Working with Women Bulletin 1.* REPLAN.

Clifford, P. (1986) *Unemployed Men and Adult Education in Milton Keynes.* Milton Keynes Community Education.

Cole, P. (1986) *Dearne Valley Project, Annual Report 1985–86.* Northern College.

Colwell, D. (1988) *Factory Project Report.* ALFA: Access to Learning for Adults. The North London Open College Network.

Cookson, P.S. (1987) The nature of the knowledge base of adult education: the example of participation. *Educational Considerations V, XIV.*

Cooper, M. & Bornat, J. (1988) Equal opportunity or special need: combatting the woolly bunny. An assessment of the work of the ILEA Education Resource Unit for Older People. *Journal of Education Gerontology, 3,1.*

Courtney, S. (1981) The factors affecting participation in adult education: an analysis of some literature. *Studies in Adult Education, 13,2, pp104–5.*

Cross, K.P. (1981) *Adults as Learners.* Jossey-Bass.

Croydon English Language Scheme (1987) *Annual Reports 1985–86 and 1986–87.* Norwood AE Centre.

Daines, J., Elsey, B. & Gibbs, M. (1982) *Changes in Student Participation in Adult Education.* University of Nottingham.

Darkenwald, G.G. (1975) Some effects of the obvious variable: teacher's race and holding power with black students. *Society of Education, 48, pp420–431.*

Darkenwald, G.G. (1988) *Comparison of Deterrents to Adult Education Participation in Britain and the United States.* SCUTREA.

Darkenwald, G.G. & Hayes, E. (1987) Assessment of adult attitudes towards continuing education. *International Journal of Lifelong Education,* March 1987.

Darkenwald, G.G. & Larson, G.A. (1980) What we know about reaching hard-to-reach adults. *New Directions for Continuing Education, 8.*

Darkenwald, G.G. & Merriam, S.B. (1982) *Adult Education: Foundations of practice.* Harper and Row.

Darkenwald, G.G. & Valentine, T. (1985) Factor structure of deterrents to public participation in adult education. *Adult Education Quarterly, 35,4, pp177–193.*

Douglas, J.A. *et al.* (1984) Return to study: access points to continuing education? *Adult Education, 57,2, pp131–134.*

Drysdale, D.H. (1973) A joint experiment to combat social deprivation. *Adult Education,* 46.

Dubar, C. (1977) Formation continue et differentiations sociales. *Revue Francaise Sociologique,* XVIII, pp543–575.

Duke, F. (1987) Degrees of experience: are the needs and expectations of mature adults and school-leavers compatible? *Journal of Access Studies,* Spring 1,1, pp54-63.

Dutch Open University (1986) *Innovations in Distance Education.* Occasional Papers of the Dutch Open University, no. 1.

Education Advice Service for Adults (1987) *Annual Report 1986 and 1987–88.* EASA.

Edwards, J. (1986) *Working-class Education in Liverpool: A radical approach.* Centre for Adult and Higher Education, University of Manchester.

Eldred, E.J. (1987) An exploration of the experiences of non-participant long-term unemployed and their attitudes towards continuing education. Unpublished dissertation, University of Sheffield.

Evan, H.H. (1984) Further education in the community. *Adult Education,* 6,4.

Evans, N. (1988) *The Assessment of Prior Experiential Learning.* CNAA Development Service Publication 17. CNAA.

Falken, G. (1988) A black model of community education. *Journal of Community Education,* 6,4, pp4–6.

Finch, J. & Rustin, M. (1986) *A Degree of Choice? Higher education and the right to learn.* Penguin Books.

Finn, J.D. & Dulberg, R. (1980) Sex differences in educational attainment: the process. *Comparative Education Review,* 24,2, pp23–52.

Ford, G. (1984) Meeting the vocational education, training and guidance needs of adults. *Adult Education,* 58,1, pp34–38.

Frame, P. (1983) ESL: is it a ghetto in your college? *NATFHE Journal,* March/April.

Fraser, A. (1988) *Access to Employment in Childcare and Nursery Education for Bengali Women.* Tower Hamlets AEI.

Fraser, L. & Ward, K. (1988) *Education from Everyday Living: An assessment of community-based courses with unemployed people.* NIACE/REPLAN.

Freire, P. (1971) *Pedagogy of the Oppressed.* Penguin.

Fulton, O. & Ellwood, S. (1989) *Admissions to Higher Education: Policy and practice.* Training Agency.

Further Education Unit (1983) *Curriculum Development for a Multicultural Society: An FEU review.* FEU.

Further Education Unit (1985) *Black Perspectives on FE Provision: Summary document.* FEU.

Further Education Unit (1985) *Marketing FE – A feasibility study.* FEU/REPLAN.

Further Education Unit (1986) *Retraining Adults: Responding to the education/training needs of unemployed adults in Coventry.* FEU/REPLAN.

Further Education Unit (1987) *Access to Further Education and Higher Education: A discussion document.* FEU.

Further Education Unit (1987) *Anxious To Work.* FEU.

Further Education Unit (1987) *Black Students and Access to HE: A summary document.* FEU.

Further Education Unit (1987) *Equal Opportunities for Ethnic Minorities in NAFE.* FEU.

Further Education Unit (1987) *FE Can Really Change Your Life.* FEU/NUS.

Further Education Unit (1987) *FE in Black and White.* FEU/Longman.

Further Education Unit (1987) *Marketing Adult Continuing Education: A project report.* FEU.

Further Education Unit (1987) *Preparing Adults: An appraisal of MSC-sponsored adult preparation courses.* FEU.

Further Education Unit (1987) *Supporting Adult Learning.* FEU.

Further Education Unit (1987) *Supporting the Unemployed in FE.* FEU.

Further Education Unit (1987) *Unemployment, Education and Training on the South Coast: A summary bulletin.* FEU/REPLAN.

Further Education Unit (1987) *Working and Unemployed Adults in Cheshire: Conference report.* FEU/REPLAN.

Geraint Evans, J. (1986) *Adult Basic Education in Powys, 1983–85. ALBSU Development Project Final Report.* ALBSU.

Ghazzali, A. (1979) Reasons for adult participation in group education activities. *Research in Education,* 21.

Goldsmiths' College (1986) *Something to Teach and Something to Learn: An initial research report on an outreach project.* Goldsmiths' College.

Gooderham, P.N. (1987) Reference group theory and adult education. *Adult Education Quarterly,* 37,3, pp140–151.

Gray, E. (1988) *First Year Report of the Open University Community Education Project, Feb 1986–Feb 1987.* Open University National Community Programme Agency.

Groombridge, B. (1982) Learning, education and later life. *Adult Education,* 54,4.

Halsey, A.H. *et al.* (1980) *Origins and Destinations: Family, class and education in modern Britain.* Clarendon Press.

Hart, M. (1982) Factors affecting adult learning. *Adult Education,* 54,4, pp349–352.

Health Education Council and Age Concern (1988) *Age Well Ideas Pack.* National Community Health Resource.

Hedoux, J. (1981) Les non-publics de la formation collective. *Education Permanente,* 61, Decembre, pp89–105.

Hedoux, J. (1982) Des publics et des non-publics de la formation d'adultes: Sallaumines-Noyelles-sous-Lens des 1972. *Revue Francaise Sociologique,* Avril-Juin, pp253–274.

Her Majesty's Inspectorate (1989) *Students with Special Needs in FE.* Education Observed 9, HMI.

Hills, A. (1987) *Link into Learning: Report on the ALBSU special development project in Richmond Adult and Community College, July 1984–March 1986.* ALBSU.

Holmes, J, & Storrie, T. (1985) Consett – A Case Study of Education and Unemployment. FEU.

Holtzclaw, L.R. (1988) Flexible admission practices for adult learners. *Lifelong Learning,* April, pp9–11. AAACE.

Hopper, E. & Osborn, M. (1975) *Adult Students: Education, selection and social control.* Frances Pinter.

Hothersall, G. (1972) Education and social growth in contrasting neighbourhoods: a study in Skipton. *Adult Education,* 45,1.

Houle, C. (1961) *The Enquiring Mind.* University of Wisconsin.

Irish, G.H. (1980) Reaching the least educated adult. *New Directions for Continuing Education,* 8.

Issitt, M. (1988) Organising women's health days – a feminist approach to community education in Coventry. *Journal of Community Education,* 6,4, pp8–10.

Issitt, M. & Spence, J. (1988) An exploration of the relationship between community education and higher education. *Journal of Community Education,* 6,4a, pp14–17.

Jarvis, P. (1982) What's the value of adult education? *Adult Education,* 54,4, pp342–348.

Jarvis, P. (1983) Education and the elderly. *Adult Education,* 55,4, pp343–350.

Johnstone, J.W.C. & Rivera, R. (1965) *Volunteers for Learning: A study of the educational pursuits of American adults.* Aldine Publishing Company.

Johnstone, R. (1987) *Exploring the Educational Needs of Unwaged Adults.* NIACE/REPLAN.

Jones, B. (1988) Educating Ritas. *Times Higher Education Supplement,* 24 June 1988.

Jones, D. (1988) *Access to the Arts: Adult education and cultural development.* Routledge.

Jones, H. & Charnley, A.H. (1978) *Adult Literacy: A study of its impact*. NIAE.

Kearney, P. (1987) *Second Chance to Learn: Final report*. WEA Berks, Bucks and Oxon.

Killeen, J. & Bird, M. (1981) *Education and Work: A study of paid educational leave in England and Wales, 1976–77*. NIAE.

Kitchen, P. (1981) Non-formal adult education: the role it could play in the inner cities. *In Adult Education in the Inner City Areas: The practice, the policy and allocation of resources*. Adult Learning Federation.

Kitchen, P. (1988) Give us more of the cake. *Journal of Community Education*, 6,4, pp19–21.

Lambers, K. (1988) *Women Returners in Education: Conference report*. Polytechnic of the South Bank/Open College of South London.

Larson, G.A. (1980) Overcoming barriers to communication. *New Directions for Continuing Education, 8*.

Lawson, A. (1988) *Older Unemployed Adults Project*. Liverpool City College/REPLAN.

Leeds Department of Education (1987) *Return to Learn: A new course for adults (curriculum development and adult basic education students in Leeds)*. ALBSU.

Lewis, L. (1988) An issue of support. *International Journal of Lifelong Education*, 4,2, pp163–176.

Liddington, J. (1988) What do you do after a "New Opportunities" course? *Adult Education*, 61,1, pp36–40.

Lovett, T. *et al*. (1983) *Adult Education and Community Action*. Croom Helm.

Lowen, D. (1986) *Barriers to Educational Opportunities for Adults. A report on the institutional barriers to educational opportunities for adults*. Central and West London Open College.

McDonald, J. (1984) *Education for Unemployed Adults*. DES.

Mace, J. (1985) *A Time and a Place: A study of education and manual work at Goldsmiths' College, 1983–84*. Lee Centre, Goldsmiths' College.

Mace, J. & Yarnit, M. (eds) (1987) *Time Off To Learn: Paid educational leave and low-paid workers.* Methuen.

McDonald, J. (1984) *Education for Unemployed Adults.* DES.

McIlroy, J. & Spencer, B. (1988) *University Adult Education in Crisis.* University of Leeds.

McPherson, J. (1986) *Development of Co-ordinated Adult Education and Training Provision in a Rural Area.* FEU.

Maloney, K. (1989) Priming the system. *REPLAN Review 4.* DES/REPLAN

Maslow, A.H. (1954) *Motivation and Personality.* Harper and Row.

Mezirow, J., Darkenwald, G.G. & Knox, A.B. (1975) *Last Gamble on Education.* AAACE.

Midwinter, E. (1982) *Age is Opportunity: Education and older people.* Centre for Policy on Ageing.

Miller, H.L. (1967) *Participation in Education: A force-field analysis.* Center for the Study of Liberal Education for Adults, University of Boston.

Millins, K. (1983) Some aspects of access studies. *NATFHE Journal,* March/April.

Millins, K. (1984) *Report on Access Courses.* DES.

Mills, J. (1986) *The Bridge Project: Training for women in Washington.* Washington Tyne and Wear Bridge Project.

Mills, J. (1988) Funding for women's courses. *Working with Women Bulletin 2.* REPLAN.

Montilbert, C. de (1973) Le public de la formation des adultes. *Revue Fran'aise Sociologique,* XIV, pp529–545.

Morstain, B.R. & Smart, J.C. (1974) Reasons for participation in adult education courses: a multivariable analysis of group differences. *Adult Education,* 24,2 pp83–98.

Morton, S. (1987) An Exploration of the Educational Circumstances and Needs of Mature Unwaged Women who are Non-participants in Continuing Education. Unpublished MEd dissertation, University of Sheffield.

Moss, W. (1987) *Breaking the Barriers*. ALFA/REPLAN.

Mullarney, P. & Lewis, L. (1984) *Resolving the Dilemma: Where do we go from here?* School of Education, University of Connecticut.

Munn, P. & MacDonald, C. (1988) *Adult Participation in Education and Training.* SCRE.

National Advisory Body (1987) *Higher Education For All – But Is It? A report on discussions held by NAB Equal Opportunities Working Group.* NAB.

National Advisory Body (1988) *Action for Access.* NAB.

National Institute of Adult Education (1970) *Adequacy of Provision.* NIAE.

Neville, C. (1986) *Education and Change: A survey of users of an education advice service.*

Nicholl, N. (1988) *Older Adults. REPLAN Project Report.* Sandown College/REPLAN.

Norris, C. (1985) Towards a theory of participation in adult education. *Adult Education*, 58,2, pp120–122.

Northern College (1983) *A New Approach to Adult Education.* Paper presented by the Academic Board to the Council of Management.

Organisation for Economic Co-operation and Development (1977) *Final Report of Tokyo World Conference on Adult Education.* OECD.

Organisation for Economic Co-operation and Development (1979) The non-participant issue. *Learning Opportunities for Adults,* 3.

Osborn, M., Withnall, A. & Charnley, A.H. (1980) *Review of Existing Research in Adult Continuing Education, Volume 3: The disadvantaged.* NIACE.

Osborn, M. *et al.* (1984) *Review of Existing Research in Adult Continuing Education, Volume 6: Mature students.* NIACE.

O'Shea, J. & Corrigan, P. (1979) Surviving adult education. *Adult Education,* 52,4.

Payne, R. (1988) *The Access Enquirer Project: From enquiry to interview.* ILEA/ALFA.

Pelissiet, C. & Smith, R. (1988) Student-centred continuing education: a county strategy for access. *Journal of Further and Higher Education,* 12.

Percy, K. (1983) *Post-initial Education in the North-west of England: A survey of provision.* ACACE.

Percy, K. *et al.* (1988) *Learning in Voluntary Organisations.* UDACE.

Pound, A., Mills, M. & Cox, T. (1987) *A Pilot Evaluation of NEWPIN: A home visiting and befriending scheme in south London.* NEWPIN.

REPLAN (1987) Breaking down the barriers. *REPLAN Review 2.* DES/REPLAN.

REPLAN (1987) *Consulting Women: Examples of educational initiatives with unwaged women.* REPLAN.

REPLAN (1987) *Curriculum Development and Institutional Change in Further and Higher Education.* REPLAN.

REPLAN (1987) *How Responsive Is Your College to the Wants and Needs of Black Unemployed People?* REPLAN.

REPLAN (1987) In search of the missing millions. *REPLAN Review 1.* DES/REPLAN.

REPLAN (1987) *Reach Out.* (REPLAN Yorkshire and Humberside Newsletter, issue 2.)

REPLAN (1987) *Working with Women Bulletin 1.* REPLAN.

REPLAN (1988) *Developing Educational Provision for Unemployed Adults.* REPLAN.

REPLAN (1988) *FATEBU Newsletter 1.* REPLAN.

REPLAN (1988) *Working with Women Bulletin 2.* REPLAN.

Rogers, D. (1985) *Life Chances: A working report on community education with single, homeless people.* Lee Centre.

Rubenson, K. (1977) *Participation of Adults in Education: A force field analysis.* Centre for the Study of Liberal Education for Adults, University of Boston.

Scanlan, C.L. (1986) *Deterrents to Participation: An adult education dilemma.* National Centre for Research in Vocational Education, Ohio State University.

Scanlan, C.L. & Darkenwald, G. (1984) Identifying deterrents to participation in continuing education. *Adult Education Quarterly,* 3.

Schuller, T. (1978) *Education Through Life.* Fabian Society.

Sinfield, S. (1987) *ALFA Adult Education and Further Education Links Project: Evaluation Report.* ALFA.

Sheffield, S.B. (1962) The orientations of adult continuing learners. Unpublished thesis, University of Chicago.

Smith, V. (1983) College democracy: it isn't working. *NATFHE Journal,* March/April, pp22–23.

Thackwray, R. (1988) *Black Opportunities Project.* UDACE.

Tough, A. (1971) *The Adult's Learning Projects: A fresh approach to theory and practice in adult learning.* Ontario Institute for Studies in Education.

Ibid. (1979) 2nd ed.

Unit for the Development of Adult Continuing Education (1986) *The Challenge of Change: Developing educational guidance for adults.* UDACE.

Unit for the Development of Adult Continuing Education (1988) *Securing Adequate Facilities: Planning for the education of adults. A development paper.* UDACE.

University of Lancaster (1987) *Evidence from the Child Development Study.* ALBSU.

Usher, R. & Bryant I. (1989) *Adult Education as Theory, Practice and Research: The captive triangle.* Routledge.

Verner, C. & Newberry, J.S., Jr. (1958) The nature of adult participation. *Adult Education* (US), 8, pp208–222.

Webster, R. (1985) Adult education and social policy in the Republic of Ireland. *Adult Education,* 58,2.

West, L. (1987) Challenging the WEA: crisis, learning and purpose. *Workers Education,* 1.

White, J. (1987) *Need to Know Project: Final report.* ALBSU.

Williams, J., Davis, L. & Cocking, J. (1989) *Equal Opportunities and Racial Equality in Higher Education.* CRE.

Woodley, A. *et al.* (1987) *Choosing to Learn: Adults in education.* SRHE/Open University Press.

Woodrow, M. (1986) Access courses: some questions and answers. *Journal of Access Studies,* 1,1, p72.

Workers' Educational Association (1987) *Report of Rural Second Chance.* WEA West Mercia.

Workers' Educational Association (1987) *The WEA and the Black Communities.* WEA.

Wylei, A. (1987) *Developing Access Routes for Unwaged Women. A review of provision developed at Sandown College, Liverpool.* Sandown College/REPLAN.

Appendix 1

During the research, a large number of people provided written information and gave up considerable time to discuss their experience and relevant issues during visits and over the telephone. To all of these people I am very grateful.

Barbara Addams, Hall Green Technical College, Birmingham
Elizabeth Adlington, formerly REPLAN, London and South East
Eileen Aird, formerly WEA, London
Chris Aldred, WEA, Aberdeen
Phillip Barker, Bristol Polytechnic
John Baillie, Newham Community College
Beryl Bateson, Erdington, Birmingham Department of Recreation and Community Services
Geoff Bateson, Erdington, Birmingham Department of Recreation and Community Services
Hal Beder, Rutgers University, New Jersey, USA
Keith Belfield, Hodge Hill area, Birmingham Department of Recreation and Community Services
Ann Bell, formerly Chelmsford AEC, Essex
Les Brook and staff of Newham Community College
Cathy Brophy, State Education Department, Hartford, Connecticut
Sue Brown, Adult Education Office, Truro, Cornwall
Jacqui Buffton, formerly REPLAN Field Officer, South and South West
Cliff Burgess and staff, Willesden College of Technology
Gloria Campbell, formerly Vauxhall Manor Community Education Project
Julia Carter, formerly Polytechnic of North London

Alan Chadwick, University of Surrey
Alan Charnley, NIACE
Barbara Cherry, Yardley, Birmingham Department of Recreation and Community Services
Sheila Clarke, South Bristol College
Sarah Clarkson, Self-help Action Project, Hereford
Paul Clifford, Unemployed Men's Project, Milton Keynes
Maggie Coats, formerly REPLAN, Midlands
Alan Cohen, Central AEI, London
Pam Cole, Northern College
Margaret Coleman, Bradford and Ilkley Community College
H.L. Cotterill, Northfields, Birmingham Department of Recreation and Community Services
Glynis Cousin, REPLAN, Northamptonshire
Jane Cowell, formerly REPLAN, North West
Gordon Darkenwald, Rutgers University, USA
Margaret Davey, Croydon LEA
Ken Davies, Wensum Lodge, Norfolk
Joyce Deere, S Nottingham FE College
Dominic Delahunt, ECA
Linda Dicks, Central and West London Open College
Judy Donovan, WEA, Yorkshire North
Rory Donovan, REPLAN, Northamptonshire
Carolyn Douglas, Exploring Parenthood
Jan Eldred, Rother Valley College
Ann Eveleigh, REPLAN, London
Susan Fey, formerly Morley College
Brian Field, Claycross Centre
Howard Fisher, NIACE
Mair Francis, Dove Workshop, Banwen

Ann Fraser, Tower Hamlets AEI,
London
Bob Fryer, Northern College Barnsley
Derryck Gent, Cambridge LEA
Russell Gibbon, Step into Education
Project, Cardiff
Janet Gordon, WEA,
Northamptonshire
Elizabeth Gray, Open University
Community Education Project
Jill Hainsworth, Rycote Centre, Derby
Penny Hempstet, Sutton Coldfield
area, Birmingham
Christine Hepplestone, Sinfin
Community School
Eric Higginson, Derbyshire LEA
Mavis Hill, Bradford and Ilkley
Community College
Gill Horsfield, Rutland
Dick Hunter, Community Services,
Milton Keynes
Tony Huntington, Derbyshire LEA
Sheila Hutchins, Truro
Heather Jackson, formerly REPLAN
London and South East
Norma Jaggon, Accredited Training
Centre, Bristol
Anne Jenkins, Newpin, London
Tricia Jenkins, University of
Liverpool
Ian Jones, South Norwood Adult
Education Centre, Croydon
Nalini Joshi, Newham Community
College
Dick Jotham, University of
Nottingham
Keith Jones, Brighton Technical
College
Carole Kettle, REPLAN, West
Midlands
Elizabeth Kidd, South Glamorgan
LEA
Tom Kinneavy, Cleveland College
Phil Kitchen, Todds Noot Education
Centre, Newcastle-Upon-Tyne
Kitty Lambers, Open College of South
London
Phoebe Lambert, Hillcroft
Residential College, Surrey

Ann Leakey, South Norwood Adult
Education Centre, Croydon
Jim Leggatt, Adult Training Centre,
Croydon
Dania Leslie, Shipley College
Mike Lieven, Fircroft Residential
College, Birmingham
Ella Lutchmeyer, Croydon English
Language Scheme
Sarah Lloyd-Jones, People and Work
Unit, Wales
Jane Mace, Lee Centre, London
Jill MacPherson, Northamptonshire
LEA
Faith Mann, formerly WEA, Fife
Robert Mark, Longland College,
Middlesborough
Harold Marks, NACRO
Liz Matthews, Norfolk County
Council
Kauser McCallum, ALBSU
Andrea McIver, WEA, Bristol
Stephanis McKnight, Mary Ward
Centre
Prafulla Modi, WEA, Leicester
Marion Molteno, Croydon English
Language Scheme
Sheila Morton and short course
organisers at Northern College
Leni Oglesby, University of Sheffield
Sarah Osborne, REPLAN, South and
South West
Elizabeth Parker, Yardley area,
Birmingham Department of
Recreation and Community Services
Sue Pedder, Access to Learning For
Adults (ALFA), London
Monique Pincon-Charlot, Centre
d'Etudes Sociologiques, Paris
Bob Pitt and the students of CLASS
South Bristol College
Eileen Powell, REPLAN, Hereford
and Worcester
Sheila Pregnall, WEA, Swindon
Ronald Pugsley, State Education
Department, Washington DC
Margaret Purdey, formerly REPLAN,
Wales
Steve Randall, WEA Manchester

Jenny Reeves, Willenhall Community Education Project, Coventry
Hilary Rimmington, formerly Vauxhall Manor Community Education Project
Viv Rivis, formerly EASA, Bradford
John Roberts Training Shop, Cleveland
David Rogers, Lee Centre
Sharon Rooper, SALP, Luton ALBSU Project
Penny Shimmin, WEA, Hereford
Alan Skinner, Friary Centre, Colchester
Jan Smithies, Health Education Authority,
Jo Stanley, Polytechnic of North London
Michael Stephens, University of Nottingham
Judith Summers, Macclesfield LEA
Pauline Sweet, NACRO, Leeds
Simon Taylor, Fircroft Residential College, Birmingham
Bob Thackwray, Luton College of Higher Education
Tony Tovell and activities promotors, City of Norwich Amenities Department
Alan Tuckett, NIACE
Ruth Van Dyke, Polytechnic of North London
Jill Vennard, Northern College, Barnsley
Phil Vowles, Ludlow Close Annexe, St Pauls, Bristol
Sue Waddington, formerly REPLAN, Midlands
Cathy Walsh, WILCOT
Liz Weightman, formerly FEU
Bob West, Temperatures, Isle of Wight
Janet White, Need-to-Know Project, Derbyshire
Eric Whittington, City Polytechnic, London
Brian Wicker, Fircroft Residential College, Birmingham
David Wilson, Northamptonshire Education Department

Maura Wilson, REPLAN, Bradford
Carolyn Winkless, NIACE
Alexandra Withnall, NIACE
Robyn Young, DHSS
Jane Zuengler, Department of Education, Washington DC

During the research visits were made to:

Aston Park Hospital
Bedfordshire ALBSU Project
Bradford REPLAN and URBAN PROGRAMME office
Bradford and Ilkley Community College
Brighton Technical College
Bristol Polytechnic
Castle Vale Community Centre
EASA, Bradford
Erdington Adult Education
Exploring Parenthood
Derbyshire LEA
Fircroft Residential College
Health Education Authority
Lee Community Education Centre
Leicester WEA
Luton College of Higher Education
Ludlow Annexe, Bristol
Mary Ward Centre, London
Need to Know Project
Newham Community College
Northern College
Northamptonshire LEA
Norwich City Council Amenities Department
North London Polytechnic
Open College of South London
People and Work Unit, Cardiff
Polytechnic of South London
Ryecroft Centre, Derby
SALP, Luton
Sinfin Community School
South Bristol College
South Norwood Adult Education Centre
University of Surrey

Tower Hamlets Adult Education Institute
Vauxhall Manor Community Education Project
Willesden College of Technology
Willenhall Community Education Project

Additional face-to-face and telephone discussions were held with staff from:

Birmingham Recreation and Community Department (Hodge Hill, Northfield, Sutton Coldfield amd Yardley area AE offices)
Bradford Women's Employment Project

Central Adult Education Institute, London
Chelmsford Adult Education Centre
Cleveland College
Hall Green College of Further Education
Hillcroft Residential College
University of Liverpool
Milton Keynes Community Services
Newpin Project
REPLAN regional offices
South Glamorgan LEA
Redcar College
Shipley College
Training Shop, Cleveland
WEA: Manchester
WEA: North Scotland
WEA: South Scotland

Appendix 2

Participation in adult education survey

The survey is being conducted to obtain information on participation in adult learning activities in the UK. It is for the use of the National Institute of Adult Continuing Education only. No names are required and all responses will be kept completely confidential.

Please answer the following questions (where there are several possible responses circle the one that applies to you).

1. Title of WEA course/day school you are currently attending:
2. Sex: M F
3. Age range: under 20 20-29 30-39 40-49 50-59 over 60
4. Marital status: married single divorced/separated widowed
5. Number and ages of children
6. Are you: employed unemployed housewife?
7. If employed, what is the nature of your job?
8. Age at which you left school?
9. Do you have any educational qualifications? Yes No
    If yes, please specify:
10. Have you been involved in any other learning activities for adults (before present participation in WEA programme)? Yes No
    If yes please specify:
11. Can you identify the reasons which led you to attend this course/day school?
12. How did you hear about the class/day school: word of mouth; personal meeting with WEA tutor; saw publicity (please add any other applicable to you).
13. Has your attitude to learning changed in any way as a result of your participation in this class/day school? Yes No
    If yes, can you describe in what way your attitude has changed
14. Do you intend to join any other learning activities after this class/day school?
    Yes No
    If yes, please indicate the type of learning activity you are intending to join.

Appendix 3

Basic interview schedule used in non-participant interviews

Please ring answers applicable
1. Sex? M F
2. Age range? 20-29 30-39 40-49 50-59 60-69 70+
3. Marital Status? married single divorced/separated widowed
4. Number and ages of children?
5. Mother tongue if not English?
6. Current employment status? employed unemployed housewife
7. If employed, nature of job?
8. At what age did you leave school?
9. Educational qualifications?
10. Since leaving school have you voluntarily participated any of the following types of activity?
    adult learning programmes including classes, courses, discussion groups, workshops
    skills training/job training
    organised activities to do with sports, hobbies or leisure activities
    community or neighbourhood group activities (e.g. to do with church, mother and toddler, playgroup, school, tenants' groups, special interest group, womens's groups, etc.)
    If yes, specify:
11. Do you know what learning opportunities for adults exist within this area?
    If yes, specify:
12. Are group activities with an education/learning element of any interest or relevance to you? If not, can you identify the reasons?
    (This question is to elicit, if possible, views/attitudes towards AE; reasons for lack of interest etc.; it can be worded at interviewer's discretion.)

Any additional comments, observations considered relevant by interviewer:

Appendix 4

Participation in adult education survey

This survey is being conducted to obtain information on participation in adult education activities in the UK. The aim is to find out:

☐ what motivates people to participate in educational activities and what deters them from participating
☐ what different sections of the community want from the service
☐ how the service might be improved to meet community needs.

Adult education is defined as any educational activities for adults (including job training) organised by local adult education centres, further education/technical colleges, polytechnics, community groups, clubs, unions, employers, churches, etc. It includes ALL subjects, job skills and hobbies and *all* ways of learning: classes, discussion groups, training workshops, conferences, etc. This survey is for the use of the National Institute of Adult Continuing Education only. No names are required and all responses will be kept completely confidential.

Please answer the following questions (where there are several possible responses circle the one that applies to you).
1. Current job description
2. Age range 16-20   20-29   30-39   40-49   50+
3. Marital Status? married   single
4. Are you a parent of school-aged children?
5. At what age did you leave school?
6. What are your educational qualifications?   (please ring any of the following that apply)
   No formal qualifications
   RSA, School Certificate or School-Leaving Certificate
   GCE O-level or CSE in one or more subjects
   GGE A-level in one or more subjects
   BTEC ONC or OND
   HNC or HND
   City and Guilds
   YTS
   Other (specify)
7. Have you engaged in any educational activities for adults since leaving school? Yes No
   If yes, please specify:
8. Have you ever considered participating in any educational activity for adults but not done so? Yes   No

If yes, can you remember what stopped you from enrolling? (for example: distance, lack of transport, lack of information, lack of time, lack of money, lack of confidence, etc.)

9. Is there any educational activity/course/topic you would like to follow if provided? Yes No
   If yes, please specify:

10. Are there any particular factors or circumstances which would lead you to participate in an educational activity that interests you?

PLEASE PLACE COMPLETED FORMS IN THE BOX PROVIDED. THANK YOU VERY MUCH FOR YOUR CO-OPERATION!

Index